Science and Patterns of Child Care

Science and Patterns of Child Care

Elizabeth M. R. Lomax
UNIVERSITY OF CALIFORNIA, LOS ANGELES

in collaboration with

Jerome Kagan
HARVARD UNIVERSITY

Barbara G. Rosenkrantz
HARVARD UNIVERSITY

One of a series of historical monographs
sponsored by the Committee on Brain Sciences,
Division of Medical Sciences, Assembly of
Life Sciences, National Research Council

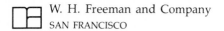 W. H. Freeman and Company
SAN FRANCISCO

The preparation of this publication was supported by the National Institute of Mental Health, of the Alcohol, Drug Abuse, and Mental Health Administration, under Contract No. N01-MH-1-0094 (ER)

Library of Congress Cataloging in Publication Data

Lomax, Elizabeth, M   R
   Science and patterns of child care.

   (A Series of books in psychology)
   Includes bibliographies and indexes.
   1. Child development. 2. Child psychology.
3. Children—Management—History. I. Kagan, Jerome,
joint author. II. Rosenkrantz, Barbara Gutmann, joint
author. III. Title.
HQ767.9.L65   649'.1   78-4972
ISBN 0-7167-0296-7
ISBN 0-7167-0295-9 pbk.

Printed in the United States of America
9 8 7 6 5 4 3 2 1

    The project that is the subject of this book was approved by the Governing Board of the National Research Council, whose members are drawn from the Councils of the National Academy of Sciences, the National Academy of Engineering, and the Institute of Medicine. The members of the Committee responsible for the book were chosen for their special competences and with regard for appropriate balance.

    This project has been reviewed by a group other than the authors according to procedures approved by a Report Review Committee consisting of members of the National Academy of Sciences, the National Academy of Engineering, and the Institute of Medicine.

Committee on Brain Sciences

Subcommittee on Importance of Early Experience in Child Development

JEROME KAGAN, Ph.D., chairman. Professor, Department of Psychology and Social Relations, Harvard University, Cambridge, Massachusetts

BETTYE CALDWELL, Ph.D., Professor, Center for Early Development and Education, University of Arkansas, Little Rock, Arkansas

VICTOR H. DENENBERG, Ph.D., Professor, Department of Biobehavioral Sciences, University of Connecticut, Storrs, Connecticut

JULIAN JAYNES, Ph.D., Professor, Department of Psychology, Princeton University, Princeton, New Jersey

AUSTIN H. RIESEN, Ph.D., Professor, Department of Psychology, University of California, Riverside, California

BARBARA G. ROSENKRANTZ, Ph.D., Professor, Department of the History of Science, Holyoke Center, Harvard University, Cambridge, Massachusetts

MARK R. ROSENZWEIG, Ph.D., Professor, Department of Psychology, University of California, Berkeley, California

PETER H. WOLFF, M.D., Professor of Psychiatry, Harvard Medical School, Boston, Massachusetts

Contents

FOREWORD   ix

ACKNOWLEDGMENTS   xiii

1

Introduction: Reflections on 19th-Century
Conceptions of Childhood   1

2

The First Empirical Studies   19
*Nineteenth-Century Studies and Theories of Infant Psychosocial
Development*   24
G. Stanley Hall   31
Arnold Gesell   36

3

Freud and His Influence   45
Early Psychoanalytic Theories of Child Development   45
Psychoanalytic Theories of Development Become Popular   73
Maternal Deprivation   76
Conclusions   96

4

Watson and the American Tradition   113

Early Behaviorist Theories of Child Development   110
Similarities and Differences between Freud and Watson   120
The Influence of Behaviorism on Developmental Psychology   125
Trends in Advice on Infant Care, 1900–1940   129
Conclusions   140

5

The Value of Recent Empirical Research   151

Longitudinal Studies   153
Experimental Studies   161
Factors Contributing to the Adoption of Early Stimulation
        Hypotheses   170
Conclusions   199

6

Conclusion   213

APPENDIX A   218

APPENDIX B   223

APPENDIX C   231

Foreword

Although the construction of theories that are systematic, satisfying, and predictive is the principal purpose of scientific work, a second function is the disconfirmation of erroneous ideas. This function of inquiry is especially important in the social and behavioral sciences, in which hypotheses often influence the everyday practices and attitudes of the average citizen. The results of research help us to check the validity of theoretical assumptions and to prevent incorrect explanations from seizing the mind of a community.

On occasion, society uses the data of the social sciences to rationalize a change in policy. The Supreme Court's decision to desegregate the public schools is perhaps one of the best contemporary examples of the complementary relation between social science and society. For the most part, the Western community is respectful of objective fact and disposed to accommodate to it. One of the major products of research in psychology, sociology, and anthropology is information that prevents incorrect, misleading, or harmful practices from dominating the minds and actions of the community for too long a time. Such information is as vital as a more efficient machine, a more powerful drug, or a more precise surgical instrument.

Parents' beliefs about what children are like and how they should be treated if they are to approach the ideal the family reveres are vulnerable to dogma. Only 60 years ago many American mothers believed that infants were fragile creatures who should not be handled frequently or overstimulated lest the stress of that intrusion damage their internal balance. Only 25 years ago millions of American mothers believed that anxiety, anger, shame, or guilt about nursing, weaning, toilet training, and masturbation could prevent a child from realizing his intellectual and emotional potential. I recall hearing of a parent who told the college girl who was sitting with her infant to make sure that the infant did not see his feces when she changed his diapers because the trauma of viewing his squashed bodily product might scar him. That story may seem amusing in the 1970s, but 20 years ago many parents worried about whether they should bottle or breast feed, and for how long, and whether they should leave the bathroom door closed or open. The fact that empirical data have failed to verify certain theoretical predictions from psychoanalytic theory is one of the reasons for the current indifference to these dilemmas.

In an important chapter written about a dozen years ago, Bettye Caldwell, after reviewing over 150 studies on the effects of infant care, concluded that there was no support for the superiority of breast over bottle feeding, and that the mother's attitude was more critical than the means of feeding the infant. She found no relation between schedule of feeding or method of weaning and the personality of a child. That conclusion could not have been reached without the efforts of hundreds of investigators, and, once written, it affected the attitudes of psychologists, magazine writers, and eventually parents.

Contemporary America broods about a new set of propositions dealing with the raising of children. It is not clear which of these are useful, which meaningless, and which false. Do infants require the physical stimulation of toys if they are to attain full intellectual development? Is day care harmful to a young child because it makes him less secure, blocks creativity and independence, and causes him to become fearful of not being accepted by his peers? Does malnutrition during infancy and early childhood prevent a child from attaining his full intellectual potential? Does permissive socialization produce a rebellious adolescent?

Strong statements have been made on each of these issues. Empirical research has separated the more true from the less true beliefs during the last quarter century, and it will, during the next, continue to assess the validity of today's controversial hypotheses.

Recently, Henry Ricciuti of Cornell University, Jerome Kagan of Harvard, and Philip Zelazo and Richard Kearsley of Tufts University found independently that group care for young infants does not necessarily produce behavioral profiles of separation anxiety that are markedly different from those displayed by children reared by their mothers at home. Studies of children growing up in isolated Third-World villages where there is minimal variety of stimulation early in life do not report irreversible retardation of intellectual abilities in older children. None of these issues is settled and each remains controversial. But that is as it should be. The product of scientific inquiry, not prejudice, phenomenology, or authoritative declaration, must be the judge of the truth of the catechism parents use to raise their children.

Elizabeth Lomax has provided a fresh, provocative, and intriguing study of the relation between empirical science and the belief, so strong in Western society, that early experience has a profound and lasting effect on a child's development. This book is not a history of the major themes of child development. Rather, Dr. Lomax has entered the archives with a particular inquiry and has tried to show how the ideas of Freud and Watson influenced beliefs and practices about childrearing that were complemented by the empirical research of the 1930s and 1940s, which was Lockean in spirit. The child was a sensitive tablet, and the experiences first imprinted on his psychic structures during the opening years of life were likely to influence the degree of health or pathology he would experience 20 years later. Parents were told, and they believed, that their children should be fed at the same hour every day and that they should not be fed when they cried. Parents were told that if they adhered to these practices, they accomplished two things for their baby at the same time: "You teach his body good habits and you teach his mind good habits."

Freudian theory posited a different set of mechanisms but arrived at the same conclusion regarding the significance of early care. John Bowlby, after reviewing the relevant literature in 1950, concluded, "Maternal care in infancy and early childhood is essential for mental health." These views, stated without qualification, were eventually supported by research on animals that seemed to affirm the significance of early experience. As a result, the belief that what happened to a child during the first two or three years of life would control him for the rest of his life became even more popular. The results of longitudinal studies that began in the early 1930s in California and Ohio, only recently published, fail to demonstrate dramatic predictive relations between the quality of early infant experience and adolescent or adult personality. These data are becoming public at a time when Piagetian theory and the results of cross-cultural inquiry emphasize the dynamic and plastic qualities of development and provide a balance to the earlier views.

Developmental psychology, now without guiding theory, needs a continuous flow of new knowledge to create fresh theoretical directions and to force examination of prejudices that harmonize with past teaching and future expectations. This is a time when empirical research in the behavioral and social sciences should have the highest priority.

Jerome Kagan, CHAIRMAN
Subcommittee on Importance of Early Experience in Child Development

Acknowledgments

This book could not have been written without the help and constructive criticism of people working in various disciplines, some of them only tangentially related to child development. First, my thanks must go to members of the advisory panel, Subcommittee on Importance of Early Experience in Child Development; to the chairman, Dr. Jerome Kagan, who has been indefatigable in organizing material and providing direction, advice, and encouragement; to Dr. Victor H. Denenberg, who has been especially helpful in pointing out inconsistencies and illogical trains of thought in the manuscript; to Dr. Julian Jaynes, who has provided detailed assessments that paid particular attention to broader historical perspectives; to Dr. Austin H. Riesen and Dr. Mark R. Rosenzweig for responding to numerous pleas for assistance on top of all the other demands made upon members of the advisory panel; to Dr. Bettye Caldwell for advice on both content and style; and to Dr. Barbara G. Rosenkrantz, who undertook to rewrite the first chapter when it obviously was not getting off the ground.

I am greatly indebted to scientists and members of the library staff at the University of California, Los Angeles, for all kinds of assistance; particularly to Dr. Arthur Parmelee, Director of the Division of Child Development in the Department of Pediatrics, for unstintingly providing advice, source material, and encouragement; and to members of his group, especially to Dr. Claire Kopp, who was willing to discuss any problem, any time.

My thanks also go to those further afield who have granted
time for interviews; to Drs. Jean Macfarlane, Mary Cover Jones,
and Marjorie Honzik whose perspectives on longitudinal research were invaluable; to Drs. Paul Mussen, Stephen Suomi,
and Richard Herrnstein, who have provided information on different aspects of the research. I am also most grateful to all who
have written to advise and comment, including Drs. H. Harlow,
Benjamin Spock, Daniel X. Freedman, Neal E. Miller, Harold B.
Gerard, and James Prescott. Finally, I am deeply indebted to Dr.
Louise Marshall, formerly staff officer for the Committee on
Brain Sciences and now with the Brain Information Service of
the Center for the Health Sciences, UCLA, without whose assistance, encouragement, and persistence through all trials and
tribulations this project would never have been completed.

Elizabeth M. R. Lomax
March 1978

Science and Patterns of Child Care

1

Introduction: Reflections on 19th Century Conceptions of Childhood

Parents must make decisions about how to raise their children. They cannot reflect too long on whether they should let a child cry when he wakes up from his nap, play with him when he's alert, or spank him when he defecates. To avoid the uncertainty and tension that follow from having too many reasonable alternatives, each society supplies a rationale for specific practices in specific situations in the form of a theory of child development. In many societies, the theory is merely an informal collection of prejudices handed down from generation to generation, supported continually by neighborly gossip. Consider the following maxims: "The child's temperament is determined by the day he is born," "Children should be kept inside for the first six months of their lives so they won't get sick," "You should never let a child cry," and "You should feed an infant every four hours." Each of these, at different times in different societies, has been accepted as a directive.

In Western society, the human sciences—primarily psychiatry and psychology—have assumed the role of counsel to parents. It is widely believed that theoreticians, in harmonious collaboration with empirical scientists, will discover the truths about human development and ensure that a faithful translation of these truths will be disseminated, in palatable form, to parents. There are two problems with this idealistic and somewhat ingenuous view. The first is that the theorist and his audience are members of the same culture and therefore tend to have the same biases and illusions. The second is that many theories of development rest on untested presuppositions. That is why empirical science is so important. Theoretical premise can withstand one or two firm facts that are inconsistent with its central thrust; but there is a critical point at which the facts overpower the theory and force us to look for new directions. Science's functions, not unlike those of the Supreme Court, are to referee ideas and to help people decide which principles are likely to be correct. In an endeavor as vital as childrearing, incorrect views must not become rigid dogma.

The purpose of this work is to trace part of the history of scientific studies in child development during the last century to document how the continued tension between a particular empirical fact and the larger theory in which it is embedded has prevented a hardening of positions regarding how children should be reared.

The physical circumstances under which children are born and raised and the expectations of parents for normal growth and development have changed radically over the last 300 years. But a concern for the relation between childhood experience and adult character has been a persistent characteristic of American society. Historians of the colonial period have shown that settlers in the New World paid a great deal of attention to the ways that the family, the church, and the community promoted the early socialization of children. Apparently, the mixture of hope and fear engendered by the mission to establish a new society in the wilderness drew attention to the special opportunities and hazards of early childhood experience in a way that caused the colonists' attitudes and practices to differ from those of the English. The warm reception for psychological theories stressing the critical importance of early childhood and the growth of pediatric medical practice in the United States from the late eighteenth century onward give testimony to the enduring conviction among laymen and scientists in America that children require special consideration.

Furthermore, in the United States the focus of attention on the impressionable nature of the child has tended to foster high expectations and optimism. The well-worn notion that "just as the twig is bent, the tree's inclined" has elicited hopes of opportunities far more often than it has elicited fears about potential hazards. Parents, teachers, and behavioral scientists have not been overwhelmed by the burdens implicit in the image of a child's plasticity, but rather have assumed that careful nurture will lead to character and habits that will determine optimal adult adjustment and productivity.

Although the risk of death in infancy and childhood was great until the second decade of the twentieth century, fears of disease and death did not shape seventeenth- and eighteenth-century attitudes toward children. On the contrary, the greatest attention was paid to the development of moral standards and character during the years when life itself was most threatened. In colonial

New England, parents fearful that too much affection for their children might make them resistant to the imposition of discipline often placed their offspring in another home, where habits and behavior might be molded more deliberately.[1] When it appeared that a relaxation of family rule might impair normative social development, American colonists consciously set about schooling the young to offset the temptations that could threaten impressionable minds and souls. So although the young were at risk, they were considered amenable to education and training.[2]

If the view of receptivity to training in early childhood has remained fairly constant, what differentiates colonial Americans from their descendants is the notion of what constitutes normal childhood behavior. The tasks of children in the seventeenth and eighteenth centuries were similar to the tasks of adults; in both dress and manner, children were expected to emulate their elders. The anticipation that this could be successfully accomplished set the mode of childrearing and dominated the picture of childhood in that period. An examination of family diaries, letters, and journals suggests that both in families of means and in those less well off there was no clear demarcation between responsibilities and behavior expected of adults and those expected of the young—once the time for indulgence generally allowed to infants had passed.[3]

In the early years of the nineteenth century concern for the social stability of the young republic may have protected young children from some of the physical threats encountered by English children through the demands of industrial development. At a time of rapid and unsettling economic growth and social change the family assumed particular importance in assuring continuity. As occupational opportunities increased for men, renewed attention was assigned to women's place within the structure of the home. The importance of the mother's role in rearing children seemed particularly critical when social values were believed threatened by a rupture with traditions that had not themselves been firmly established. The appearance of the first texts on child nurture written by Americans provides a sense of the importance children assumed. If visitors from abroad found Americans peculiarly child-centered, it may well have been because the visitors did not appreciate how precarious the social order seemed to Americans. Symbolically as well as practically, the molding of childhood had special significance for a tempestuous society.

The Maternal Physician (1811), written by an anonymous American matron, dealt with both the physical care and the character training of the infant and young child. As in the colonial period, concern was expressed for the guidance and discipline of childish will. The author related how her little son "gave evident signs of an obstinate and passionate temper" in babyhood. Worried about his turbulence of spirit when the child was nine months old, she "began a course of discipline which, in a few years, so entirely subdued a refractory spirit, which did bid fair to cause his friends and himself great trouble, that now I have not a more amiable child, or one who renders more prompt obedience to the commands of his parents; and this was accomplished before he was four years old, so that I have had no occasion to use the least severity since."[4] The view that natural propensities to evil must be corrected early and the infant prevented from acquiring bad habits found easy acceptance in a society concerned with self-control and orderly development. Although the infant was equally prone to good and evil, there was an implicit expectation that plasticity offered the opportunity to encourage the former tendency and eliminate the latter. The resonance of optimism inevitably placed the child in a favored spot for observation and attention.

During the latter part of the nineteenth century, texts of advice to parents began to emphasize that the good and innocent qualities of childhood required more understanding and gentle care and less stringent discipline. Jacob Abbott was the author of numerous popular texts that reflected this gentler view of the child's innate nature and encouraged a more lenient parental role. The benevolent attitude toward children found in the childrearing literature in the years after the Civil War was in part a reflection of a growing secularization of American values and the increased enjoyment of material prosperity. But, in addition, children were the beneficiaries of widespread reevaluation of the relationship between a person's behavior and the aspects of the social and physical environment.

Before the Civil War, poverty, illness, intemperance, and criminality were viewed primarily as failures of individuals—as weaknesses that could be corrected only by the imposition of a discipline awakened by personal commitment to improvement. In the last half of the nineteenth century, the causes and consequences of dependence came to be looked on more sympathetically. Personal failings came to be attributed to the inadequacies of the surroundings in which the delinquent and dependent person lived. In large measure, this was a reflection of the increased heterogeneity of society and a recognition that conditions beyond the control of the individual might determine personal behavior. One consequence of this attention to the environmental etiology of personal failure was the creation of institutions to care for the indigent, the sick, and the disorderly. Another consequence was a more kindly view toward dependence itself and a concern with providing the resources to promote social readjustment. As the individual was seen as less culpable, the society assumed additional responsibilities. At the same time, when individuals were found less in control of their personal lives, new reasons for the success of some and the failure of others were sought.

The perception that the status of dependence legitimatized specific requirements for growth and adjustment placed the child in a new position. Not only did it become justifiable to see childhood as a period in which adult responsibility could not be assumed, but a rationale was provided for the establishment of special institutions to care for the unique needs of children. In Michigan, for instance, a public school was opened in 1874 to support and instruct children between the ages of four and 16 who had previously been placed with indigent adults in poorhouses. Childhood victims of society's inequities must be separated from adults, it was held, inasmuch as childhood needs required special attention. The establishment of institutions in which children were the specific focus of concern awakened further interest in the special developmental characteristics of children.

Acknowledgement of the dependence of children led to the possibility of special remedial attention. In a report to the National Conference of Charities and Correction in 1892, H. H. Hart noted that, among the 25 million children in the United States under the age of 16, nearly 100,000 did not receive sufficient attention from their families. In the course of the debate between those who argued for placing these neglected children in institutions and those who argued for placing them in the homes of stable families, the idea emerged that both the physical status and the psychological status of children needed evaluation. In Hart's opinion, "wherever the dependent child is, whether in a foster home or in an institution, he will make little headway if left to himself and his environment. He must have the society, or better, comradeship, as well as the instruction of older people who are interested in him. He must be known and trained according to his personal and individual characteristics and not merely by a name or number."[5] The importance of assessing individual differences in order to effect optimal rehabilitation rested on a new sense of obligation to the child. With very few tools available for measurement and little established knowledge on developmental stages, most remedial efforts were based on long-held assumptions about the wholesomeness of work within a well-regulated environment in which both affection and discipline were displayed in appropriate proportions.

In those days, many people expected that children would work alongside adults and would keep pace with them. An English survey reflecting contemporary notions of child development was undertaken by several physicians in 1833. A survey of 28 professional colleagues drawn up by Dr. Bissett Hawkins showed that only two considered a 12-hour work day excessive for the young. The 20 who suggested that a 10-hour day was more appropriate did so out of concern for the children's moral instruction; because many worked a 6-day week, they did not attend Sunday school, and those who did were too fatigued to concentrate. Although such working conditions were less common in America at the time, their absence was a reflection of the slow development of industry rather than of expectations for an appropriate childhood environment. In this country, as in England, children's work was more likely to be determined by their parents' social standing than by their chronological age. Whenever labor shortages have made it plausible to recruit the young, the children have been part of the work force. In the United States, the need for agricultural labor drew children to the fields and canneries throughout the nineteenth century. Right up to the present, the persistent aura of romantic attitudes toward work outdoors has exempted the children of the poor and migrant workers from protective legislation.

Where work was deemed valuable in strengthening physical and social well-being, the focus of regulation was on allowing sufficient time for schooling rather than on protection from hazards or exploitation. According to the United States census reports of 1870, one of every eight children between 10 and 15 years old was gainfully employed. Only after the turn of the century did child-labor reformers examine the consequences of work for the physical and psychological health of the child. The reformers examined the work of students of child development, such as G. Stanley Hall, for evidence that normal development proceeded slowly and through definable stages. According to Hall, play, as well as work and learning, had its place in the growth and development of the normal child. Hall's warning that interference with appropriate growth stages would not only injure the individual but also impair the evolution of society was cited. Although it was argued that from both the biological and the educational points of view work might well be damaging to children, attempts to establish state and federal laws failed to change the conditions under which children could work. In 1900, 24 states and the District of Columbia did not restrict children's work in any way, and, although 45 states had some regulatory statutes by 1915, the nature of these provisions made it easy for employers and workers to avoid confrontation with the law. Children who worked on farms or in industries related to the production of food were ordinarily not protected by any legislation because these workplaces were believed inherently "healthy" or because their work was done within the context of family occupation.

A small group of educated men and women devoted to the growing movement for "child conservation" cited the work of Hall, John Fiske, and other scientists studying human development and social organization to bolster their demands for protective laws and institutions. [6] Those arguing against such regulation continued to refer to the desirable benefits of work and to defend the rights of parents, as opposed to the state, to control the employment of their children. One must conclude that in the long run neither the study of child development nor the explication of the stages of normal childhood maturation benefited the movement to restrict child labor; the protection of children from the damaging consequences of work has come about only when work was unavailable. Unemployment of adults, particularly during the economic depression of the 1930s, has had a far greater effect on eliminating child labor from fields and factories than have empirical studies of child growth and development. [7]

Continued reliance on the family to provide the best environment for growth effectively removed the child from some of the advantages sought by social-welfare reformers at the beginning of the twentieth century. Parental prerogatives to raise and educate children supported arguments against outside intervention, whether by private agencies or by the state. Except for schooling, the family remained, in the eyes of most Americans, the proper locus for early socialization. Throughout the nineteenth and early twentieth centuries the schoolroom itself was treated by many as an extension of the home environment. The schoolteacher was regarded as a surrogate parent, rather than as an expert in his or her own right. The elevation of the mother's status as disciplinarian, moral adviser, and model made it entirely reasonable for children of both sexes to be trained almost always by women. In the schools, the demand for women teachers increased until, by 1870, women constituted almost 60 percent of the teaching force—a proportion that rose to over 70 percent by 1900. Stressed though the schools were by the influx of children from foreign backgrounds and by the expectation that they would give children the skills and models necessary for adjustment to adult life, they were an acceptable setting for the management of childhood.

At a time when scientific knowledge was growing rapidly and the application of knowledge derived from science was expected to have widespread social utility, results of empirical studies of child development could be legitimately incorporated into pedagogy. One must, therefore, look to the school for evidence of a new perception of the importance of childhood in the formation of character. In the texts for teachers there is evidence of interest in the importance of the environment and the implications of evolutionary biology for understanding and shaping human development. In the United States, the reception of Darwin's hypothesis on evolution had important implications for social practices and institutions. The question of whether natural selection through the struggle for survival implied the abdication of responsibility for the weak and deficient was debated. The special characteristics that distinguished human infancy from that of animals inevitably attracted attention. "It will appear that it was the lengthening of infancy which ages ago gradually converted our forefathers from brute creatures into human creatures," said John Fiske in a lecture delivered at Harvard in 1871 on "The Meaning of Infancy." In an introduction to the published version of Fiske's lecture, Professor Henry Suzzalo, of Teachers College, Columbia University, noted the special contribution of evolutionary biology to educational precepts:

If the democratic movement emphasized the factor of social adjustment in the school's function, it was the scientific movement of the last half-century which drew attention to infancy as a superior opportunity to sculpt final adjustment. Among all the contributions of modern evolutionary science to educational thought, none is more striking or more far-reaching in its implications than that special group of generalizations which states that the biological function of a prolonged infancy in man is to educate the child. By interpreting this period of helpless dependence as one of plasticity and opportunity, it implied that man's power to adjust to the varied and complex conditions of life was due to his educability, which in turn was the result of his prolonged childhood. [8]

The relative importance of the environment and heredity—the assessment of whether nurture or nature is more important in determining adult potentialities—was to be of practical import in the education of the young.

Science had something to say about the role of experience in two critical respects—intellectual growth and character formation. For Fiske and other students of evolution, the interaction between experience and the gradually maturing person replaced the notion of the mind as a *tabula rasa*. Fiske wrote,

As mental life [becomes] more complex and various, as the things to be learned [keep] ever multiplying, less and less can be done before birth and more and more must be left to be done in the earlier years of life. So instead of being born with a few simple capacities thoroughly organized, man came at last to be born with the germs of many complex capacities which were reserved to be unfolded and enhanced or checked and stifled by the incidents of personal experience in each individual. In this simple yet wonderful way there has been provided for man a long period during which his mind is plastic and malleable, and the length of this period has increased with civilization until it now covers nearly one-third of our lives.[9]

The implications of this outlook for the individual child were of extraordinary significance. Furthermore, in Fiske's view, it was the educability of the infant that assured the progress of civilization itself. The dependence of childhood created the necessity of the family, and in family "the rude beginnings of human morality" were fashioned. Evolutionary theory brought a new dimension to infancy and to the nurturing role of the family as the source of social stability. The school, as the other major influence on children, attained additional importance.

Not only was the school an important locus of institutional socialization: it also provided a potential laboratory for the observation and study of children and an environment in which children "at risk" could be identified. During the last two decades of the nineteenth century, discussion of the school's philosophy and daily examination of children to discover physical defects and signs of impending illness were endorsed by forward-looking communities as part of an effort to improve health through the application of scientific knowledge. A report from the physician who directed medical inspection of Boston schoolchildren in 1897 stated that the youngsters were often "unaware of the fact that they were suffering from infectious diseases." He described the advantages of the program that had recently been instituted:

There are about 85,000 pupils and over 1,500 teachers in the public schools and about 13,000 in the parochial schools of Boston which furnishes a wide field and the best opportunity for the exercise of professional observation and sanitary precautions against the diseases of childhood incident to school attendance. This work has now been in successful operation in Boston for over two years and seven months, has constantly grown in favor in the medical profession, among school teachers and in the community at large. There is every reason to suppose that under the influence of this daily medical attention every teacher will become more interested and expert in the outlook for and detection of any existing illness among the children under his or her care. [10]

This program for medical inspection was complemented by other systematic observations of children in school.

In general medical practice, the life experience of the infant and young child also assumed a new importance at the end of the nineteenth century. Medical texts on the care of infants gave much attention to their physical needs. These needs were seen as relatively precise and measurable, and the standards established were believed applicable to all normal infants, with little consideration of individual differences. L. Emmett Holt's *The Care and Feeding of Children,* first published in 1894, provided a good example of the systematized approach to infant care. Everything possible was regulated, including the times and numbers of feedings; the quantity of food given; the temperature of the nursery; the precise time of bathing and the order in which its face, body, and limbs were washed; and the amount of sleep required. [11]

As the practice of pediatrics grew, other facets of infant development increased in importance. Abraham Jacobi reminded a St. Louis audience in 1904 that, "in infancy and childhood, before the dangerous period of puberty sets in, the character is formed, altruism inculcated, or criminality fostered." Jacobi, too, was interested in establishing criteria for the major determinants and stages of maturation. The period of infancy represented an unparalleled opportunity for observation of normal growth and for the generation of scientific hypotheses that would aid medicine to provide adequate and effective treatment of the sick. "Infancy and childhood," wrote Jacobi, "do not begin with the day of birth. From the conception to the termination of fetal life evolution is gradual. The result of the conception depends on parents and ancestors. Nowhere are the laws of heredity more perceptible than in the structure and nature of the child." Reflecting the influence of his American environment more than his own European heritage, Jacobi continued: "Hereditary degeneracy is often caused by social influences. The immoral conditions created by our financial system make women select not the strong and hearty and the young husband, but the rich and old, with the result of having less, and less vigorous, children."[12] As a physician, Jacobi had an additional reason to focus on the infant. Disease itself could be better understood, he believed, when studied in the very young. Altogether systematic comparison of pathology in immature and mature organisms seemed a useful method for the development of scientific medicine. It seemed to Jacobi that disease might appear in its simplest form in the infant or young child: "A great many diseased conditions cannot be thoroughly understood unless they be studied in the evolving being," he said. It seemed likely that study of the infant would also reveal a new functional concept of immaturity that would illuminate the complex process of growth. Different kinds of behavior had different implications when they appeared at early stages of development. Masturbation, the ubiquitous cause of all manner of mental, physical, and moral aberration to the nineteenth-century diagnostician, appeared less indicative of pathology and less potentially damaging in the young child: "In the large majority of instances masturbation, frequent though it be, has not in the very young the same perils that are attended with it later on when the differentiation of sex has been completed and is recognized," Jacobi reported. His pronouncement was unusual for his time, and his influence on the developing field of pediatrics proved to be significant. Although the specific influence of early childhood experience on later life could not be precisely described, child behavior began to be established as a legitimate subject for scientific investigation.

It is impossible to assess accurately how influential these first studies of infancy and childhood were outside the sickroom and the classroom. The larger implications derived from observational studies stimulated little support in the United States during the first decades of the twentieth century. The notions of the plasticity of the infant and the malleability of the young child did not easily assuage fears about the influx of foreign "degenerates" and the possibilities of "race suicide" as a result of the reduction of native white fertility. Yet some of the lessons implied by studies of the child supported practices that had become part of an American tradition. Parental guidance from within the family retained its honored place. Learning theory brought scientific confirmation of common sense and affirmed the desirability of providing the infant and young child with consistent love and response appropriate to age. From Edward Thorndike's laboratory at Teachers College, Columbia, came evidence to support parents' efforts to educate their children through rewards and punishment. Furthermore, Thorndike's work encouraged attention to the infant, as well as the school-age child, and legitimized pleasurable experience as an aid to later learning and development. Such notions lent scientific credibility to the popular hope that all children might attain some degree of accomplishment.

Evidence that an infant's experience was critical for later development in no way contradicted the importance of the parent as the primary influence in the child's life. Scientific study confirmed, rather than disputed, the belief that opportunity lay ahead for each infant at birth. Scientific study also seemed to indicate that the child should not be overly protected, but should be exposed to a variety of experiences.

Notes and References

1. Morgan, E. S. *The Puritan Family: Religion and Domestic Relations in Seventeenth-Century New England.* New York: Harper and Row, 1944.

2. Bailyn, B. *Education in the Forming of American Society. Needs and Opportunities for Study.* Chapel Hill, N.C.: University of North Carolina Press, 1960. See also: M Vinovskis and D. Mean. A ray of millenial light: Infant education in Massachusetts, 1820–1840. In T. K. Hareven, Ed. *Families and Kin in Urban Communities, 1700–1930.* New York: Watts, 1977.

3. Demos, J. *Little Commonwealth: Family Life in Plymouth Colony.* New York: Oxford University Press, 1970.

4. An American matron. *The Maternal Physician; A Treatise on the Nurture and Management of Infants, from the Birth Until Two Years Old. Being the Result of Sixteen Years' Experience in the Nursery.* pp. 159–160. New York: Arno Press, 1972. As noted in the introduction by Charles E. Rosenberg, the "approved medical authors" were all British: William Buchan, Michael Underwood, Hugh Smith, and George Wallis.

5. Hart, H. H. "The economic aspect of the child health problem." *Proceedings of the National Conference of Charities and Corrections*, 1892. In Robert H. Bremner, Ed. *Children and Youth in America*, Vol. II, p. 283. Cambridge, Mass.: Harvard University Press, 1971. *See also:* R. Reeder. *How Two Hundred Children Live and Learn*. New York, 1910. Quoted in Bremner, *Children and Youth in America*, p. 303.

6. See, for example, Raymond G. Fuller. "The psychological approach to the child labor problem." *The American Child, 2*, 119–127, 1920. Fuller was an editor of *American Child*, which was the official bulletin of the National Child Labor Committee dedicated towards the amelioration of poor living and learning conditions for all American children.

7. Felt, J. *Hostages of Fortune: Child Labor Reform in New York State*. Syracuse, N.Y.: Syracuse University Press, 1965. See also: A. M. Platt. *The Child Savers: The Invention of Delinquency.* Chicago: University of Chicago Press, 1969.

8. Fiske, J. *The Meaning of Infancy.* Teachers College, Columbia University, 1871. H. Suzzalo, Ed. Cambridge, Mass.: Riverside Educational Monograph, 1909. p. viii.

9. Ibid., p. 10.

10. Durgin, S. H. *Medical Inspection of Schools* (Boston, 1897). In R. H. Bremner, *Children and Youth in America*, Vol. II, p. 906. Cambridge, Mass.: Harvard University Press, 1971.

11. The booklet, in question-and-answer form, provided instructions without detailed explanation—e.g., "How can a baby be taught to be regular in habits of eating and sleeping? By always feeding at regular intervals and putting to sleep at exactly the same time every day and evening." L. E. Holt. *The Care and Feeding of Children,* pp. 1–46. New York: D. Appleton, 1894.

12. Jacobi, A. "The history of pediatrics and its relation to other sciences and arts." Address to the Congress of Arts and Sciences, St. Louis, Missouri, 1904. *Amer. Med.* 8:795–805, November 1904; and *Contributions to American Pediatrics*, Vol. I, ed. W. J. Robinson, pp. 55–93, New York, 1909.

2

The First
Empirical Studies

Although concern for the child and uncertainty about complexities of childhood were probably as strong in Puritan New England as they are today, a major change occurred in the middle of the nineteenth century, when the child changed from an issue for discussion to an object of scientific observation. Children began to be measured, weighed, observed, and described, in the hope that the collected information could be used to facilitate understanding of their growth. It was agreed that investigation pertaining to children would be pragmatic in its intention, nontheoretical, and focused primarily on their educational progress. Thus, the studies of children still had the marks of Puritanism and were riddled with the philosophical views that we have come to call materialistic, pragmatic, and empirical. Early studies rested on the assumptions that children—separate from their parents, their kin, and their community—could be deciphered and that objective knowledge would benefit their status, health, and progress.

As might be expected, the first observations to be made were dictated by relatively practical considerations—namely, what variables were easy to measure and in what places could they conveniently be measured. The emergence of new pediatric hospitals, public schools, and industries brought together large numbers of children under one roof, which seemed to create ideal situations for quantitative evaluations. The first extensive survey, conducted by the 1833 Factories Inquiries Commission in England, was designed to answer economic rather than scientific questions. Its main goal was to discover whether children could work 12 hours a day without obvious physical damage. Their religious and moral education was of some concern to the commissioners of inquiry, but no attention was paid to the influence of full-time factory employment on intellectual or emotional development. However, buried deep in the voluminous medical reports was perhaps the first attempt to demonstrate environmental effects on physical growth.[1] In his report to the Factories Inquiries Commission, John W. Cowell, a surgeon, included tables of heights and weights showing that children employed in the mills were shorter and lighter than local nonworking children of corresponding ages.

Growth studies of children of elementary school age did not get under way until about 1870, when public education had become the norm in most Western countries. The aim of these anthropometric studies was to discover whether heredity or environment was the major determinant of growth and whether physical measurements could be used to predict mental ability.[2] It was thought that the outcome would be of practical as well as scientific interest because it might give educators reliable methods of categorizing their pupils to avoid placing children of disparate ability and disposition toward schoolwork in the same classroom. Several decades later, large, unmanageable classes brought Binet and Simon to invent the first intelligence test that categorized children through intellectual assessments rather than physical measurements.

But, in the 1870s, growth studies seemed the obvious way to proceed and they were enthusiastically undertaken in America, Germany, France, Sweden, Denmark, England, Austria, and elsewhere. Researchers soon discovered that many variables other than sex and age needed to be considered. It was suggested that race, social and nutritional environment, occupation, and climate might influence growth, but there was little agreement as to which variable was dominant. Given the novelty of such studies, one difficulty was that there was little uniformity in measurement; direct comparison of results was usually impossible. There was no common standard even for such a variable as age. Some researchers took the average figure for the children in a given grade, some specified the exact age for each child, and some rounded it off to the nearest whole number.

Studies to determine growth variables and their interdependence were nevertheless launched in many countries. In the United States, Henry P. Bowditch, assistant professor of physiology at Harvard Medical School, had over 24,000 Boston schoolchildren weighed and measured during 1875.[3] In his first report, published in 1877, he showed that children of American parentage tended to be both taller and heavier at any given age than those of Irish parentage. He concluded that their superior size was due in part to a more favorable environment because the

American families usually enjoyed a more varied diet and better housing than the poorer immigrants, and in part to the inheritance of more beneficial racial characteristics. (In the late nineteenth century, the term *race* was commonly used to denote a nation of people considered of common stock.) Bowditch then tried to determine which was the more important factor by tabulating the observations for each nationality—in this instance, American- or Irish-born—according to the occupation of the parents. Although the results indicated that rate of growth of a child depended more heavily on racial origin than on whether parents were professionals, merchants, or skilled or unskilled laborers, Bowditch was not convinced of their general validity. He noted that an English surgeon, Charles Roberts, had found that social status was distinctly associated with growth rate, and he concluded that this influence must have been masked in the Boston survey because of the difficulty in classifying people accurately according to occupation. Classification was much easier to accomplish in England, because there the population was relatively homogeneous and static. Taking this consideration into account, Bowditch concluded that "the importance of mode of life, as a factor in determining the size of growing children in this community [Boston] is at least equal to, and possibly even greater than, that of race."[4]

The possibility of a relation between physical size and mental development was of great interest to researchers. From his extensive examinations of St. Louis schoolchildren, William Porter, a physiologist, obtained data showing that at any given age the precocious children tended to be heavier and the dull children lighter than the average child. From this he concluded that there was a "physical basis of precocity and dullness."[5] The anthropologist Franz Boas disagreed with this interpretation, arguing that the less favorably developed children should be labeled "retarded," rather than "dull," because they might undergo rapid development later and become quite intelligent. He also pointed out that Porter's data showed only "that mental and physical growth are correlated, or depend on common causes; not that mental development depends on physical growth."[6]

Porter and Francis Warner in England proposed that a child's physical condition could be used to predict mental development, implicitly suggesting that the rate of change in both mental and physical growth remained constant for each individual.[7] Boas opposed this theory, showing that Porter's growth curves could be better interpreted by assuming that the rate of physical growth varied throughout childhood:

As a matter of fact, three factors condition the rate of growth: hereditary influences, the preceding life story of the individual and the average conditions during the period under consideration, and it is quite unlikely that these factors should always be found to stand in such a relation as to result in general stability of percentile grades.[8]

Boas further pointed out that physically fit children would make more rapid intellectual progress because they would attend school more often than those children who were frequently ill. This did not mean that they were inherently brighter than those who were less healthy. (This debate has its modern form in contemporary inquiries into the relation of malnutrition and mental development.)

Boas seems to have realized the limitations of statistical studies more clearly than most. He repeatedly pointed out that a positive correlation between a pair of growth factors did not necessarily imply a causal relation between the two. At a time when most scientists assumed that development was mainly influenced by either heredity or environment, he stressed that it was far more likely to be the complex product of both factors acting over time. In the same vein, he later argued that culture reflected the social and historical experiences of its constituent people, and not merely their hereditary racial endowments, as assumed by many anthropologists and by eugenicists.[9]

Nineteenth-Century Studies and Theories of Infant Psychosocial Development

Although groups of schoolchildren provided a unique opportunity for statistical growth studies, some researchers elected to solve developmental problems in a different manner—namely, by observing the changes that occurred in individual infants. Most then made a more or less detailed description of the behavior of the baby, but some psychologists, notably Wilhelm Preyer and James Mark Baldwin, went further and presented developmental theories based in part on the observations made on their own infants—a technique Jean Piaget was also to use years later.

The more descriptive sketches are called by many "the baby biographies." The first such diary to be published (1787) was written by Dietrich Tiedemann, a German historian of philosophy. From it we can gain hints of late eighteenth century concepts of the nature of childhood.

Tiedemann noted actions that seemed to demonstrate the superiority of the child over the young animal of a similar age. Soon after birth, the infant followed moving objects with his eyes; his father then interpreted this as evidence that "man, being ordained for higher purposes, seeks from the beginning to expand his ideas without regard to his physical needs, and finds entertainment even when he is not driven by sensuous desires."[10] Tiedemann attributed the cause of this difference to the higher degree of activity of the human soul. He found evidence of this in the fact that infants gradually required less and less sleep, whereas animals "if they have abundance of food, so they are not moved to action by hunger and thirst, sleep the live-long day."[11] Tiedemann concluded that the older human infant remained awake longer, in contrast with most animals, because his mind was constantly gathering ideas and thus not permitting his body to rest. At first, the differences between animal and child nature were quantitative, rather than qualitative. Later, when such faculties as memory, thought, and judgment, the truly human properties of the mind, appeared in the child, Tiedemann no longer compared him with lower animals.

Few baby biographies were published in the early nineteenth century, but more were published after about 1875[12]; then Hippolyte Taine published his observations on the acquisition of language by a little girl. He drew attention to the differences in mental capacities between this child and animals, but treated these variations as matters of degree and not of kind. "Delicacy of impressions and delicacy of expressions are in fact the distinctive characteristics of man among animals and . . . are the source in him of language and of general ideas."[13] Taine ended his sketch with a brief reference to recapitulation theory, which was then finding extensive theoretical biologic application:

Speaking generally, the child presents in a passing state the mental characteristics that are found in a fixed state in primitive civilizations, very much as the human embryo presents in a passing state the physical characteristics that are found in a fixed state in the classes of inferior animals.[14]

The reading of Taine's report in *Mind* (1877) stimulated Charles Darwin to publish an account of his infant son's development, which he had written 37 years earlier.[15] His main object had been to observe emotional development and the time of appearance of the various faculties. Thus, he kept a record of the earliest discernible signs of anger, fear, pleasure, affection, moral sense, shyness, the association of ideas implying rational thought, and so on. At one point in the account he said, "The facility with which associated ideas due to instruction and others spontaneously arising were acquired, seemed to me by far the most strongly marked of all the distinctions between the mind of an infant and that of the cleverest full-grown dog that I have ever known." Clearly, Darwin did not consider intelligent behavior peculiar to human beings, but he noted that they showed signs of their greater potential early in life.[16]

Incidentally, Darwin seems to have believed that children were fundamentally social beings, not wild animals that needed to be tamed. He related that by the age of 2 years his son had never been punished in any way but rather had been "educated solely by working on his good feelings." And, according to the kindly father, this method worked, for the child "soon became as truthful, open, and tender, as anyone could desire."[17]

Darwin's contribution prompted the publication of more baby biographies. Some, such as Millicent Shinn's *Notes on the Development of a Child* (1893), were voluminous, but almost entirely descriptive.[18] Most were concerned with the development of one or two children as observed by a relative, usually the father. The first full-length book of this nature to be published, Bernard Perez's *The First Three Years of Childhood* (1878), was unusual in that it was based on observations of several presumably middle-class French children rather than on the usual one or two.[19] Like Darwin, he noted the timing of the appearance of the various faculties and sentiments, observing that Tiedemann's child seemed "much too precocious." He observed that the faculties were not of the same intensity in each child, and he suggested that physiognomy (the determination of character and disposition from facial features) might provide a means of discovering, even before the child could speak, whether he had a good or bad memory. If bad, it could be improved by special exercise and training:

Then, too, it will be possible, and very useful, to be able from the first months of life to distinguish between the original aptitudes of the memory and those acquired under the influence of various circumstances, to mark the union and the conflict of the one with the other, in a word, to determine how far exercise and education modify the memory, as a whole and in its special adaptions.[20]

Neither the doctrine of innate ideas nor that of pure associationism was held by Perez, Preyer, or Baldwin. Instead, they seem to have subscribed to evolutionary associationism, a compromise doctrine first suggested by Herbert Spencer. (The process by which he reached his theory has recently been detailed by Robert M. Young.[21]) In brief, Spencer objected to sensationalism because it could not explain individual and species differences and it "ignored the fundamental importance of the biological endowment of varying brain structures."[22] With a simple *tabula rasa* view of the mind, all animals should be as educable as man.

Spencer solved the problem, while retaining associationism, by positing that the accumulated experiences of the race could be inherited and thus become the instincts or innate ideas of the individual.

By replacing the *tabula rasa* of the individual with that of the race, Spencer was able to retain the basic position of sensationalism while recognizing the inherited biological endowments in the nervous system, and avoiding the risk of the rationalist belief in innate ideas.[23]

Admittedly, Spencer implied a Lamarckian mode of inheritance, but at the time the transmission of acquired characteristics seemed the most likely method of adaptive change. It was acceptable to Hall, Preyer, and Baldwin, who to some extent adopted evolutionary associationism as an underpinning to their writings on child development. Apparent confirmation for this evolutionary interpretation of mental development was provided by recapitulation doctrine. All in all, Spencer's thesis was most attractive to the biologically oriented developmentalist.

Its influence on Preyer can be detected in the preface of his first biographic work, *The Mind of the Child*:

The mind of the new-born child, then, does not resemble a *tabula rasa*, upon which the senses first write their impressions; so that out of these the sum-total of our mental life arises through manifold reciprocal action, but the tablet is already written upon before birth, with many illegible, nay, unrecognizable and invisible, marks, the traces of the imprint of countless sensuous impressions of long-gone generations. . . . But the more attentively the child is observed, the more easily legible becomes the writing, not at first to be understood, that he brings with him into the world. Then we perceive what a capital each individual has inherited from his ancestors—how much there is that is not produced by sense-impressions, and how false is the supposition that man learns to feel, to will, and to think, only through his senses.[24]

In his later work, *Mental Development in the Child,* Preyer suggested that the observation of savage as well as of civilized infants would probably reveal a remarkable similarity between the first concepts they formed, whatever their culture or race. This would not prove the existence of innate ideas, but rather the similarity of the early environment enjoyed by all neonates.

In consequence of external impressions acting always in the same way during countless generations in the human race, and even in the mammals, in the very first period of life, the child has in every instance adjusted his brain to the same way of receiving nourishment through milk, and to what goes along with that; and hence it cannot seem strange that all human children in their very first period of human life think precisely the same thing. [25]

Each baby's environment would become more specific later in infancy, when, with education, it would act "to modify the condition and character of the human being."

The most complete genetic theory of development was offered by Baldwin in *The Mental Development of the Child and the Race* (1894). Being of philosophical bent, he decried the use of observation or experiment without a theory as directive:

That most vicious and Philistine attempt in some quarters to put science in the strait-jacket of barren observation, to draw the life blood of all sciences—speculative advance into the meaning of things—this ultra-positivistic cry has come here as everywhere else, and put a ban on theory. On the contrary, give us theories, theories, always theories. [26]

In *Mental Development of the Child and the Race,* Baldwin set out a developmental theory that explained how the young child adapted to novel experience and in the process ac-

quired new and useful habits. His synthesis was remarkably prophetic of the two major theories of the twentieth
century, in that he combined what were to become the
firmest principles of behaviorism with the essentials of
Piaget's ideas.[27] He defined habit as "the tendency of an
organism to continue more and more readily processes
which are vitally beneficial."[28] Through accommodation,
more complex habits would be formed or old ones disin-
tegrated and replaced by more appropriate ones—the
seminal principle of learning theory.

　　Baldwin defined his two most vital concepts—accommodation and habit—repeatedly.

The two great principles of Habit and Accommodation have
been noted, simply, and we have intimated incidentally that by
them two great gains are made possible to the organism: first,
the repetition of what is worth repeating, with the conservation
of this worth: this is Habit; and, second, the adaption of this
organism to new conditions, so that it secures, progressively,
further useful reactions, which at an earlier stage would have
been impossible: this is Accommodation.[29]

But continued accommodation was possible only "because
the other principle, *Habit*, all the time conserves the past
and gives *points d'appui* in solidified structure for new ac-
commodations."[30] Furthermore, these habits imprinted as
mental structures could be revived as memories to become the basis of "volition." Learning also occurred
through imitation, in which the memory of a model's actions served as repetitive stimulation for motor movement, until by trial and error the child had acquired the
requisite skill.

　　Baldwin saw the infant as an active organism that
matured under genetic influences while adapting to the
environment through accommodation, acquisition of use-

ful habits, and distintegration of habits that were no longer functional. He realized that sensation and stimuli formed part of the learning process, but he did not stress them because he, like Hall and Preyer, assumed the existence of a normal supportive environment. Instead, he emphasized the phylogenetic nature of development and the idea that mental growth was primarily the consequence of the organism's own activity, and thus provided a functional psychology to replace the traditional belief that the various mental faculties simply appeared during development.

In the main, Baldwin was ignored because his ideas were too speculative to impress contemporary psychologists.[31] True, he had provided some data, based on observations of his two daughters, but the links between this meager empirical evidence and his generalizations were too tenuous to be persuasive. He was a theorist, his writing style was often complicated, and he would probably make little sense, even today, had it not been for Piaget's massive contributions in the same tradition.

G. Stanley Hall

The first major child psychologist who not only retained the concern with growth and pragmatic goals but combined it with a new emphasis on gathering scientific data about large numbers of children was G. Stanley Hall.[32] The child-study movement that Hall initiated in 1891 was designed to provide as complete a description as possible of the child from birth through adolescence. Nothing was to be excluded: thought, emotions, and behavior were to be charted and listed by drafting the citizenry to aid in

this monumental task.[33] Parents and teachers from all
parts of the United States and later Europe were asked to
make as many observations as possible of child behavior
and report them to Hall. It was a census of children, with
Hall assuming that asking about hitting, crying, and pout-
ing was essentially no different from asking, "How many
people sleep in this house?" Hall and his associates at
Clark University would be the demographers, examining
the corpus of information and from it constructing a composite picture of the mental and physical development of
children. It was assumed that these data, when processed
through the minds of Hall and his colleagues, would yield
a small number of general concepts that could be disseminated to teachers and parents as guidelines for
changes in educational and childrearing methods. The survey was descriptive and atheoretical, and was intended
to follow Baconian principles.[34]

Hall proposed two ways to study children.[35] Interested citizens were to send in case studies on individual children, both normal and retarded or delinquent.
These letters were to describe the behavior as fully as
possible. Parents were to keep a daily log, a kind of "life
book," of their children's acts, desires, and diseases. In
addition to these diaries, experts were to send out a series
of questions—perhaps the first questionnaires about
children—on single topics, such as children's fears or
their anger. These questionnaires would be circulated
widely (see Appendix A). The respondent, whether teacher or parent, was to obtain as many answers as possible according to a format that Hall had suggested. Hall
was enthusiastic about the questionnaire, and he issued
194 between 1894 and 1915 (see Appendix B). Because he
did not have the resources to create an experimental laboratory school at Clark—one existed at Columbia Univer-

sity Teachers College and another at the University of Chicago[36]—he was confined to this less expensive method of learning about children. However, his unwillingness to set rigid criteria and firm definitions for the behavior that he wanted his unpaid assistants to code led the surveys to degenerate into accumulations of ambiguous, anecdotal information that was essentially uninterpretable. By 1923, Hall realized that his choice of method had been poor and ruefully admitted that it had been a mistake to proceed without firmer ground rules. "In such ways vast bodies of data were accumulated and sent to us in response to some of the more popular questionnaires and it was a very perplexing question how to make the net result of it all into anything like a composite photograph of the subject point by point," he said.[37] Hall's hope that child study would provide the data to support the genetic psychology to which he was so firmly committed was not realized.[38]

Hall based his work on the popular doctrine of recapitulation, which has been mentioned earlier, known also as the biogenetic law. In summary, this assumption stated that a higher organism, such as a child, passed through developmental stages that were apparently identical with those of lower forms—such as fish, reptiles, and primates—from which human beings had evolved. In a sense, the infant was expected to show the behavior of an adult amphibian, inasmuch as the actions of a young member of a higher form should resemble the more mature behavior of a lower form. In this way, the assumption of continuity could be satisfied. This view was originally formulated by comparative embryologists. After its popularization by Ernst Haekel in the 1860s, it was believed to have wider applications and to be a general law of nature.[39] Hall extended recapitulation doctrine into child psychology, viewing postnatal development as a series of distinct stages representing the evolutionary history of man. On this principle, human infancy represented the higher vertebrate period, early childhood the simian stage, middle childhood the savage stage, and adolescence "the infancy of man's higher nature, when he receives from great all-mother his last capital of energy and evolutionary momentum."[40] Natural or more primitive mental patterns were adduced to explain why children enjoyed myth and melodrama, primitive colors, crude ways of eating, fighting, climbing, and running, and even why children tended to lie, steal, and bully. If atavistic behavior was not obvious, although one could find it in lower forms of animal life, it was because of adaption to a more civilized modern social and cultural environment. In a sense, children fight because animals fight—a doctrine that was recast in different words years later, in Lorenz's book on aggression.

The child, uncivilized and to some extent even savage, is precociously thrust into an environment saturated with adult influences because of language and accumulated grown-up customs, traditions, and ideas; and for this reason as well as because of its intense, imitative propensities tends to be very early stripped of many of its psychic rudiments and recapitulatory traces. Yet the more we know the child, the more clearly do we see the germs of many atavistic tendencies nipped in the bud, though many of them have so long been.[41]

Hall's writings and lectures revitalized Rousseau's view of childhood as a series of discrete mental and physical stages culminating in adolescence. A scientific theory —recapitulation doctrine—made the notion of stages more persuasive and less speculative. This attractiveness was short-lived, for by the late nineteenth century, embryologists had collected enough empirical evidence to render a literal interpretation of recapitulation theory improbable. Early in the twentieth century, the doctrine was rejected by most child psychologists, except perhaps those at Clark University.[42] The loss of support from biology removed the spine of Hall's genetic psychology, and the data he had gathered were seen by more objective researchers as subjective and sentimental.

Hall was not particularly concerned with the infant because his methods required that children be able to express their motives and feelings. He assumed that some of the primitive traits present in the newborn infant would persist through life, although overlaid by more recent phylogenetic characteristics acquired throughout childhood. He believed to some extent that early experience influenced later emotional development, and this belief was one reason for his enthusiastic support of Sigmund Freud and the theory of infantile sexuality.[43] Hall did not ignore the influence of environment in attenuating or accentuating natural impulses, but in his scheme of development the most recent experiences were the most important ones. The pragmatic goal of his research was to discover and understand feelings of the child at each stage of development and to determine the environment suitable for each age group, especially the right kind of schooling. (Hall was concerned with school reform. Notice the contrast between the concern with the emotional basis of good schooling in the 1890s and the cognitive basis of good schooling almost a century later in contemporary America. The criteria have not changed, but our theory about what is vital for educational progress has undergone a reversal.)

Hall was the first American psychologist to study the mental development of the child scientifically. In the main, he failed because he attempted to solve too complex a problem with too crude a method. The parents and teachers that he used as assistants lacked the objectivity necessary to generate useful information, and unfortunately he based his child psychology on a scientific premise that soon became outdated. He shunned statistics and experiment at a time when these methods were deemed essential to scientific inquiry.[44] His eagerness to generalize broadly from meager observations appealed to lay audiences, but irritated scientists.[45] His massive effort did, however, indicate the hitherto unsuspected complexity of the enterprise.

Arnold Gesell

Hall and Baldwin had been the outstanding exponents of the organismic concept of growth in America, and both had deplored the reductionist approach of the newer generation of experimentalists. When behaviorism came to the fore, both had already retired from active participation in academic psychology, but their developmental theories were epitomized in the work and teaching of Arnold Gesell. He had obtained a doctorate in psychology at Clark in 1906 and he confessed great admiration for Hall, whom he considered an intellectual genius, "a naturalist Darwin of the mind, whose outlook embraced the total phylum, and lifted psychology above the sterilities of excessive analysis and pedantry."[46]

Gesell saw human beings as tough organisms whose inherent maturational pattern could not easily be deformed by environmental stress or emotional pressure.

Genetic sequence is itself an expression of elaborate pattern. And the relative stability of both prenatal and postnatal ontogenesis under normal and even unusual conditions must be regarded as a significant indication of the fundamental role of maturational factors in the determination of behavior.[47]

In his mind, genetic equipment determined the sequential phases of development, which were merely modified or accentuated by environmental factors. Thus, extreme conditioning, whether favorable or not, could have only limited effects, and the integrity of the organism was safeguarded by a system of maturational checks.

A physician as well as a psychologist, Gesell supported his views with both clinical and experimental evidence. Indeed, he raised the observational study of children to a degree of sophistication undreamed of at the turn of the century. In 1919, he began a systematic longitudinal investigation of normal children from birth to the age of 6. In 1927, he directed a more detailed study, using the movie camera as an additional means of recording behavior. He also set up a homelike nursery unit with one-way viewing arrangements, so that mothers could be observed while they were interacting with their infants in as natural a manner as possible. Through such work over the years, Gesell became the leading expert on normative development.

The following kinds of evidence led Gesell to emphasize the primacy of biological maturation, rather than experience, in determining behavior. First, he noted the regular appearance of such skills as grasping, sitting, standing, and walking. Not only did all normal infants exhibit the capacity to perform these activities at approximately the same time and in the same order, but they also went through similar stages in perfecting such skills. Second, he observed a general correspondence in the development of behavior patterns in identical twins, in spite of different training.[48] Third, he pointed out sequential changes in an infant's emotional behavior that could be better explained by the action of maturation than by that of conditioning. For example, although 10-week-old infants would not protest when put into a small enclosed space, at 20 weeks they would display mild apprehension and restlessness, and at 30 weeks they would cry loudly in extreme fear or intolerance. "Is not this a genetic gradation of fear behavior which is based upon maturational sequence rather than upon an historical sequence of extrinsic conditioning factors?" he asked. [49]

Yet, by 1943, Gesell was acknowledging that early environmental influences play a larger part in determining future personality. Although not concurring with any Freudian hypothesis, Gesell now suggested that early emotional experiences determined the child's future capacity of acculturation:

We wish to avoid the suggestion that the personality of infant and child is a product of emotions which operate in some mysterious way through the subconscious or otherwise. We should prefer to think of personality in less mysterious and more realistic terms as a structured end product of the child's developmental past. As such, it bears the imprint of the patterns of the culture in which he was born and reared. The early impression of the family life during the first five years leaves the most fundamental and enduring imprint. Acculturation begins in the home and the influence of the larger social groups is limited by the trends initiated through the family. [50]

The point was made, but not labored. All in all, Gesell was proposing that psychological development was constrained by biological factors—a posture that is now popular again: heredity sets a pattern that can be altered by environmental influences, but organisms lose their plasticity after a few years as permanent structures evolve.

Notes and References

1. *British Parliamentary Papers,* XX, D 1, p. 87, 1833.

2. Burk, F. "Growth of children in height and weight." *Amer. J. Psychol.* 9:253–326, 1898. Review and analysis of the major growth studies carried out in the United States and Europe.

3. Bowditch, H. P. "The growth of children." *Eighth Annual Report of the State Board of Health of Mass.* 8:275–323, 1877; "The growth of children." *Tenth Annual Report of the State Board of Health of Mass.* 10:35–62, 1879; "The growth of children studied by Galton's method of percentile grades." *Twenty-Second Annual Report of the State Board of Health of Mass.* 22:497–522, 1890.

4. Bowditch, H. P. *Tenth Annual Report,* p. 54.

5. Porter, W. T. "The relations between the growth of children and their deviation from the physical type of their sex and age." *Trans. Acad. Sci. St. Louis,* 6:243–250, 1893.

6. Boas, F. "On Dr. William Townsend Porter's investigation of the growth of the school children of St. Louis." *Science* (N.S.) 1:225–230, 1895.

7. Warner, F. *The Children: How to Study Them,* p.v. (2nd ed.) London: Francis Hodgson, 1896. Francis Warner had been engaged "in an inquiry as to the visible signs by which we may study mental states and brain action." Between 1888 and 1894, with the help of other physicians, Warner examined 100,000 schoolchildren with a view to finding correlations between physical condition and mental ability as assessed by the teacher. The results were published as a report by the Committee for the Scientific Study of the Mental and Physical Conditions of Childhood in 1885. Warner became one of the leaders of the child-study movement in England.

8. Boas, F. On Dr. William Townsend Porter's investigation, p. 229.

9. Boas was an early and persistent opponent of the eugenicist notion that some races were biologically fitter than others. See: K. M. Ludmerer. *Genetics and American Society: A Historical Appraisal,* p. 126. Baltimore: Johns Hopkins University Press, 1972.

10. Tiedemann, D. "Observations on the mental development of a child" (1748–1803), pp. 11–13. In W. Dennis, Ed. *Historical Readings in Developmental Psychology.* New York: Appleton-Century-Crofts, 1972.

11. Ibid., p. 17.

12. For a review of the early baby biographies, see: W. Dennis, "Historical beginnings of child psychology." *Psychol. Bull.* 46:224–235, 1949.

13. Taine, H. "The acquisition of language by children." *Mind* 2:252–259, 1877. First published in the *Revue Philosophique*, 1876.

14. Ibid.

15. Darwin, C. "A biographical sketch of an infant." *Mind* 2:285–294, 1877. Darwin's biographical sketch of his infant son is reprinted in W. Kessen's *The Child*, pp. 118–129. New York: John Wiley, 1965. This book contains many other readings from early works on early development and an analysis of their authors' contributions to the growth of child psychology.

16. Ibid., p. 290.

17. In his autobiography (intended for his family, not for publication), Darwin stated that not one of his children had ever given him one minute's anxiety, except on the score of health, and that they had all been pleasant, sympathetic, and affectionate to their parents and to each other. He added that he had always enjoyed playing with them when they were little. N. Barlow, Ed. *The Autobiography of Charles Darwin, 1809–1882*, p. 97. London: Collins, 1958.

18. Shinn, M. (1859–1940). "The biography of a baby" (1900). Extracts may be found in W. Dennis, Ed. *Historical Readings in Developmental Psychology.* New York: Appleton-Century-Crofts, 1972, pp. 160–167.

19. Perez, B. *The First Three Years of Childhood.* (Translated by A. M. Christie.) Chicago: A. N. Marquis & Co., 1885.

20. Ibid., p. 129. The belief that mind and body developed in parallel and that an examination of the nervous system would provide indications of mental function was implicit, as with Francis Warner.

21. Young, R. M. *Mind, Brain, and Adaptation in the Nineteenth Century: Cerebral Localization and its Biological Context from Gall to Ferrier.* Oxford: Clarendon Press, 1970.

22. Ibid., p. 173. Young has pointed out that these were the same objections that Gall made to sensationalism.

23. Ibid., p. 178.

24. Preyer, W. *The Mind of the Child. Part I. The Senses and the Will,* p. xiv. New York: D. Appleton and Co., 1890. Also quoted in W. Kessen's *The Child,* p. 132. Kessen sees Preyer as a maturationalist with a lack of enthusiasm for empirical epistemiology, but Preyer may also be interpreted as a believer in evolutionary associationism.

25. Preyer, W. T. *Mental Development in the Child,* pp. 137–138. (Translated by H. W. Brown.) New York: D. Appleton and Co., 1907.

26. Baldwin, J. M. *Mental Development in the Child and the Race.* p. 35. New York: The Macmillan Co., 1906.

27. When using a term previously employed by Baldwin, such as "circular reaction," Piaget usually carefully defined differences in semantics between himself and his predecessor. J. Piaget and B. Inhelder. *The Psychology of the Child.* (Translated from the French by H. Weaver.) New York: Basic Books, Inc., 1969.

28. Baldwin, J. M. *Mental Development in the Child and the Race,* p. 452.

29. Ibid., p. 161.

30. Ibid., p. 455.

31. Kessen, W. *The Child,* p. 165. New York: John Wiley, 1965.

32. A recent extensively documented biography of Hall is Dorothy Ross's *G. Stanley Hall: The Psychologist as Prophet* (Chicago: University of Chicago Press, 1972), which considers the child-study movement in detail (pp. 113–133, 279–394).

33. Hall hoped that the data collected would confirm his recapitulation theory of development. "The synthetic method for Hall consisted of the encyclopedic marshaling of facts in the support of a single hypothesis," according to E. G. Boring. (Boring. "The influence of evolutionary theory upon American psychological thought," p. 279. In S. Persons, Ed. *Evolutionary Thought in America*, New Haven: Yale University Press, 1950.)

34. For example, E. Harlow Russell, principal of the State Normal School, Worcester, Mass., defended the child study carried out by students on the principle that they were providing material that could be manipulated by the psychologist to yield generalizations. "If this great science is to be changed over from the deductive to the inductive side, and thus 'fall into line in the great Baconian change of base,' then we may be sure there is work cut out for more than one generation." He advocated a method of work "such as to postpone rather than hasten conclusions, and this feature is deliberately and confidently put forth as a recommendation of its character. It is expressed in the motto printed at the head of our blanks, a sentence from Darwin's autobiography: 'I worked on true Baconian principles, and without any theory collected facts on a wholesale scale. . . .' " E. H. Russell. "The study of children at the State Normal School," Worcester, Mass. *Pedagogical Seminary* 2:343–357, 1893.

35. Hall, G. S. "The methods, status, and prospects of the child-study of today." *Transact. Illinois Soc. Child-Study* 2:178–191, 1897.

36. Ross, D. G. Stanley Hall, p. 290.

37. Hall, G. S. *Life and Confessions of a Psychologist*, p. 390. New York: D. Appleton, 1923.

38. In 1894, Paul Hanus of Harvard University informed the Executive Committee of the Illinois State Teachers Association that, in his opinion, "the organized study of children to which you refer has not thus far yielded any results, not previously known, that would cause the abandonment of some prevailing methods in 'the teaching and treatment of children.' " This was in reply to a question asked by the Association, and circulated among prominent scientists, as to what teaching methods should be altered to comply with the findings of child study. (Hanus. "Results of child-study applied to education." *Transact. Illinois Soc. Child-Study* 1:30–32, 1895.) Hugo Münsterberg criticized unenlightened experimentation with children by teachers in "The danger from experimental psychology" (*Atlantic*

Monthly 81:159–167, 1898). In September 1898, in reply to the re-
futations and the praise aroused by the earlier article, Münsterberg wrote a more detailed condemnation of child study.
(Münsterberg. "Psychology and education." *Educational Rev.*
16:105–132, 1898.) In 1895, Baldwin replied, in some detail and
without derogatory implications, to the queries circulated by the
Illinois State Teachers Association. (Baldwin. "Results of child-
study applied to education." *Transact. Illinois Soc. Child-Study*
1:14–17, 1895.) However, by 1898 he was convinced that questionnaires were of little value, both by his own experience (he
had issued a syllabus on "Social Sense") and by reading of the
results of others. "They lack the first requisites of exact method;
and moreover they are often further vitiated by a certain speculative philistinism and crudity of results." (Baldwin. "Child-
study." *Psychol. Rev.* 5:218–220, 1898.)

39. For the influence of recapitulation theory on concepts
of child development and later reasons for its abandonment,
see: P. E. Davidson. *The Recapitulation Theory and Human Infancy.*
New York: Columbia University Teachers College, 1914. *Also:*
R. E. Grinder. *A History of Genetic Psychology. The First Science of
Human Development.* New York: John Wiley, 1967.

40. Hall, G. S. *Adolescence; Its Psychology and Its Relations to
Physiology, Anthropology, Sociology, Sex, Crime, Religion and Education,* Vol. 2, p. 71. New York: D. Appleton and Co., 1904.

41. Strickland, C. E., and C. Burgess, Eds. *Health, Growth,
and Heredity: G. Stanley Hall on Natural Education,* p. 45. New
York: Teachers College Press, 1965.

42. Embryology was being transformed from a descriptive
to an experimental science during the last decades of the
nineteenth century. See: W. Coleman. *Biology in the Nineteenth
Century: Problems of Form, Function, and Transformation,* pp. 47–56.
New York: John Wiley, 1971.

43. At Hall's invitation, Freud attended the Clark University Conference of 1909. For Hall's initially enthusiastic and later
more restrained endorsement of Freudian ideas, see D. Ross, *G.
Stanley Hall,* pp. 368–394.

44. Hall considered that A. C. Ellis, who collaborated with him in "A study of dolls" (*Pedagogical Seminary* 4:129–175, 1896), relied too much on statistical treatment. Hall. *Life and Confessions of a Psychologist*, p. 390.

45. Hall's most scientifically acceptable study was probably his first major one: "The contents of children's minds." *Princeton Rev.* 11:249–272, 1883. Reprinted in W. Dennis, Ed. *Historical Readings in Developmental Psychology*, pp. 119–137. New York: Appleton-Century-Crofts, 1972. For a recent reevaluation of this study, see: J. C. McCullers. "The contents of children's minds: A partial replication." *J. Hist. Behav. Sci.* 7:169–176, 1971.

46. Boring, E. G., Ed., *A History of Psychology in Autobiography*, Vol. IV, p. 127. New York: Russell and Russell, 1952.

47. Gesell, A. "Maturation and infant behavior pattern." *Psychol. Rev.* 36:307–319, 1929.

48. Gesell, A., and H. Thompson. "Learning and growth in identical infant twins: An experimental study by the method of co-twin control." *Genet. Psychol. Monogr.* 6:1–124, 1929.

49. Gesell, A. "Maturation and infant behavior pattern," p. 317.

50. Gesell, A. L., F. L. Ilg, and L. B. Ames. *Infant and Child in the Culture of Today. The Guidance of Development in Home and Nursery School*, p. 37. New York: Harper & Row, 1943.

3

Freud and
His Influence

Early Psychoanalytic Theories
of Child Development

Sigmund Freud's writings constituted the boldest attempt
to compose a comprehensive theory of psychological development. His theory was gleaned, not from long hours
of observing children, but, oddly enough, from conversa-
tions with middle-class adult patients. Of course, Freud
had some direct experience with children, having six of
his own. Furthermore, during the period of his children's
birth (1887–1895), he was working as director of the
neurology department at the Institute for Children's Diseases in Vienna.[1] But he himself discounted any effect
that his encounters there may have had on this thinking,
stating in 1914 that:

In the beginning, my statements about infantile sexuality were founded almost exclusively on the findings of analysis in adults which led back into the past. I had no opportunity of direct observations on children. It was therefore a very great triumph when it became possible years later to confirm almost all my inferences by direct observation and analysis of very young children. . . .[2]

(These observations were carried out by others, not by Freud, as will be discussed later.)

Influenced by Charcot's idea that trauma was the cause of hysteria, Freud at first believed that this disease was the result of early childhood seduction, usually by the father. He thought that in contrast, obsessional neurosis was caused by the memory's repression of gratifying sexual acts carried out during childhood.[3] By 1897, he had abandoned this hypothesis about hysteria because it seemed unlikely that Vienna harbored so many perverted fathers. Freud now assumed that the memories recalled by his hysterical patients during free association were only fantasies. Yet he remained convinced that the sexual quality of these fantasies was of primary importance. Freud solved this puzzle by postulating a broadly based autoeroticism common to all young children which, however, only induced traumatic experiences in those with vulnerable constitutions. In such persons, the later fantasies "were intended to cover up the autoerotic activity of the first years of childhood, to gloss it over and raise it to a higher plane."[4]

FREUD'S THEORY OF PSYCHOSOCIAL DEVELOPMENT

With consummate skill, Freud used his idea to explain what he considered the almost universal rejection of an obvious phenomenon—the child's sexuality. In the late

nineteenth century, it was thought, at least conventionally, that the child was asexual until puberty.[5] Although
this attitude was not as general as Freud implied, he
hardly exaggerated when he noted that signs of precocious sexual activity, such as erections and masturbation,
were "always quoted as exceptional events, as oddities or
as horrifying instances of precocious depravity."[6] Physicians commonly regarded masturbation in the child as a
sign of degeneracy or of impending mental disintegration.
According to Freud, the refusal to consider early eroticism
as normal was due to "considerations of propriety, which
the authors obey as a result of their own upbringing,"
and to a psychological phenomenon whereby most people had no memory of their early childhoods (before
the sixth or eighth year).[7] He labeled this phenomenon "infantile amnesia" and suggested that the forgotten impressions leave "the deepest traces on our minds and have a
deterministic effect upon the whole of our later development."[8] Here the essence of Freud's faith in continuity is
revealed. To him, it seemed that the memories of significant childhood experiences were not lost but merely
excluded from consciousness—in his word, repressed.
The task was to discover the cause of repression, for
Freud believed that the same mechanism could lead to
hysterical amnesia.

Thus, the discovery of the etiology of adult neuroses
depended on a prior understanding of the sexual development of the child. Freud's earliest interpretations of
this process were most clearly laid out in the essay "Infantile sexuality" (1905) and briefly reiterated in the fourth of
the five lectures he gave at Clark University in 1909.[9] Although he was later to downplay the part played by sexual instincts in determining personality development, at
this point (until 1910) he thought that these were the only
biological instincts subject to repression and hence capa-

ble of causing future neurosis. This view accounted for
his preoccupation with the sexual aspects of child development and his ability to find a sexual basis for the child's
enjoyment of such activities as walking, running, wres-
tling, riding in trains, and even intellectual work.[10]

Freud believed that "the germs of sexual impulses"
were present at birth. One early sign of this activity was
thumb-sucking, the mouth being the first erotogenic
zone. Freud observed that the infant initially derived pleasure from feeding at the breast, not only because it
gratified his hunger, but because of its link to the primitive sexual drive.

No one who has seen a baby sinking back satiated from the
breast and falling asleep with flushed cheeks and a blissful smile
can escape the reflection that this picture persists as a prototype
of the expression of sexual satisfaction in later life.[11]

Freud made an error common in science: he classified two
events that appeared similar as being reflections of the
same process. Because the child wanted to repeat his
pleasant experience, he sucked anything available—most
commonly his thumb. The initial incentive for sucking,
which was hunger, seemed to Freud to be replaced by a
sexual incentive. Not all infants indulged in excessive
sucking, and Freud assumed that those who did probably
possessed "a constitutional intensification of the erotogenic significance of the labial region." If this intensification disposition persisted,

these same children when they are grown up will become epi-
cures in kissing, will be inclined to perverse kissing or, if males,
will have a powerful motive for kissing and smoking. If, however, repression ensues, they will feel disgust at food and will

produce hysterical vomiting. The repression extends to the nutritional instinct owing to the dual purpose served by the labial zone.[12]

Freud also emphasized the importance of the anal area as an erotogenic region. "The intestinal disturbances which are so common in childhood see to it that the zone shall not lack intense excitations," he wrote. According to Freud, children most susceptible to this type of gratification would hold back their stools until the accumulated fecal material caused violent muscular contractions. They would enjoy the contractions and the stimulation of the mucous membrane of the anus that accompanied passage of the mass.

One of the clearest signs of subsequent eccentricity or nervousness is to be seen when a baby obstinately refuses to empty his bowels when he is put on the pot—that is, when his nurse wants him to—and holds back that function till he himself chooses to exercise it. He is naturally not concerned with dirtying the bed, he is only anxious not to miss the subsidiary pleasure attached to defecating. Educators are once more right when they describe children who keep the process back as "naughty."[13]

More dramatic revelations were to come. "A bombshell," according to Ernest Jones, "that aroused more derision than anything he had hitherto written" was Freud's description of the evolution of an anal personality.[14] This was set forth in "Character and anal eroticism," an essay first published in 1908. Freud's opinion was that adults who were exceptionally orderly, parsimonious, and obstinate had been reluctant as children to empty their bowels in a regular orderly manner, and instead had held back their stools and had defecated at their own convenience. This constitutionally intensified anal eroticism did not persist, however, because of the cultural unacceptability of expressions of anal sexuality. Instead, they sublimated their desires, which led them to develop the three permanent character traits mentioned before. Freud suggested at the end of his essay that infantile erotogenic activity might be related to the development of other specific types of personality. He proposed three mechanisms that he thought influenced personality development: "the permanent character-traits are either unchanged perpetuations of the original impulses, sublimations of them, or reaction-formations against them."[15]

The notion that the oral and anal regions are early erotogenic zones, destined to be abandoned later during normal development, was first made public by Freud in *Three Essays on the Theory of Sexuality*. Yet, as revealed in his letters to Fliess, ever since 1896 Freud had been considering the idea of consecutive psychosexual stages in infancy and of their causal relation to repression or perversion.[16] That the first two stages should be oral and anal seemed reasonable, in that taste and smell were the principal senses that aroused sexual and other drives in lower animals. In human beings, as the upright carriage was adopted, and the "nose raised from the ground," formerly "interesting sensations attached to the earth" became repulsive.[17] The mouth and anus no longer produced a release of sexuality in the normal human adult, but did so for a transient period during infancy. The biological analogy made this idea attractive: not only did the infant recapitulate a stage of development known to persist in lower animals in accord with Haeckel's recapitulation theory, but the extinction of the initial sexual zones in man had "a counterpart in the atrophy of certain internal organs in the course of development."[18]

Here we have an example of Freud's preference for creating analogies between principles or processes in two different scientific fields to reinforce his arguments. With considerable dexterity, but without much sound evidence, he used late nineteenth-century biological and physical models to lend credence to his psychological theories. Such a technique might convince laymen, but it irritated experimental psychologists. Many of these, including Karl Lashley and Knight Dunlap, objected to Freud's free use of speculative analogies, fearing that he was reintroducing a scientifically outdated method of procedure.[19]

According to Freud, the genital area was the third autoerotic region to emerge in human development. This assumption, so obvious to all, needed no supportive biological model to gain acceptance. According to Freud, the genital organs became the center of autoerotic activity in late infancy, marking the "beginning of what is later to become 'normal' sexual life."[20] Of necessity, this region was washed and rubbed, so the infant soon became aware of the pleasurable nature of genital stimulation. Infantile masturbation, "which scarcely a single individual escapes" established "the future primacy over sexual activity exercised by this erotogenic zone."[21] Freud observed that masturbation recurred intermittently until puberty and sometimes persisted through life.

According to Freud's theories, a child's first sexual instincts were fully satisfied by autoerotic activity. But although the erotogenic zones remained the dominant sources of libidinal satisfaction during childhood, sooner or later other people became sexual objects. By the end of puberty, object choice—the selection of another person as the source of libidinal gratification—had prevailed over self-stimulation, "so that now in the sexual life all components of the sexual impulse are satisfied in the loved person."[22] In the meantime, social and cultural pressures had caused the repression of many of the early libidinal impulses.

The child's attachment to his parents, at first dictated by physical needs, soon acquired a sexual component. Usually, one of the parents was favored—a process encouraged by the presumed tendency of the father to prefer his daughter and a mother her son. This situation led the boy to want to displace the father and the girl, the mother. "The feelings awakened in these relations between parents and children," Freud suggested, "and as a resultant of them, those among the children in relation to each other, are not only positively of a tender, but negatively of an inimical sort."[23] Freud believed that the resulting emotional state in the child, the *Oedipus complex*, would be repressed and yet would exert a permanent effect on the unconscious, to form the basis of any future neurosis.

According to Freud, the Oedipus complex appeared at about three to five years of age, at the stage of maximal infantile sexual activity, when the genital area represented the dominant autoerotic zone. During this peak of sexuality, the child began to formulate his own sexual theory, which, although incorrect, was closer to reality than an adult might imagine. The child usually failed to discover only two sexual facts—the role of the semen and the existence of the vagina.[24] This lack of knowledge led to a distorted and incomplete understanding of sexuality, which created a fear of castration in a boy and penis envy in a girl. Although bewildered by his sexual theories and fears, the child did not confide in his parents, but kept his ideas to himself. The normal child repressed his sexual preoccupations as he became absorbed with school and peer activities. The genital period gave way to the latency stage, a period of sexual quiescence which persisted until puberty. It was inevitable, and normal, Freud believed, for a child first to become attached to his parents, but it was also essential for him to break the tie and make other object choices later in childhood; otherwise, he would not gain independence to become integrated in a wider society.

During the time that the represented activity is making its choice among the partial sexual impulses and later, when the influence of the parents, which in the most essential way has furnished the material for these repressions, is lessened, great problems fall to the work of education, which at present certainly does not always solve them in the most intelligent and economic way.[25]

In this remark Freud was making one of his relatively few allusions to the importance of environmental factors. Perhaps rendered cautious by his earlier mistaken attribution of hysteria to actual seduction by the father, he now produced a theory in which parents played a less active role in their children's development.[26] Nevertheless, he repeatedly stated that both hereditary and environmental factors must be taken into account in determining the possible causes of neurosis:

Neurosis will always produce its greatest effects when constitution and experience work together in the same direction. When the constitution is a marked one it will perhaps not require the support of actual experiences; while a great shock in real life will perhaps bring about a neurosis even in the average constitution.[27]

* * *

A good proportion of the deviations from normal sexual life which are later observed both in neurotics and in perverts are thus established from the very first by the impressions of childhood—a period which is regarded as being devoid of sexuality. The causation is shared between a compliant constitution, precocity, the characteristic of increased pertinacity of early impressions and the chance stimulation of the sexual instinct by extraneous influences.[28]

Freud implied that a dynamic interaction between biological and environmental factors during the first few years of life determined the course of personality development. Yet, on balance, he seems to have favored constitution, or biological makeup, as the more potent determinant. Later generations of American psychoanalysts would criticize his failure to emphasize cultural and familial influences.

Freud's theory of development could be interpreted as predeterministic. In his essay on "Infantile sexuality," he stressed the role of individual constitutional factors. He postulated that at birth, each person possessed different but fixed quantities of sexual energy, or *libido*, a biological "given" that restricted the degree of satisfaction or trauma derived from future experience. This idea was derived from Maxwell's concept of energy. Later, when Freud revised his theory of motivation, he defined the libido as the energy reservoir for all of the life-preserving instincts (not merely the sexual instincts), but not for the newly postulated death instinct. Always a broad concept (far broader than that usually implied by the term "sexual"), the libido now became to him the source of energy for nearly all mental activity.

The fate of the sexual drives, or "the use to which they were put during the course of development," could not, however, be predicted, but only determined retrospectively. Freud first set out some of the possible outcomes in his paper, "Character and anal eroticism," and later in, "Instincts and their vicissitudes," an article first published in 1915. He surmised that an infantile instinct could persist unchanged into adult life, when, if socially unacceptable, it was labeled a perversion. There are four other possibilities, according to his view: reversal into its opposite, turning around upon the subject, repression, and sublimation.[29] By the term *reversal into its opposite*, Freud implied that an active instinct—for example, the desire to inflict pain—could become passive in its aim, leading to self-torture. Thus he explained sadomasochism, insisting that the masochistic element was never primary. The enjoyment of self-torture was also an example of an instinct turning around on the subject. Freud defined sublimation, which entailed the redirection of libidinal energy into culturally acceptable channels rather than obviously sexual ones, as the basis of creative and intellectual endeavor and of love for a person as an outgrowth of sexual attraction. To him repression was the undeliberate exclusion from consciousness of the mental presentation of an intolerable instinct. This process was accompanied by fixation, whereby the instinct remained attached to this primitive mental picture, both persisting unaltered from then on. Repression prevented awareness of anxiety associated with an unacceptable instinct. But often repression was only partially successful, in that as a rule it created a *substitute formation*, and left psychological symptoms in its wake. Consciousness continued to be bombarded with ideas sufficiently dissimilar from those associated with the primitive instinct for their origin not to be recognized, and thus energy was discharged in disguised form. But the substitute itself could be the cause of anxiety, as Freud demonstrated in his descriptions of animal phobia. (According to Freud, the original erotic impulse could be sexual attraction to a parent accompanied by anxiety. A boy might fear retaliation from his father. After repression, the libidinal object and the source of fear might become some animal equally capable of provoking anxiety. The result is "fear of a wolf, instead of a demand for love from the father."[30] If the animal phobia becomes crippling, nothing short of full awareness of the original repressed material can lead to a cure of the anxiety neurosis.) Freud did not suggest that repression inevitably had a bad outcome. On the contrary, at times it was an essential mechanism for psychological adaptation—for example, in the passing of the Oedipal phase of development. It was forgotten by many who read his theories that Freud had put forward an explanatory theory that did not always make very specific predictions of outcome. Instead, many assumed that Freud had implied that all situations that lead to conflict and repression in early childhood could and should be avoided, at any cost. When these ideas became public knowledge, many middle-class parents worried about the anxiety that their children were experiencing and tried to avoid practices and encounters that would promote repression.

FREUD'S REVISIONS
OF HIS THEORY OF DEVELOPMENT

Confusion was indeed inevitable, for Freud was constantly revising and supplementing his ideas. By 1914, he had become less certain that neurosis could be caused only through the agency of repressed libidinal instincts. This premise had been a major reason for the rejection of his ideas first by Alfred Adler and then by Carl Jung. Although Freud considered their revised theories as heresies, he was probably more deeply influenced by their dissent than he cared to admit.[31] Between 1915 and 1925 he wrote numerous papers and monographs, revising various aspects of psychoanalytic theory, and finally producing a new hypothesis of mental development that complemented the libido theory. [32]

Of the many revisions undertaken during these crucial 10 years, only a few can be summarized here. One concept Freud introduced was that self-preservation drives could also contribute to neurosis and that the development of the ego therefore could not be ignored in a complete theory of personality. Freud came to this conclusion after studying the anxiety neuroses exhibited by some World War I combatants, for their diseases seemed to be caused by the ego's fear of being damaged rather than by any repression of the libido. Nor could this latter mechanism account for narcissism, aggression, or repetition compulsion (the tendency to ruminate over or actively repeat early experiences, especially unpleasant ones.) To encompass these objections, Freud proposed a revised theory of instincts in *Beyond the Pleasure Principle* (1920). Here, he suggested a new group of ego drives— the death instincts—that he said were opposed to the sexual or life instincts. The latter included the old libido and newly formulated self-preservation ego instincts. Freud now concluded that the ego was the original reservoir of psychic energy, and that libido could only be invested in objects and persons (object cathexis) through the ego. The death instincts tended toward self-destruction and a return to an inorganic state, whereas the libidinal drives exerted pressure toward prolongation and enjoyment of life.

Further new concepts of mental operations were proposed in *The Ego and the Id* (1923), which has been described as the last of Freud's major theoretical works. He revised his relatively simple idea of mental structure: that the mind consisted of the unconscious, the preconscious, and the conscious, with the ego belonging to the latter. He now postulated that some of the ego might be unconscious and introduced two new divisions of the mind, the id and the superego. The id corresponded to what had earlier been described as the "unconscious," and the term "unconscious" was now used to refer to all the mental processes that could not be brought into awareness by normal means. The superego represented Freud's earlier concept of the ego ideal "the heir to the Oedipus complex."[33] As this complex became resolved, part of the ego identified itself with either the mother or the father figure to become the superego, an amalgam of ego ideal and conscience.

Freud had now provided the material for the construction of a second maturational process that paralleled and interacted with psychosexual development. He proposed that at birth, the mind consisted entirely of the unconscious id, which contained all inherited dispositions, including the instincts. The id was amoral, operating according to a primary process, or pleasure principle, which entailed gaining immediate satisfaction of instinctual desires. Under the influence of the external world, one portion of the id became differentiated into the ego, which operated according to a secondary process, or reality principle, and sought to preserve the organism by acting as an intermediary between the id and the world outside. The ego began to separate from the id early in infancy, but the superego did not become differentiated from the ego until the fifth or sixth year of age, gradually emerging as the Oedipus complex was brought under control. It was to become the inner representative of discarded parental authority and of social awareness, operating both consciously and unconsciously. Note the implication of continuity here and the embryological analogy: primordial "structures" give rise to succeeding structures, but there is always the assumption of a continuity between them, the past never being lost.

By the mid-1920s Freud had produced a massive theory whose internal consistency was obscured by the cumulative, unsystematic method of its production over the years. This led to much confusion, even among analysts, and to frequent misrepresentations of Freudian concepts by nonspecialists. One difficulty was that the theory was structured on models derived from both the physical and biological sciences.[34] But a synthesis was lacking, in that at no point did Freud unite the models into a single explicit theory. Furthermore, because his analogies were drawn from late nineteenth-century scientific sources, they depended heavily on outdated concepts and so carried little conviction to the active researcher.[35] His theory of psychosexual development and his concept of inborn instincts showed the influence of what David Rapaport has called "the Darwinian or genetic model." Accepting the Lamarckian postulate of inheritance of characteristics acquired by the parental generation, Freud visualized the organism as capable of withdrawing from external events through a variety of movements, the most appropriate of which was "thenceforward transmitted as a hereditary disposition." But this mechanism was useless in dealing with instinctual stimuli arising from within the organism. The central nervous system could not simply ward off these stimuli, but had to react to them in a more complex manner. It was these persistent internal stimuli, rather than external ones, that had promoted maximal structural adaptation of the brain:

We may therefore well conclude that instincts and not external stimuli are the true motive forces behind the advances that have led the nervous system, with its unlimited capacities, to its present high level of development. There is naturally nothing to prevent our supposing that the instincts themselves are, at least in part, precipitates of the effects of external stimulation, which in the course of phylogenesis have brought about modifications in the living substance. [36]

In the letter to Fliess mentioned earlier, Freud had noted that the oral and anal erotogenic zones were retained in lower animals. Their elimination during normal human development was a prerequisite for higher achievement, their retention a basis for neurosis. He felt that the model for infantile sexual development could be found in biology; the model for the adolescent phase and the preceding latency period probably had its inception in the early history of mankind.

The fact that the onset of sexual development in human beings occurs in two phases, i.e., that the development is interrupted by the period of latency, seemed to call for particular notice. This appeared to be one of the necessary conditions of the aptitude of man for developing a higher civilization, but also of their tendency to neurosis. So far as we know, nothing analogous is to be found in man's animal relatives. It would seem that the origin of this peculiarity of man must be looked for in the prehistory of the human species. [37]

The scientific models were a legacy from Freud's earlier career as a neurophysiologist, but he did not keep abreast of changes in biological theory once he became absorbed in psychoanalysis. Orginally a reductionist, as clearly expressed in the introduction to "Project for a scientific psychology" (1895), Freud lost interest in the search for physiological bases of behavior. [38] He retained the certainty that behavior was rigidly determined, but became progressively more convinced that only psychological causes could be uncovered by the human observer. In his more optimistic moments, he expressed confidence that physiology, when more advanced, would confirm the validity of his postulates, but by the end of his life was most skeptical about this possibility:

We have adopted the hypothesis of a psychical apparatus, extended in space, appropriately constructed, developed by the exigencies of life, which gives rise to the phenomena of consciousness only at one particular point and under certain conditions. . . . In our science the problem is the same as in the others: behind the attributes (i.e., qualities) of the object under investigation which are directly given to our perception, we have to discover something which is more independent of the particular receptive capacities of our sense organs and which approximates more closely to what may be supposed to be the real state of things. There is no hope of our being able to reach the latter itself, since it is clear that everything new that we deduce must nevertheless be translated back into the language of our perceptions, from which it is simply impossible for us to set ourselves free. . . . Reality will always remain 'unknowable.'[39]

Thus, we may assume that over the years Freud intended his scientific analogies as metaphoric aids to the understanding, and progressively less as actual models of underlying biological structure.

To a growing body of psychologists dedicated to objective research, Freud was guilty of far more cardinal sins than the excessive use of metaphor and symbolism. His very method was suspect, inasmuch as there was nothing to prevent him from interpreting his patients' experience according to his own preconceived notions. Given the almost endless data presented to him during psychoanalysis, he apparently sifted out relevant material intuitively. From this, he constructed internally consistent

theories that required the acceptance of numerous unveri-
fiable postulates: the existence of the unconscious, of innate drives, of psychic energy; the development of the
ego and superego; repression, cathexis, and so on. To
take anything on trust was contrary to the basic canons of
scientific objectivity. Given this impasse, experimental
psychologists favored Freud with a passing nod of interest, but initially were not concerned with testing his proposals in the harsh empirical arena. It was not until the
1940s that serious empirical work began, and, as we shall
see, it was instrumental in sifting useful from less useful
ideas.

REFLECTIONS ON FREUD'S INFLUENCE
ON PATTERNS OF CHILD CARE

But Freud's ideas did attack cherished beliefs held by
many American parents, particularly the belief in strict
discipline.

In the nineteenth and early twentieth centuries, those
who stressed the importance of early training assumed
that habits learned in infancy would persist throughout
life. Toilet training was begun as soon as possible, not
only for convenience in the era before washing machines,
but also because it seemed that permanent bowel regular-
ity would thus be ensured.[40] This was an important consideration, in that even physicians then considered con-
stipation to be the cause of many ailments and a state to
be guarded against if at all possible. Similarly, regular
sleeping and eating habits were recommended for the
immediate benefit of the household and the lifelong benefit of the child.

The rationale of strict early training was undermined
by Freud's theories and those of Arnold Gesell. According
to Freud, denial of an infant's instinctive needs was likely

to injury his psyche permanently. Gesell wrote that it was a waste of time to attempt to "condition" a baby until his nervous system had reached the requisite stage of differentiation or maturity. In the 1930s this argument sounded convincing to parents; today it is the basis of much neuroanatomical research.

Freud's theory was so broad and rich and it encompassed so many facets of personality development that it was hard to reject it outright. Everyday experience seemed to confirm much of what he said, especially the phenomena of slips of the tongue (parapraxes) and infantile sexuality. Scientific opinion was divided, but clinicians, especially those who were concerned with child guidance, were sympathetic toward Freudian concepts. To some parents, the consequences of ignoring psychoanalytic precepts of childrearing were too devastating to be contemplated with equanimity. Conversely, following such precepts promised to ensure that children would develop into well-balanced, effective adults. It was worth a try, inasmuch as apparently nothing much could be lost, and a great deal could be gained by allowing a child to have freer expression.

The emphasis on personality development was new, a reflection of Freudian influence that had been latent for so many decades. But the interest in character formation was not quite so new; as shown by Celia B. Stendler, it had been a major preoccupation in the late nineteenth century, in the "pre-aseptic" childrearing era.[41] To judge by the content of articles in women's magazines, parents had been very concerned with the moral development of their children. Conventionally, "motherhood" was idealized; the mother was not only the source of love and inspiration, but also the model of "proper" behavior to be imitated by her offspring. And not such vaguely defined products as well-adjusted and secure children were sought, but rather child-training practices were designed to produce children who would exemplify the Victorian ideals of courtesy, honesty, orderliness, industriousness, and generosity. [42]

All generations of parents hold some ideal for their children. What changes with time and culture is the stereotype of the ideal adult, male and female. In the late nineteenth-century America, the ideal parent was a person of strong moral fiber; by the mid-twentieth century, a well-balanced flexible personality had become more important. Many factors probably contributed to this change, including the impact of Freudianism, a gradual revulsion against Victorian hypocrisy, the ever-increasing mobility of people in the United States (which required adaptability, rather than rigidity, of personality), and the decreasing influence of religion and its moral imperatives.

Freud's contribution to this new outlook was imponderable but considerable. Implicit in his theories, at least from the American viewpoint, was the promise that, if a child's early experiences were pleasurable and if he suffered a minimum of frustration and was given a maximum of encouragement and understanding, he would develop into a well-adjusted person. Freud himself had stated that "the application of psychoanalysis to education, to the upbringing of the next generation," was perhaps the most important of all the activities of child analysis. [43] He suggested that development would be enhanced if all children were analyzed, as a prophylactic measure. At least, educators should have undergone analysis, and any parents that had done so would surely treat their children with greater understanding.

But Freud still had reservations about human perfectibility. Even with parents and teachers prepared for the task in hand, childrearing would remain a complex undertaking. According to Freud, a major purpose of education was to teach the child to control his impulses, which for social reasons could not be allowed completely free expression. Yet, because this suppression of the instincts carried the risk of producing neurosis, education had to find its way "between the Scylla of noninterference and the Charybdis of frustration." Freud foresaw that this might prove an insoluble problem and that at best there could be only a compromise enabling "education to achieve the most and damage the least." By such means, accidental trauma to the immature psyche could be avoided, but the other factor that could lead to neurosis—"the power of an insubordinate instinctual constitution"—would remain unaffected. [44] Freud stressed that only persons who had themselves been set straight through analysis could provide the child with the relative proportions of discipline and love required by his specific constitution.

Freud's implication that a child's constitution set limits to his perfectibility, no matter how favorable the environment, was too pessimistic to find much favor in America. This aspect of Freudian theory was not incorporated into the content of popular articles dealing with childrearing; instead, the mother was given the impression that if she did right by her child, all would be well. The onus was on parents, especially mothers, to find out about problems likely to occur, to recognize them when they did appear, and then to cope in an enlightened and adult manner. *Parent's Magazine,* for example, contained numerous rather smug articles explaining how the authors had successfully dealt with such problems as sibling jealousy, sex education, and the loss of a parent through death or divorce. No difficulty was insurmountable. This was encouraging, but perhaps less commendable were the explicit assertions that, if a mother became irritated in dealing with her offspring, the fault lay in her own immaturity. This left the mother in a more helpless condition than before she began to read the article. For example, in an article entitled "Don't be afraid of strong feelings," mothers were told that they must learn to face and accept all types of emotional outbursts on the part of their children, so that the children would not become fearful of their own feelings.[45] Angry and "hostile" thoughts must be expressed, not repressed. A mother who would not permit her child to call her improper names might be expressing "her own fears and insecurities." Seeing her own success as a parent threatened and feeling ashamed and humiliated, she would be overreacting to such outbursts on the part of her child. According to the author of the article: "We should feel suspicious of ourselves when we react strongly to something as absurdly simple, for example, as a child calling us names."[46]

This was not quite what Freud had intended. On the contrary, he had expected parents, by virtue of their greater experience, to assume responsibility for setting limits to the antisocial manifestations of a child's instinctual urges. The difficulty was that Freud had never translated theory into practical childrearing advice. Nor, except in the case of "Little Hans," had he ever engaged in child therapy. These more mundane tasks were left to his successors. In the meantime, scattered among Freud's writings were the concepts for the most comprehensive theory of child development ever proposed. Small wonder that those interested in child welfare did not wait for a systematic exposure by psychoanalysts, but interpreted Freud's writings as they saw fit.

For decades, beginning at least as early as the 1920s, Freudian ideas were informally popularized. Psychoanalysts did not write texts on infant and child care that could serve as comprehensive guides for parents, for the simple reason that the experts—Anna Freud, Melanie Klein, and others—were only slowly gathering the necessary evidence from direct child study.[47] Also, because they lived in Europe, perhaps they did not recognize the need in the United States for a simply written text to disseminate psychoanalytic ideas among the public. After all, behaviorism had been popuiarized through Watson's *Psychological Care of Infant and Child* (1928), and maturational theory through Gesell and Ilg's *Infant and Child in the Culture of Today* (1943).* The sales of Benjamin Spock's *The Common Sense Book of Baby and Child Care* have demonstrated the almost insatiable demand for professional advice. But the psychoanalysts remained aloof, at least until E. Erikson wrote *Childhood and Society* (1950). By then the pioneering work had been done, informally and chattily by Spock.[48]

Freudian concepts of child development, as applicable to child care, were also propagated by social scientists, psychiatrists, and pediatricians, especially those who worked in child guidance. Their outlook tended to be practical, rather than theoretical; consequently, they presented to the public a simplified working knowledge of psychological development in the child. An example of the type of book produced was *Psychosocial Development of Children* (1948), written by Irene M. Josselyn, a practicing psychiatrist, for the benefit of both parents and social workers.

On the whole, Josselyn adhered closely to classic Freudian concepts of development, emphasizing the relevance of the psychosexual phases of maturational con-

*The earliest book by Gesell seems to have been *The Pre-school Child* (1923), followed by *Infancy and Human Growth* (1928), Gesell and Thompson, *Infant Behavior: Its Genesis and Growth* (1934), and Gesell, et al, *The First Five Years of Life: The Preschool Years* (1940).

cepts. She deliberately avoided more recent controversial pyschoanalytic issues, and attempted to discuss "only those portions of psychiatry which, at the present stage of development, lend themselves to simplification."[49] Convinced by her clinical work that the emotional stability of adults depended on their having been reared according to Freudian precepts, rather than strictly disciplined, she aimed at providing an unambiguous digest of psychoanalytic theories of child development.

One difficulty was to differentiate between concepts that had been experimentally shown to have probable validity and those that were only conjectural. Josselyn was well aware of this problem, remarking that,

because psychiatry is a young science at the present, its literature is composed not only of sound material but also of much material that further research and investigation will determine to be of little or no real value; and much that we labor over in current writings, will, in time, without doubt prove to be of only pseudoprofundity. It is not always possible at the present time to differentiate the false from the true, to discard the unsound and to preserve the valuable.[50]

But how many readers would remember this warning given in the preface, when coming across statements like: "It is recognized that breast milk is better for babies than formulas. The breast-fed baby gains better, seems more contented, and is not as subject to colic."[51] Josselyn also perpetuated the Freudian postulate that unresolved conflicts occurring during the period of anal eroticism would lead to the development of an anal personality or (worse) to obsessional neurosis. Faced with such an unattractive prospect, parents would tend to discontinue efforts to toilet train their children, assuming that "nature" would win out in the end. This would seem a reasonable solution, given easy access to a washing machine and a social environment that tolerated untrained children three years old or older. However, matters were not this simple, according to analytic theory, because an anal personality could also develop in children whose training had been put off too long.

The contention that mother's milk was better for infants than anything out of a bottle was certainly reasonable at the turn of the century, when cow's milk was often contaminated and the powdered preparations lacked vitamins. But, by 1948, this proposition was of doubtful validity, and it was no longer inevitable that the breast-fed infant gained weight more rapidly than the bottle-fed one. On the contrary, the converse was often true. Furthermore, an infant getting insufficient milk at the breast would neither gain weight nor be contented, and this would lead a mother to resort to complementary bottle-feeding. Then, as if in defiance of psychoanalytic theory, the infant would often reject the breast in favor of the bottle.

In 1964, Bettye Caldwell reviewed the research literature on "The effects of infant care." Her conclusions were these:

1. The bottle-breast dilemma had remained unresolved.[52] The best solution seemed to be to ask the mother where her preferences lay, on the grounds that an anxious and tense mother or a modest one might have more success with bottle feeding.

2. It was difficult to demonstrate any consistent relationship between oral gratification, defined to include type and scheduling of feeding and time of weaning, and either child or adult personality.[53]

3. Research seemed to show that a prolonged period of nutritive sucking ensured easy transition to other techniques of obtaining nourishment and prevented the development of habits of nonnutritive sucking, such as thumb sucking.

4. The atmosphere in which bowel training was conducted seemed more important than either the timing or the method. Orderliness, obstinacy, and parsimony did seem to coexist in some adults, to form the "anal personality," but there was "no consistent evidence that the strength of the trait was related to elimination training."[54]

5. The underlying attitude of the mother—warmth, coldness, acceptance, etc.—might be more important than her overt behavior in determining the influence of any particular method of child care.

6. There were social differences in patterns of childrearing, middle-class parents apparently being the most permissive in the decade studied.

Caldwell suggested that researchers should investigate other aspects of infant behavior and avoid retrospective methods, with all their inherent disadvantages: "Only prospective longitudinal studies can provide the answers to many of the perplexing problems in this area, and there is need for more and better research of this type."[55] she said.

Now, in the 1970s, pediatricians and psychologists are again strongly recommending breast feeding as more beneficial to both mother and child. The medical viewpoint depends on studies showing that artificially fed infants tend to gain weight faster than their breast-fed counterparts, and on even more recent research suggesting that the obese infant is more likely to develop into an obese adult than is the baby of average weight. From a psychological perspective, breast feeding seems preferable because it allows for more subtle interactions between mother and child. [56]

In the meantime, whatever the state of the science, some kind of advice had to be given to parents and others in charge of small children. Pediatricians and psychologists could hardly avoid this responsibility inasmuch as it was the publication of their research findings that had initiated the general disenchantment with traditional modes of childrearing. Other factors, such as increased ease of mobility (which led to ever greater numbers of young parents being geographically isolated from former friends and relatives), helped to make the experts indispensable. But it was difficult for the mother to recognize the tentative or provisional nature of such "expert" advice, especially when it was provided by articles in popular journals. Often, the authors implied contemporary scientific omniscience with phrases like "now we know a great deal more than Grandma did" or "everybody is agreeing that" or "it is now known that."

Unfortunately, psychoanalytic concepts dealing with unconscious motivation and emotional interaction between parent and child could easily be misinterpreted. The complex theory, built on the premise that adult neurosis was the result of unresolved childhood mental conflict, was both reassuring and threatening to parents. If it were adhered to, the child would acquire a healthy, well-integrated personality; if it were ignored, he would become maladjusted, neurotic, and perhaps even perverted and delinquent. Driven by fear, as well as hope, parents were inclined to interpret literally what they imagined to be Freudian theory, perhaps unaware that this was too complex and tentative to be reduced to a few practical directives.

The problem was aptly stated by Anna Freud in 1956:

Unfortunately, the pathways leading from insight into the etiology of psychological disorders to their prevention are not straightforward ones. There is a multitude of external and internal factors which combine their influence to cause mental suffering; with the best will in the world, not all of them can be eliminated from the child's life. Some are anchored in the very traditions of the society in which the child grows up, are part and parcel of it, and as such immovable. Some, though harmful from certain aspects, are beneficial from others and therefore indispensable for normal life. Some are the results of development itself, i.e., inextricably tied up with the complexity of the child's growing personality, his moral demands on himself, his attempts at adaption to the environment. In fact, nothing that we learn in this respect from psychoanalysis entitles us to expect more than a reduction in the number of these pathogenic agents. [57]

An understanding of analytic theory might help in the prevention of gross errors of childrearing—that is, those almost bound to result in permanent distortion of the personality—but could contribute little to the evaluation of the effects of subtler behavioral interactions between the child and his environment.

What the public expected was no less than a revolutionary but systematic, well-integrated guide to the rearing of a new, healthier and happier generation. What they received, in fact, were isolated, hard-won insights, highlighting sometimes one, sometimes another area of the child's mind, frequently transmitted without the relevant guidance to their proper application. These resulted, it is true, in some significant successes, but not without an almost equal number of significant failures and disappointments. [58]

Psychoanalytic Theories
of Development Become Popular

Psychoanalytic theories of child development had their greatest impact in the United States between 1940 and 1960.

The incidence of mental illness, brought to the fore by war experiences, promised to be reduced by careful attention to emotional development. Furthermore, analytic theories were supported by a vast body of literature and enough research to warrant the publication of an annual series: *The Psychoanalytic Study of the Child*, from 1945 onward. There was no other competitive theory of personality development. The concepts of social learning theory, themselves partially derived from psychoanalytic postulates, were only beginning to be formulated,[59] and cognitive development was not to attract much attention until later.

ERIK ERIKSON'S THEORY OF DEVELOPMENT

Some indication of the dominance of psychoanalytic ideas may be gained by surveying the *Fact-Finding Report to the Midcentury White House Conference on Children and Youth*, the final version of which was published as *Personality in the Making*. The theme of the White House conference was "How can we rear an emotionally healthy generation?"[60] The difficulty was obtaining a consensus among psychiatrists, anthropologists, psychologists, and pediatricians as to the factors that influenced the development of a healthy personality. An answer, satisfactory to most on the fact-finding committee, was provided by Erik H. Erikson's descriptive systematization of the ego qualities that needed to emerge at critical periods of development to ensure an integrated personality. These ideas were first spelled out in *Childhood and Society* (1950) and expounded at greater length for a Macy Foundation symposium on the healthy personality held in the same year.[61]

Like Freud, Erikson provided a biologically determined stage theory of development, but one that conformed better with more recent psychoanalytic, ethological, and anthropological findings. Erikson's stages were not set by the child's psychosexual needs, but rather by "the organism's readiness to interact with the opportunities offered in the environment."[62] Each stage represented a critical period during which a specific ego component became apparent, met its crisis in dealing with the environment, and finally came to terms with the requirements of the culture, which were transmitted at first by the attitudes of the parents. The final emergence of a healthy personality, or ego integrity, depended on significant and satisfying interaction between the child and those who tended him at each point in his development. "While such interaction varies from culture to culture, it must essentially consider the *proper rate and the proper sequence* which govern the *growth of a personality* as well as that of an organism," Erikson insisted.[63]

The first component of a healthy personality, according to Erikson, was a sense of basic trust—an attitude derived from the experiences of the first year of life. If that attitude were impaired, the result would be a basic mistrust seen at its most extreme in paranoid schizophrenics. The second component was a sense of autonomy that developed around the ages of one to three years: "From a sense of *self-control without loss of self-esteem* comes a lasting sense of autonomy and pride; from a sense of muscular and anal impotence, of loss of self-control, and of parental over-control comes a lasting sense of doubt and shame."[64] The third component, which emerged between the ages of four and five years, was a sense of initiative. During this period, the child discovered not only what he was able to achieve, both physically and intellectually, but also what he was permitted to do, in his particular culture. "The danger of this stage is a sense of guilt over the goals contemplated and the acts initiated in one's exuberant enjoyment of new locomotor and mental power," Erikson said.[65] It was at this stage of initiative that conscience became established, at best to act as a regulator of personal enterprise, at worst to act as an inhibitor by fostering an overpowerful sense of guilt. The next stage, the final one belonging to childhood itself, occurred after the age of five years or so, when in most cultures some kind of schooling was initiated. Then a child must learn to work not only with his mind, but also with his hands. If all was well, he developed a sense of industry and persevering diligence; if ill-prepared for systematic instruction, he became prey to a sense of inadequacy and inferiority. The next crisis was that of puberty, when the child either developed a sense of personal integrity, of ego identity, or became confused and lost.

Erikson's stages coincided with those of Freud, except that his emphasis was on ego, rather than psychosexual, development. This trend, launched by Heinz Hartman, had been pursued by other psychoanalytic theorists, including Ernst Kris, David Rapaport, and Anna Freud, who no longer assumed that the ego was derived from the id, but that both arose from undifferentiated processes.[66] To these theorists the ego had a primary autonomy and was influenced by heredity. Environmental factors, to which the id was immune, could act on this immature ego, allowing learning to occur earlier in infancy than had previously been posited. The neonate was no longer considered merely a mass of instinctual drives, but rather an organism with some capacity to respond to environmental influences. Erikson, while retaining the framework of Freud's developmental stages, stressed the importance of early socialization in influencing personality development, thus helping to make analytic theory more acceptable to social learning theorists and more reflective of cultural differences in childrearing.

Nevertheless, Erikson's hypotheses of ego development were, like Freud's, untestable and thus unacceptable to the scientist. Furthermore, the old problem remained: the intuitive method of generalizing from the analysis or observation of a few clinical cases remained unconvincing to the academically trained researcher. Most analysts continued to ignore the principles of objectivity in collecting data; consequently, their work was either disregarded or severely criticized by experimental psychologists.[67] Naturally, criticism was most likely when analysts popularized developmental concepts of fundamental social importance.

Maternal Deprivation

The effects of early maternal deprivation or even separation became such an issue. Between 1943 and 1951 psychoanalysts suggested that children who were reared in an institution were bound to become emotional cripples because of early lack of maternal love. The contents of their articles, which we will discuss in this section, were so shocking and frightening that for a while there was an extreme reaction against even short-term separations of mothers and infants. Gradually, other developmental psychologists began to contribute a more restrained assessment of the problem, suggesting that the crucial cause of abnormal development was not the lack of a loving mother but the absence of adequate social and cognitive experience within an institutional setting.

To this day, the debate continues: most psychoanalysts remain convinced that a mother is essential during infancy, and their critics argue that there is no conclusive evidence that the mental and physical deterioration sometimes found in institutionalized children is due to lack of adequate maternal care itself. The maternal deprivation question is important and fascinating and it illustrates how psychoanalytic and experimental research complement each other, for the ultimate benefit of society at large. Without the relatively unlimited perspectives of psychoanalysis, the possible dangers of "maternal deprivation" might never have become a subject of general concern. Without the rigorously disciplined approach of academic psychology, the extreme view that an infant required the sole and constant attention of one caretaker might have prevailed and led to the mutual enchainment of mother and child.

THE EMERGENCE OF THE CONCEPT
OF MATERNAL DEPRIVATION

The earliest report of a "maternal deprivation syndrome," in Margaret Ribble's *The Rights of Infants*, was highly speculative, being based on a presumed interaction between physiological and psychological factors without supporting evidence.[68] She assumed that marasmus in the infant was in the "nature of a general disorganization of functions and a deterioration of primary body reflexes due in large measure to lack of [mothering] or stimulation."[69] Although Ribble went beyond her facts, her vigorous writing served to revive the suspicion that marasmus, or failure to thrive, might often have primarily a psychological rather than physical cause.

The work of William Goldfarb and Rene Spitz was directed at determining the effects of early institutionalization on mental and physical development. Goldfarb's studies were retrospective.[70] He selected two samples of children of similar hereditary background who lived in foster homes and were 10 to 14 years old. One group consisted of children who had been directly handed over to the foster parents by their mothers and who had therefore not undergone prolonged maternal deprivation (in the usual sense). The second group of children had spent almost the whole of their first three years of life in an institution. The children were subjected to a battery of psychological and IQ tests; the previously institutionalized group had a significantly lower mean score.

Spitz relied on direct observation and executed a series of studies. The first study was directed at four groups of infants: one group were in a foundling home without their mothers; the second, of similar sociocultural background, were reared at home; the third were cared for in a nursery, by their mothers; the fourth was a matched control group for the third, reared at home.[71] All three groups of infants who had contact with their mothers showed average or above-average developmental quotients by the end of their first year, whereas the foundling children exhibited an astonishing deterioration, according to tests, and were in poor physical health and extremely susceptible to infection. During Spitz's observation in the foundling home, there was an epidemic of measles, "with staggeringly high mortality figures," notwithstanding liberal administration of convalescent serum and globulins, as well as excellent hygienic conditions.[72] Of a total of 88 children up to the age of two and one-half years, 23 died. (Intercurrent infections continue to cause problems in institutions for infants, including day-care centers.) Although the foundling infants were isolated in their cots, Spitz did not think that their progressive mental deterioration was mainly due to lack of perceptual stimulation. Rather, he believed "that they suffer because their perceptual world is emptied of human partners, that their isolation cuts them off from any stimulation by any persons who could signify mother-representatives for the child at this age."[73]

During the course of this study, Spitz encountered a striking syndrome, which he labeled *anaclitic depression*. [74] This occurred between the ages of six and 11 months in 19 infants out of 130 in the foundling home and in the nursery, after separation from the mother had taken place. The mothers of the nursery children were only temporarily absent, usually for three months; but during this time, striking evidence of depression was noted. These children seemed to recover fully when reunited with their mothers. But this never happened to the foundling children, who became progressively more remote, apathetic, and unable to eat or sleep. To Spitz, this syndrome signified more than simple mourning; it was a true infantile depression with a poor prognosis, unless the mother returned within three months.

BOWLBY'S REPORT ON
THE EFFECTS OF MATERNAL DEPRIVATION

In 1951, Bowlby (as a contribution to the United Nations program for the welfare of homeless children) reviewed all the earlier studies on maternal deprivation. He added his own recommendations for the improved care of such children, as a matter of common humanity and to prevent the perpetuation of mental sickness, saying that "when their care is neglected, as happens in every country of the western world today, they grow up to reproduce themselves.[75] Children under the age of two and one-half years, according to Bowlby, should not be institutionalized, but should be cared for by their own mothers, with help from social workers if the stresses are great, or by adoptive or foster parents. "Mother-love in infancy and childhood is as important for mental health as are vitamins and proteins for physical health," he said.[76]

Bowlby's report had an immense and varied influence. As intended, it led to changes in the institutional care of young children in many countries. It stimulated research into the effects of maternal deprivation—in its most extreme form, as when a child was institutionalized or his mother died, and in its modified form, as when a child or his mother was hospitalized. There was also criticism of many aspects of the report.[77] Much of the evidence adduced by Bowlby rested on inadequately controlled studies and was therefore unconvincing.[78] Some of his conclusions were unwarranted. For example, there was no firm evidence (Goldfarb's was retrospective and therefore open to doubt) that early confinement to an institution necessarily led to specific forms of personality maladjustment. Nor was there any proof that the mental and physical retardation so often noted in orphanage children was inevitably permanent.[79] Furthermore, Bowlby's central thesis was questioned; physical and psychological deterioration might be due not to maternal deprivation itself, but to the consequent lack of variety in environmental stimulation.[80] Because it was normally the mother who provided care for an infant on a 24-hour basis, it was easy to assume that her personal presence, rather than the stimuli that she provided, was essential to normal development.

THE MATERNAL DEPRIVATION HYPOTHESIS
UNDER SCRUTINY

This debate, as to whether the crucial factor was lack
of maternal care, on the one hand, or lack of variety in
experience and opportunity to practice developing skills,
on the other, was of far more than mere theoretical interest. Bowlby implied that every degree of maternal separation—brief, prolonged, or permanent—was potentially
dangerous if it occurred in early childhood. Consequently, if he were taken literally, mothers should not
work during their children's infancy, nor should babies be
left temporarily in the care of friends or relatives. Some,
usually the more psychoanalytically oriented, did interpret maternal obligations that way, and this led Edelston
to recall Margaret Mead's comment that "the campaign
against maternal deprivation has become a subtle form of
antifeminism in which men, under the guise of exalting
the importance of maternity, are tying women more
tightly to their children."[81] Potentially more dangerous
was the tendency for social workers now to consider that
young children were better off with their mothers, whatever the home conditions, than in any institution.[82] This
idealized concept of the virtues of family life *per se* received a sharp setback in the 1960s with the publication of
reports on child abuse, specifically those on the "battered
child syndrome."[83] It became apparent that the problem
created by unwanted children (a problem that has existed
throughout mankind's history) cannot be resolved by the
application of simple formulae.

Yet few would deny that a strong bond normally de-
velops between infant and mother and usually becomes
apparent in the infant between the ages of six and eight
months. Bowlby reasoned that any rupture of this bond

could cause damage and, furthermore, that any separation lasting more than five months would certainly be harmful. An uninterrupted bonding with a single person during infancy enabled the child to form affectionate relations with others in later life. An affectionless personality developed if this bond had never been formed or if it was disrupted too early in life.

His critics differed from him on a few or many points. Most agreed that bonding occurred, but believed that an affectionless personality resulted only if permanent maternal separation took place before bonding—that is, before six months of age, and if no permanent mother substitute were provided.[84] Others proposed that a single attachment figure was not essential and that effective bonding could occur between the infant and several caretakers. Childrearing experiences in Israeli kibbutzim seemed to bear this out, but even there a main bond seemed to develop between the infants and their natural parents, even if they were together only on weekends.[85] As pointed out by Rutter, well-controlled studies are still needed to confirm or refute the tentative conclusion that multiple mothering need have no adverse effects, so long as it is "of high quality and is provided by figures who remain the same during the child's early life."[86]

Moderate critics of Bowlby held that, whereas early bonding to one or many persons was essential to emotional development, an attachment was not necessarily tied to cognitive growth, which was a product of hereditary factors and environmental stimulation. "Maternal deprivation" was a misleading term, in that it was commonly used to subsume the inhibition of both processes. The critics insisted that the disruption of bonds should be seen as a factor separate from stimulus privation, although the two commonly coexisted. However, evidence has accumulated that increased attention to the provision of stimulation among institutionalized children results in improved intellectual functioning, even in the continued absence of the parents.[87] One of the earliest of such studies was initiated by Harold M. Skeels in the late 1930s, and he has since published progress reports on his subjects.[88]

Skeels's experimental group consisted of 13 children—10 girls and three boys, all under the age of three years—who were transferred from an orphanage for presumably normal children to an institution for the mentally retarded where the young children were cared for by residents of the institution. All 13 children were considered to be intellectually retarded at the time of their transfer, for their mean IQ was 64.3 (range of 35 to 89). At the new institution for the mentally retarded, the young children experienced more varied social interaction with older persons and were able to form attachments to a particular person. During the experimental period, which varied from 5.7 to 52.2 months, all children showed some increases in IQ score (from 7 to 58 points). At the end of the period 11 of the children were considered suitable for adoption and only two remained institutionalized.

Skeels's study was not well designed and has been subjected to much criticism. Skeels himself has admitted that it was originally intended as a project "to rescue for normalcy, if possible, those children showing delayed or retarded development" and was therefore not well controlled. Further studies have shown that an institutional environment need not lead to obvious intellectual deprivation. But, on the whole, there has been a paucity of such direct studies.

Instead, most researchers have concentrated on demonstrating the perceptual or social deprivation, or re-

striction, common to most institutions that provide full-
time infant care. As mentioned earlier, Casler, after reviewing the relevant literature twice, in 1961 and in 1968,
concluded that "the human organism does not need maternal love in order to function normally."[89] Social stimulation was probably secondary in importance and did not
need to be provided by a single figure, whether mother or
surrogate. Indeed, using Harlow's studies of infant monkeys as evidence, Casler suggested that socialization with
a peer group might be the indispensable factor for later
adjustment.

Animal research has been used to support both sides
of the debate. For the last 20 years or so, Bowlby has continued to stress the importance of the mother-infant
bond, using ethological findings and cybernetic models to
support his theory. In the process, he has diverged from
conventional analytic theory, which has continued to
support the Freudian postulate that the infant initially
sucked to satisfy his hunger and in so doing derived erotic oral gratification. The mother, by gratifying this two-
fold need, became the infant's first love object. Bowlby,
greatly influenced by Harlow's findings that monkeys
preferred a terrycloth surrogate mother to one who supplied food, argued that it was a mistake to regard sucking
and feeding as the preeminent causes of attachment. Other
primary instinctual responses, at first relatively independent of each other, also played a part in creating
the bond between child and mother.

Those which I am postulating are sucking, clinging, following,
crying, and smiling, but there may well be many more. In the
course of the first year of life, it is suggested, these component
instinctual responses become integrated into attachment behavior. How this process of integration is related to the parallel process in the cognitive sphere is difficult to know. It seems not

unlikely, however, that there are significant connections between the two and that a disturbance in the one will create repercussions in the other.[90]

According to Bowlby, sucking, smiling, clinging, crying, and following were instinctual responses that had survival value, in that they served to ensure maternal care. From comparative studies, however, it seemed probable that each of these responses could become focused on some object other than the mother. "The clearest examples of this in real life are when sucking becomes directed towards a bottle and not to the mother's breast, and clinging is directed to a rag and not to the mother's body," he said. Bowlby was not suggesting that several different objects or persons should be supplied to fulfill the infant's multiple needs. On the contrary, he thought that the mother became the central figure in the infant's life because of her common role as universal provider. His point was that at least five instinctual responses led to attachment behavior and that it was not yet known which, if any, was the most significant. "However, the ease with which sucking is transferred to objects other than the mother's breast leads me to think it will not prove the most important. Clinging and following seem more likely candidates for the role." From clinical observation, he had concluded that there is little or no relation between the type and degree of mental disturbance and whether the child has been breast-fed. However, rejection of clinging and following was apt to lead to emotional disturbance, even if breast-feeding had occurred. If this hypothesis was correct, he said,

we shall no longer regard it as satisfactory to equate breast and mother, to identify good feeding and good mothering, or even to speak of the earliest phase as oral and the first relationship as anaclitic. To some these may seem revolutionary consequences, but, if the hypothesis advanced here is correct, terminological change is inescapable.[91]

Eleven years later, Bowlby expounded his theory in far greater detail in *Attachment and Loss*.[92] He emphasized the reciprocal nature of attachment behavior: mother and infant continuously interact, so that normally by the age of nine months the child shows clear signs of firm attachment to his primary caretaker. Evidence that environmental variables—specifically, the amount and quality of maternal care—influence the development of attachment has been provided by Mary Slater Ainsworth. The variables that she considered important, as a result of observations of infants in both Uganda and North America, were:

the sensitivity of the mother in responding to the baby's signals of need and distress and to his social signals, and the promptness and appropriateness of her response; the amount of interaction she has with him and the amount of pleasure both derive from it; the extent to which her interventions and responses come at the baby's timing rather than her own; the extent to which she is free from preoccupation with other activities, thoughts, anxieties, and griefs so that she can attend to the baby and respond fully to him; and finally and obviously, the extent to which she can satisfy his needs, including his nutritional needs.[93]

Nevertheless, Ainsworth also concluded that "there is no evidence that care by several people necessarily interferes with the development of healthy attachment"— an opinion not really at variance with Bowlby's emphasis on the essential nature of the monolithic tie. He has accepted the implications of Ainsworth's findings: namely, that multiple mothering need not interfere with attachment to a principal figure, but that, conversely, a weak primary bond might delay the formation of secondary attachments. [94]

The question of the relation between attachment behavior and cognitive development, essentially avoided by Bowlby, was investigated by Ainsworth and Sylvia Bell. Their studies form part of a continuing research program. It should also be mentioned that Bettye M. Caldwell reported in 1969 the results of an investigation testing the hypothesis that "an appropriate environment can be programmed which will offset any developmental detriment associated with maternal separation and possibly add a degree of environmental enrichment frequently not available in families of limited social, economic, and cultural resources." [95]

Since 1965, Caldwell and her colleagues had operated a day-care center for infants. When examined at the age of 30 months, the enrolled children showed no important differences from a control home-reared group in patterns of mother-child attachment. The developmental quotients (DQ) of each group of children were measured at 12 months and again at 30 months. The home group of children, who had a significantly higher mean DQ at 12 months, showed the decline over time that has been consistently reported for disadvantaged children. "The Day Care children, while not showing any astronomical rise in developmental level, have managed to avoid decline and have, in fact, shown a slight rise." [96] Although the difference in DQ between the two groups at 30 months was not statistically significant, the findings did show that day-care programs could be designed to prevent development

decline while not damaging attachment bonds between
parent and child.

In contrast with enrichment studies, those involving
systematic deprivation could not be undertaken with
human babies. The closest alternative was infant monkeys, and extensive research with them has been carried
out by Harlow and his associates at the University of Wisconsin. At first, Harlow's findings seemed to support the
psychoanalytic dictum that an infant required loving maternal care for satisfactory emotional adjustment.[97] Further
research revealed more complex issues, which may be
summarized as follows:

§   Monkeys raised in total social isolation for three
    months were socially incompetent on release, but soon
    adjusted to agemates.

§   Those reared in total isolation for six months showed
    only very limited recovery after 32 weeks of interaction
    with peers.

§   Infant monkeys mothered normally but deprived of
    peer relations for four months showed increased ag-
    gression, but otherwise normal behavior, when al-
    lowed to interact with other infants; after eight months
    of deprivation, these antagonistic responses were
    more frequent.

§   Infant monkeys raised without the benefit of either
    real or surrogate mothers, but allowed to interact with
    their peers, showed surprisingly good long-term social
    adjustment. Monkeys raised as a constant group of six
    in some ways resembled the six World War II refugee
    children studied by Freud and Dann. According to
    Harlow: "Both situations, limited as they are in scope,

do certainly point to the important role agemates may play in the development of affection and socialization, but they both leave untested the potential adjustment of the members to the larger, more heterogeneous social group."[98] (Anna Freud and Sophia Dann had studied six small children orphaned during World War II. Although these children had not had any adult specially to care for them for the first three and a half years of their lives, and could be considered to have suffered unusual emotional deprivation, they were not retarded, delinquent, or psychotic. Freud and Dann concluded that this unexpectedly good outcome was due to the unusually strong affection the six children had developed for one another.)

§ Rhesus monkeys reared on cloth surrogate mothers and allowed to interact with their peers showed remarkably good social and sexual adjustment.[99]

§ Total isolation for six months apparently had little permanent effect on the intellectual capacity of rhesus infants; once they adapted to the learning test situations, these monkeys solved problems as rapidly as the normally reared ones. (Later, Harlow and his colleagues found the monkeys were impaired in their ability to solve very difficult problems as compared with rhesus monkeys reared in an enriched environment. See p. 188.)

§ Finally, rhesus monkeys reared in complete isolation for six months could be rehabilitated by being allowed to interact with normal monkeys three months younger than they were. At first, the younger monkeys initiated social stimulation; later, the isolates became able to reciprocate and then to initiate play behavior. After six months of therapy, the isolates seemed normal. In Harlow's words:

> Apparently, adequate adaption is required for adequate performance. With respect to social behavior, it may well be that previous studies have reported performance deficits only, that social capability remains viable despite the isolation experience, and that the requirement for rehabilitation is merely appropriate social stimulation. If this finding generalizes not only to other forms of early experience but also to other species, then the implications of the present experimentation for reversal of psychopathological behavior attributed to inadequate early experience become enormous. [100]

As Harlow himself has pointed out, the justification for interspecies generalizations will always remain questionable; such generalizations should not be taken at face value, but tested by experimentation. However, because total-deprivation studies are out of the question for human babies, interested researchers have had to rely on more circumstantial evidence, as provided by the behavior of children reared in institutions or in isolated "primitive" communities. The latter approach has been used by Jerome Kagan to investigate the extent to which "psychological structures" shaped by early experience have continuity in later childhood.

Kagan had long been interested in determining the extent to which early behavior was predictive of adult personality and intellectual functioning. A longitudinal approach to the problem seemed the most adequate, and, during the late 1950s and early 1960s as a member of the Fels Research Institute team, he sought evidence of the stability of behavioral patterns through childhood. [101] On the whole, although he persisted in this search for 15 years, Kagan had found only "fragile lines that seem to travel both backward and forward in time [;] the continuities are not overwhelming in either breadth or magnitude, and each seems to be easily lost or shattered."[102]

The findings did not necessarily indicate that no traits were permanent, but rather that those usually subjected to long-term study were "inherently relativistic in definition and quantification." In other words, such characteristics as passivity, dependence, and verbal ability could not be measured as absolutes for a given individual, but only described according to the extent to which they were exhibited by other members of the group under consideration. For such characteristics, permanence could be expected only if the social environment remained essentially unchanged over time, which was unlikely. Other traits, such as lability of mood, might be more independent of social interaction and therefore exhibit continuity. However, Kagan said,

at present the dimensions that comprise the most valued compounds of self cannot be isolated from the social context the subject or the evaluator assumes as primary referent. Hence, one cannot discuss long term stability of the most human characters without specifying the context of development. Nor can one talk of an identity apart from an individual's network of relationships.[103]

Kagan and Klein provided research findings on cross-sectional samples of children growing up in an isolated Indian village to support their hypothesis that infant behavior may not necessarily be a sensitive indicator of future behavior and competence. In the isolated village of San Marcos la Laguna in northwest Guatemala, infants under one year of age were retarded in the emergence of the standard milestones of infancy compared with American infants. Confined to a dark hut, close to the mother but rarely spoken to or played with, babies received very little variety of experience until they were able to walk and provide themselves with new encounters. The 1-year-old children were inhibited and quiet, and the appearance of object permanence, language, and the enhancement of short-term memory that characterizes late infancy was delayed in them. By the age of 10, however, when children were expected to perform adult tasks and had been at school for a few years, they were alert, competent in tasks of perceptual analysis and memory, and effectively vital.

Observations in poor, isolated Indian villages have led me to reorder the hierarchy of complementary influence that biological and environmental forces exert on cognitive development. Maturation seems to set the general time of emergence of basic functions, given a reasonably natural environment. Experience can speed up or slow down the time of emergence by six months or three to four years, but nature will win in the end. The capacity for perceptual analysis, influence, deduction, symbolism and memory will eventually appear in sturdy form, for each is an inherent competence in the human program. [104]

The recent findings of Kagan and of Harlow indicate a degree of developmental plasticity, in opposition to the critical-period hypothesis put forward by the ethologists and espoused by Bowlby. Kagan and Harlow have indicated that, although early deprivation has an immediate influence on behavior, its effects need not be permanent. When placed in a suitable and more benign environment, the young organism may be able to recover from emotional and cognitive deficiencies induced by lack of variety in stimulation. The capacity for development has remained latent, requiring activation by appropriate stimulation. This was provided by the younger "therapist" monkeys in the Harlow study and by the normal environment that included peer group interaction in the Kagan-Klein cross-cultural study.

Recent research—although it has undermined the validity of his essentially monotropic attachment theory —cannot detract from the social and heuristic value of Bowlby's 1951 report, *Maternal Care and Mental Health,* or of his more recent work. There was dire need for a full investigation of the antiquated conditions in which orphans and unwanted children were reared. Nor would anyone have been likely to suggest that such infants should be deprived of intellectual and social stimulation on the slight chance that they would later be reared in an adequate "therapeutic" environment. As Kagan has stressed, the psychological traits of the individual are measured as relative to those displayed by the society in which he lives or, for the "deprived" child, as relative to those exhibited by the larger society in which he will later have to interact. Potential remains unmeasurable; only performance can be observed and measured. Whatever standards of achievement are the norms for our society, the relatively disadvantaged child will require assistance to meet these standards as soon as possible in his life.

SHORT-TERM MATERNAL DEPRIVATION

Another consequence of Bowlby's report has been a realization of the potentially serious effects of temporary maternal deprivation, especially between the ages of six months and two and one-half years, when attachment is normally growing most rapidly. Bowlby has suggested that an infant separated from its mother, perhaps owing to hospitalization, goes into a state of depression akin to

adult mourning. Again, his warning of the dire consequences, although perhaps exaggerated, has had a salutary
effect on the attitude of pediatric hospital staff members
toward young children and their families. Previously, it
was thought that small children rapidly adapted to hospital conditions and suffered stress only when their parents
visited them and thus reminded them of the world they
had lost. Therefore, the aim was to restrict visiting as
much as possible, often down to two 1-hour visits each
week. That children should be afraid of pain or mutila-
tion, especially before a surgical procedure, was accepted.
What was not understood was the potential strength and
duration of separation anxiety. This was brought home to
many by means of the film, *A Two-Year-Old Goes to the
Hospital*, made by James Robertson as part of a Tavistock
Clinic study on separation and reunion. A paper interpreting the psychodynamic processes illustrated in the
film was published in the *Psychoanalytic Study of the Child*,
by Bowlby, Robertson, and Rosenbluth.[105] Later, many
physicians and psychologists, but especially psychiatrists,
investigated the effects of this type of separation.[106] By
the middle 1960s, most hospitals in England and America
that admitted young children had extended daily visiting
hours, and many encouraged mothers to sleep at the hospital and care for their children. This solicitude to preserve the mother-child relationship would have been inconceivable 20 years earlier.

　　An earlier measure adopted by hospitals to foster the
infant-mother relationship was "rooming-in"—allowing
the newborn infant to spend the day with his mother,
rather than in a central nursery. The term "rooming-in"
was first used by Gesell, Ilg, and Ames in *Infants and
Child in the Culture of Today*, in which they laid out the
details and benefits of such an arrangement.[107] The main

advantage of the practice was that it allowed the neonate to be fed on demand, rather than to be left to cry unheeded in a communal nursery.[108] Also, the mother would be helped by the hospital staff to learn to care for her child, instead of being faced on her return home with a comparative stranger, and a very demanding one at that. In some instances, rooming-in was introduced for pragmatic rather than psychological reasons. Many hospitals experienced an acute nursing shortage during the war years, and the new system promised to ensure continued adequate supervision for each infant.

On the whole, "rooming-in" was well received by mothers, pediatricians, and psychiatrists, the main skeptics being obstetricians, who were more concerned with the care of the mother and were not convinced that suitably aseptic conditions could be maintained.[109] In this connection, as pointed out by Wilfred Gaisford, it should be remembered that "this 'new' fashion [rooming-in] was certainly a very old one which had been temporarily abandoned in maternity hospitals because of the bugbear of infection."[110] Before 1900, most babies in the United States were delivered at home; by 1940, most obstetricians were insisting on hospitalization, for reasons of safety and convenience. The shift had been accompanied by a significant decrease in maternal and infant mortality, but it had also led to a mechanization of the delivery process and a strict but necessary emphasis on asepsis. As the mortality figures fell and antibiotics were introduced, physicians became a little less concerned about physical hazards and a little more aware of the emotional factors involved in childbirth. Natural delivery, demand feeding, and "rooming-in" were all examples of relaxation of early twentieth century maternity-unit routine to satisfy pediatric and psychiatric objections.

Conclusions

Psychoanalytic ideas of child development and infant care came into their own during the 1940s and early 1950s. These ideas had been around for decades, slowly gathering momentum for their implementation from the findings of European clinicians and child guidance practitioners in America. A restrictive form of child care was replaced by practices that reflected Freud's influence. That these did not quite tally with the intent of either Freud or his followers was unfortunate but perhaps unavoidable because of the very diffuseness and intangibility of analytic theory.

Nevertheless, on one point there could be no misunderstanding—namely, the importance that all analysts ascribed to the early mother-infant relationship. Their precise theories varied, but all stressed the importance of breast-feeding, prompt attention to the infant's needs, gradual weaning, and toilet training at the child's own pace to ensure emotional stability. Such requirements seemed so obvious and so natural that they were accepted without demur; mothers perhaps little realized that they were being more tightly bound to their infants than ever before in history (the larger households of the past had provided multiple secondary caretakers). For a while, it was up to the skeptical experimental psychologist to show that empirical research did not support the more extreme psychoanalytic viewpoint. Controlled observations showed that infants who had been bottle-fed or abruptly weaned or toilet-trained early did not suffer greater emotional maladjustment than those reared according to analytic principles. Other factors—such as the attitude of the mother, her tenseness, or her warmth—seemed more relevant than the actual mechanics of child care.

In the United States, the influence of psychoanalytical concepts was probably maximal during the fifties. It began to wane in the sixties, particularly among citizens who regarded campus riots and draft-card burning as the results of an over-permissive upbringing. Furthermore, children brought up on analytic principles still had emotional problems, and the attempt to remove repression of sexual impulses among adolescents and adults did not appear to be accompanied by improved mental health. Other theories of development—for example, Jean Piaget's —began to attract attention. For these and other reasons, an erosion of the persuasive power of psychoanalytic theory gradually set in. It was to become one of the many ways to interpret early development, rather than the only one.[111]

Notes and References

1. Jones, E., *The Life and Work of Sigmund Freud*, p. 141. (Edited and abridged by L. Trilling and S. Marcus.) New York: Basic Books, Inc., 1961. *Also:* H. F. Ellenberger. *The Discovery of the Unconscious. The History and Evolution of Dynamic Psychiatry*, p. 443. New York: Basic Books, Inc., 1970.

2. Freud, S. "On the history of the psychoanalytic movement" (1914). *Standard Edition of the Complete Psychological Works of Sigmund Freud*, James Strachey, ed. Vol. 14, p. 18. London: Hogarth Press, 1953–1974.

3. Ibid., p. 17.

4. Ibid., p. 18.

5. H. F. Ellenberger *The Discovery of the Unconscious*, pp. 502–507; I. Bry and A. H. Rifkin "Freud and the history of ideas: Primary sources," 1886–1910. *Sci. Psychoanal.* 5:6–36, 1962; and S. Kern "Freud and the discovery of child sexuality." *Hist. Childhood Quart.* 1:117–141, 1973. These four authors have adduced much evidence that the ramifications of childhood sexuality were being freely discussed before 1905. That this occurred in intellectual and professional circles does not necessarily mean that the same attitude prevailed generally.

6. Freud, S. Three essays on the theory of sexuality, (1905). Standard Edition, Vol. 7, p. 173.

7. Ibid., p. 174.

8. Ibid., p. 175.

9. Freud, S. "The origin and development of psychoanalysis." *Amer. J. Psychol.* 21:181–218, 1910; also as "Five lectures on psychoanalysis." *Standard Edition*, Vol. 11, pp. 9–55.

10. Freud, S. Three essays on the theory of sexuality, *Standard Edition*, Vol. 7, pp. 201–202.

11. Ibid., p. 182.

12. Ibid., p. 182.

13. Ibid., p. 186.

14. Jones, E. Sigmund Freud: *Life and Work*, Volume II, p. 59. London: The Hogarth Press, 1955.

15. Freud, S. Character and anal erotism, (1908). *Standard Edition*, Vol. 9, p. 175.

16. Freud, S. *The Standard Edition*, Vol. 1. Pre-Psycho-Analytic Publications and Unpublished Drafts (Extracts from the Fliess Papers, Letter 52 (Dec. 6, 1896), p. 239; Letter 55 (Jan. 11, 1897), p. 241; Letter 75 (Nov. 14, 1897), pp. 268–270).

17. Ibid., Letter 75, p. 268.

18. Ibid., p. 269.

19. K. S. Lashley argued that the distributions of nervous energies and their interactions, as postulated by Freud, were not consistent with any organismic process known to biologists. "The mental mechanisms of the psychoanalysts resemble more closely the behavior of liquids under pressure than they do any physiological process and, indeed, the similarity is so exact that we might justly call the Freudian dynamics a system of psychohydraulics." (Lashley. "Contributions of Freudism to psychology. III. Physiological analysis of the libido," p. 194. *Psychol. Rev.* 31:192–202, 1924.) Knight Dunlap suggested that the feud between academic psychology and psychoanalysis was

but a revival of the age-old struggle between science and mysticism. (Dunlap. *Mysticism, Freudianism and Scientific Psychology.* St. Louis: C. V. Mosby Co., 1920. 173 pp.)

20. Freud, S. "Three essays on the theory of sexuality," *Standard Edition*, Vol. 7, p. 187.

21. Ibid., p. 188.

22. Freud, S., "The origin and development of psychoanalysis." *Am. J. Psychol.* 27:181–218, 1910.

23. Ibid.

24. Freud, S. "Three essays on the theory of sexuality." *Standard Edition*, Vol. 7, p. 197.

25. Freud, S. "The origin and development of psychoanalysis." *Am. J. Psychol.* 21:181–218, 1910.

26. Rapaport, D. "The structure of psychoanalytic theory." *Psycholog. Issues* 2(Monogr. 6):47–52, 1960. Rapaport discusses the extent to which the drives may be considered as the ultimate determinants of behavior. *See also:* C. Thompson. *Psychoanalysis: Evolution and Development*, p. 26. New York: Hermitage House, Inc., 1950.

27. Freud, S. "Three essays on the theory of sexuality." *Standard Edition*, Vol. 7, pp. 170–171.

28. Ibid., pp. 242–243.

29. Freud, S. "Instincts and their vicissitudes" (1915). *Standard Edition*, Vol. 14, p. 126.

30. Freud, S. "Repression" (1915). *Standard Edition*, Vol. 14, p. 155.

31. Freud, S. "On the history of the psychoanalytic movement" (1914). *Standard Edition*, Vol. 14, p. 52. E. Jones' account of the rift with Adler is given in *Sigmund Freud: Life and Work*, Vol. II, pp. 145–151, and of the break with Jung in the same volume, pp. 155–171.

32. An analysis of the reasons for Freud's alterations in his instinct theory is provided by Clara Thompson's *Psychoanalysis: Evolution and Development*, pp. 46–48; and by H. F. Ellenberger's *The Discovery of the Unconscious*, pp. 512–518.

33. Freud, S. *Standard Edition*, Vol. 19, p. 36.

34. In "The structure of psychoanalytic theory" (pp. 20–33),

David Rapaport has pointed out that Freud used four distinct models: the reflex arc or topographic model, the entropy or economic model, the Darwinian or genetic model, and the Jacksonian or neural integration hierarchy model.

35. Thus, Freud's hypothesized instinctual energy system (based on the entropy model) was a closed one within which energy was conserved (i.e., had a fixed quantity during the lifetime of the individual concerned), could be distributed by the mechanism of cathexis, and had both kinetic and potential form. Kinetic or free energy was used in such processes as sublimation, whereas potential or latent energy was the source of tension in repression. The libido, and later the id, was conceived as the permanent reservoir of psychic energy. The Freudian energy system, based on Maxwell's model of physical energy distribution, was quite acceptable at the turn of the century; but, by the 1920s, it was incompatible with known physiological theory. Freud never revised his instinctual energy model, although it so clearly belonged to the science of his youth.

36. Freud, S. "Instincts and their vicissitudes." *Standard Edition*, Vol. 14, p. 120.

37. Freud, S. "Three essays on the theory of sexuality." *Standard Edition*, Vol. 7, p. 234.

38. "The intention is to furnish a psychology that shall be a natural science: that is, to represent psychical processes as quantitatively determinate states of specifiable material particles. . . ." S. Freud. *Standard Edition*, Vol. 1, p. 295. See: P. Amacher. "Freud's neurological education and its influence on psychoanalytic theory." *Psychol. Issues* 4:(No. 4, Monogr. 16):1–87, 1965.

39. Freud, S. "An outline of psychoanalysis" (1940). *Standard Edition*, Vol. 23, p. 196.

40. A good account of the extremes to which toilet training could be carried is given in J. Gathorne-Hardy's *The Rise and Fall of The British Nanny* London: Hodder and Stoughton, 1972.

41. Stendler, C. B. "Sixty years of child training practices. Revolution in the nursery." *J. Pediat.* 36:122–134, 1950. Stendler scanned every issue of *Ladies Home Journal, Woman's Home*

Companion, and *Good Housekeeping* for the first year in each decade from 1890 to 1948 (instead of 1950) and analyzed the concepts presented in the articles dealing with child-training practices.

42. Ibid., p. 125. *See also:* C. E. Vincent. "Trends in infant care ideas." *Child Develop.* 22:199–209, 1951.

43. Freud, S. "New introductory lectures on psychoanalysis" (1933). *Standard Edition,* Vol. 22, pp. 146–151.

44. Ibid., pp. 146–151.

45. Read, K. H. "Don't be afraid of strong feelings." *Parents' Mag.* 25:44–45, 116–118, May 1950.

46. Ibid., p. 118.

47. An exception was Susan Isaacs' *The Nursery Years,* published first in England in 1929 and then in the United States in 1938. Isaacs opposed the current emphasis on strictly disciplinarian modes of child-training, advocating instead an amalgam of psychoanalytic, maturation and common sense methods. Isaacs. *The Nursery Years. The Mind of the Child from Birth to Six Years.* New York: Schocken Books, 1968. (Reprint of the 1929 American ed.).

48. We are differentiating here between the full-time professional psychoanalysts and those like B. Spock who had some analytic training, but did not consider themselves experts in the field.

49. Josselyn, I. M. *Psychosocial Development of Children,* p. 6, New York: Family Service Association of America, 1948.

50. Ibid., p. 6.

51. Ibid., p. 34.

52. Caldwell, B. M. "The effects of infant care." In M. L. and L. W. Hoffman, Eds. *Review of Child Development Research,* Vol. I. New York: Russell Sage Foundation, 1964, pp. 9–87.

53. Ibid., p. 79.

54. Ibid., p. 55.

55. Ibid., p. 81.

56. See, for example, "Editorial: The origins of obesity," *Am. J. Dis. Child.,* 1976, *130,* 465–467 and Beverley Winikoff, "Changing public diet," *Human Nature,* 1978, *1,* 60–65.

57. Freud, A. *The Writings of Anna Freud. Vol. V: Research at the Hampstead Child-Therapy Clinic and Other Papers: 1956–1965,* p. 266. New York: International Universities Press, Inc., 1969.

58. Ibid., p. 267.

59. Two major works on social learning theory were published after 1949: J. Dollard and N. E. Miller. *Personality and Psychotherapy: An Analysis in Terms of Learning, Thinking, and Culture.* New York: McGraw-Hill, 1950, and R. R. Sears, E. E. Macoby, and H. Levine. *Patterns of Child-Rearing.* New York: Harper & Row, 1957.

60. Witmer, H. L., and R. Kotinsky, Eds. *Personality in the Making: The Fact-Finding Report of the Midcentury White House Conference on Children and Youth.* New York: Harper, 1952.

61. Erikson, E. H. *Childhood and Society,* pp. 247–274. New York: W. W. Norton, 1963. *And:* Growth and crises of the "healthy personality." In M. J. E. Senn, Ed. *Symposium on the Healthy Personality, Supplement 2: Problems of Infancy and Childhood,* pp. 97–146. New York: Josiah Macy, Jr. Foundation, 1950. For biographies of Erikson, see: Robert Coles, *Erik H. Erikson: The Growth of his Work,* Boston: Little, Brown & Co., and Paul Roagen, *Erik H. Erikson: The Power and Limits of a Vision,* New York: Free Press, 1976.

62. *Symposium on the Healthy Personality, Supplement 2,* p. 98.

63. Ibid., p. 97.

64. Ibid., p. 112.

65. *Childhood and Society,* p. 255.

66. Freud, A. The mutual influences in the development of ego and id: Introduction to the discussion (1952 [1951]), pp. 230–244. In *The Writings of Anna Freud.* Vol. IV.

67. Kubie, L. S. Problems and techniques of psychoanalytic validation and progress. In E. Pumpian-Mindlin, Ed. *Psychoanalysis as Science; The Hixon Lectures on the Scientific Status of Psychoanalysis.* Stanford: Stanford University Press, 1952, pp. 46–124. Kubie suggested methods whereby "mature" research on psychoanalytic postulates might be carried out (pp. 113–123), including the use of controls.

68. Margaret Ribble, *The Rights of Infants* (New York, Columbia University Press, 1943); and, "Infantile experience in relation to personality development," in *Personality and the Behavior Disorders*, Vol. II, ed. J. McV. Hunt (New York, Ronald Press, 1944), pp. 621–651. Ribble's publications were extensively criticized by S. R. Pinneau, "A critique on the articles by Margaret Ribble," *Child Develop.*, 1950, *21*, 203–228; and by H. Orlansky, "Infant care and personality," *Psychol. Bull.*, 1949, *46*, 1–48.

69. Ribble, M. A. *Personality and the Behavior Disorders*, Vol. 2, p. 36. It is of interest that Ribble attributed the deterioration to lack of stimulation, as well as to lack of mothering itself.

70. Goldfarb, W. Effects of early institutional care on adolescent personality (*J. Exp. Educ.* 12:106–129, 1943); Infant rearing and problem behavior (*Amer. J. Orthopsychiat.* 13:249–265, 1943); and Effects of early institutional care on adolescent personality: Rorschach data (*Amer. J. Orthopsychiat.* 14:441–447, 1944).

71. Spitz, R. A. "Hospitalism: An inquiry into the genesis of psychiatric conditions in early childhood." *Psychoanalyt. Study Child* 1:53–74, 1945. *And:* Spitz. "Hospitalism: A follow-up report on investigation described in Volume I, 1945." *Psychoanalyt. Study Child* 2:113–117, 1946.

72. Spitz, R. A. "Hospitalism: An inquiry into the genesis of psychiatric conditions in early childhood." In U. Bronfenbrenner, Ed. *Influences on Human Development*. Hinsdale, Ill: Dryden Press, 1972, pp. 202–203.

73. Ibid., p. 212.

74. Spitz, R. A., and K. M. Wolf, "Anaclytic depression: An inquiry into the genesis of psychiatric conditions in early childhood: II." *Psychoanalyt. Study Child* 2:313–342, 1946.

75. Bowlby, J. *Maternal Care and Mental Health*, p. 157. New York: Schocken Books, 1966.

76. Ibid., p. 158.

77. For example, see: M. D. Ainsworth, R. G. Andry, R. G. Harlow, S. Lebovici, M. Mead, D. G. Prugh, and B. Wootton. *Deprivation of Maternal Care. A Reassessment of its Effects.* New

York: Schocken Books, 1966. *And:* M. Rutter. *Maternal Deprivation Reassessed*, pp. 99–106. Harmondsworth, Eng.: Penguin Books, 1972.

78. Spitz's papers were extensively analyzed and criticized, mainly for their inconsistencies and the lack of significance of many of the findings, in S. P. Pinneau's "The infantile disorders of hospitalism and anaclytic depression," *Psychol. Bull.* 52:429–452, 1955.

79. The lack of firm evidence of the permanence of the effects of separation is discussed by N. O'Connor, Children in restricted environments. In G. Newton and S. Levine, Eds. *Early Experience and Behavior. The Psychobiology.* Springfield, Ill.: Charles C Thomas, 1968, pp. 530–572.

80. Casler, L. "Perceptual deprivation in institutional settings." In G. Newton and S. Levine, Eds. *Early Experience and Behavior.* Springfield, Il.: Charles C Thomas, 1968, pp. 573–626. Casler suggested that "the human organism does not need maternal love in order to function normally" and offered the hypothesis of perceptual deprivation "as an explanatory principle preferable to that of maternal deprivation for the study of the ill effects of institutionalization" (p. 612).

81. Lebovici, S. "The concept of maternal deprivation: A review of research." In M. D. Ainsworth *et al. Deprivation of Maternal Care. A Reassessment of its Effects.* New York: Schocken Books, 1966, pp. 267–287.

82. Howells, J. G. "Separation of mother and child" (Letter to the editor). *Lancet* 1:691, March 29, 1958. Howells pointed out that the exaggerated emphasis on separation as an evil in itself had led to disturbing tendencies in child care; "there is reluctance, in some quarters, to rescue a child suffering privation in his own home; there is some loss of confidence in the day nursery, nursery school, and fostering. Great opportunities for preventive psychiatry appear to lie in the antithesis of Dr. Bowlby's thesis."

83. Helfer, R. E., and C. H. Kempe, Eds. *The Battered Child.* Chicago: University of Chicago Press, 1968. *Also:* D. Bakan. *Slaughter of the Innocents.* San Francisco: Jossey-Bass, 1971.

84. Rutter, M. *Maternal Deprivation Reassessed,* pp. 99–106. Harmondsworth, Eng.: Penguin Books, 1972. Rutter discusses the idea that the failure to form bonds may have different effects from the disruption of bonds and the idea that bonding with agemates, rather than with a mother-figure, may be sufficient for later adjustment.

85. Ainsworth, M. D. "The effects of maternal deprivation: A review of findings and controversy in the context of research strategy." In M. D. Ainsworth, et al. *Deprivation of Maternal Care,* pp. 289–337, 1966. Ainsworth stated that the evidence suggested that kibbutz children made close attachments to their parents, but that they made much stronger identifications with their group age-peers than did family children. (p. 316)

86. Rutter, M. *Maternal Deprivation Reassessed,* p. 25.

87. Tizard, B. O., A. J. Cooperman, and J. Tizard. "Environmental effects on language development: A study of young children in long-stay residential nurseries." *Child Develop.* 43:337–358, 1972. Tizard and her co-workers studied 85 children aged two to five years in 13 residential nursery groups. No "institutional retardation" was found, and the mean test scores on both verbal and nonverbal tests were average. Significant correlations were obtained between the language-comprehension scores of the children and both the quality of the talk directed to them and the way in which the nursery was organized.

88. Skeels, H. M. "Adult status of children with contrasting early life experiences: A follow up study." In U. Bronfenbrenner, Ed. *Influences on Human Development,* pp. 224–255. Hinsdale, Ill.: Dryden Press, 1972. In the middle 1930s, at a time when intellectual development was generally considered to be determined by hereditary factors, Skeels began what has since become a longitudinal study of the effects of environmental influences on mental development.

89. Casler, L. "Perceptual deprivation in institutional settings." In G. Newton and S. Levine, Eds. *Early Experience and Behavior.* Springfield, Ill.: Charles C Thomas, 1968, p. 612.

90. Bowlby, J. "The nature of the child's tie to his mother." *Int. J. Psychoanal.* 39:350–373, 1958. Even in his more recent work, *Attachment and Loss* (New York: Basic Books, 1969), Bowlby has not accounted for the assumed relation between cognitive development and attachment behavior.

91. Ibid., p. 371. Bowlby's ethologically based concepts did not find much favor among more orthodox psychoanalysts. See: "Discussion of John Bowlby's work on separation, grief, and mourning." In *The Writings of Anna Freud, Volume V*, pp. 167–186, 1969.

92. J. *Attachment and Loss: Volume I. Attachment*, p. 308. New York: Basic Books, Inc., 1969.

93. Ainsworth, M. D. S. "Variables influencing the development of attachment." In C. S. Lavatelli and F. Stendler, Eds. *Readings in Child Behavior and Development*. New York: Harcourt, Brace Jovanovich, Inc., 1972, pp. 193–201.

94. Bowlby, J. *Attachment and Loss*, p. 308.

95. Caldwell, B. M., C. M. Wright, A. S. Honig, and J. Tannenbaum. "Infant day care and attachment." *Amer. J. Orthopsychiat.* 40:397–412, 1970.

96. Ibid., pp. 408–409.

97. Harlow, H. F. "The heterosexual affectional system in monkeys." *Amer. Psychol.* 17:1–9, 1962.

98. Harlow, H. F., and M. K. Harlow. "Effects of various mother-infant relationships on rhesus monkey behaviors." In B. M. Foss, Ed. *Determinants of Infant Behavior IV.* London: Methuen, 1969, pp. 15–36. The reference is to A. Freud and S. Dann, "An experiment in group upbringing" (*Psychoanalyt. Study Child* 6:127–168, 1951).

99. Evidence for these first five points is given in the Harlow paper in *Determinants of Infant Behavior IV*, pp. 15–36.

100. Suomi, S. J., and H. F. Harlow. "Social rehabilitation of isolate-reared monkeys." *Develop. Psychol.* 6:487–496, 1972.

101. A summary of a comprehensive assessment of a group of young adults who had been members of the Fels Research Institute's longitudinal population since birth was provided by J. Kagan and H. A. Moss in *Birth to Maturity; A Study in Psychological Development* (New York: John Wiley, 1962). "The findings of this study point to islands of continuity amidst the changing response patterns of the growing child and suggest that some popular hypotheses about development need revision." (p. vii).

102. Kagan, J., and R. E. Klein. "Cross-cultural perspectives on early development." *Amer. Psychol.* 28:947–961, 1973.

103. Kagan, J. "Cross-cultural perspectives on early development: A progress report." Unpublished manuscript, 1972.

104. Kagan, J., and R. E. Klein. "Cross-cultural perspectives on early development."

105. Bowlby, J., J. Robertson, and D. Rosenbluth. "A two-year-old goes to hospital." *Psychoanalyt. Study Child* 7:82–94, 1952.

106. The problem of the emotional effects of hospitalization, especially for surgery, had been explored earlier by psychiatrists. See: L. Jessner and S. Kaplan. "Observations on the emotional reactions of children to tonsillectomy and adenoidectomy—A preliminary report." In M.J.E. Senn, Ed. *Problems of Infancy and Childhood.* (Transactions of the Third Conference, March 7–8, 1949, New York, N.Y.) New York: Josiah Macy, Jr. Foundation, 1949, pp. 97–118.

107. Gesell, A. L., F. L. Ilg, and L. B. Ames. *Infant and Child in the Culture of Today. The Guidance of Development in Home and Nursery School,* pp. 82–87. New York: Harper & Row, 1943.

108. For a historical background and account of the development of rooming-in in the United States, see: E. B. Jackson and G. Trainham, Eds. *Family Centered Maternity and Infant Care.* (Report of the Committee on Rooming-In of the Josiah Macy, Jr. Foundation Conference on Problems of Infancy and Early Childhood.). New York: Josiah Macy, Jr. Foundation, 1950.

109. Josiah Macy, Jr. Foundation. Report of the Subcommittee on Rooming-In. In: *Seventh Conference on Problems of Infancy and Childhood.* New York: Josiah Macy, Jr. Foundation, 1954, pp. 141–168.

110. Gaisford, W. "Changing fashions in infant care." *J. Pediatrics* 64:913–922, 1964.

111. See, Ann M. Clarke and A. D. B. Clarke, Eds., *Early Experience: Myth and Evidence* (New York: Free Press, 1976), for a recent review and evaluation of studies questioning the validity of the hypothesis that early maternal, and other forms of severe, deprivation inevitably lead to later personality and cognitive deficits.

4

Watson and
the American Tradition

While Freud's ideas were gaining ground
in America among physicians, psychologists, social workers, and better-educated citizens, a more distinctively
American point of view was growing under the intellectual leadership of John Watson. This movement, known
as behaviorism, was and continues to be more in accord
with America's preference for pragmatism and simplicity
that was Freudianism. Watson's message could be summarized succinctly to an American parent in a single
one-hour lecture: reward the behavior that you want your
child to maintain and punish him for the behavior that
you do not want him to maintain; apply that principle
consistently for 10 years and you will have produced your
"dream child."

It is common for a new theory to gain ascendancy by
attacking a dominant point of view that is beginning to

show decay. In this instance, the movement that Watson
was trying to subdue was not Freud's psychoanalytic
theory (which was itself still immature) but a tradition in
the academy of experimental psychologists that had led to
subjective introspection and a foundering of the new science of psychology. Watson wished to scuttle that approach to psychology, rather than to prescribe childrearing practices. But his theory had repercussions in
both education and childrearing.

Early Behaviorist Theories
of Child Development

At the turn of the century many academic psychologists
were trying to understand mental activity by evaluating
subjective responses to various stimuli. The original aim
was to devise simple laws of perception, but this was
found to be impossible because reaction times varied from
person to person. To explain such differences, psychologists required each subject to describe his thought processes during an experiment, which caused the method
to lose in objectivity and gain in complexity. To some,
psychology seemed to be going nowhere as a science,
and the resulting dissatisfaction was encapsulated
in John B. Watson's manifesto, "Psychology as the behaviorist views it," published in 1913.[1] He stated that
publicly observable phenomena must replace consciousness as the subject of research, the theoretical goal of
psychology being "the prediction and control of behavior." A method suitable for this new approach had already
been suggested by animal experimentation, which was
implicitly behavioristic, in that results depended on the
observation of responses to stimuli, not on appeals to pri-

vate consciousness. Watson's idea was to extend this type of research to humans, using infants as favored subjects because they would exhibit natural rather than learned behavior.

At first, the theoretical justification for the new psychology was somewhat indefinite, as Watson himself recognized. He postulated that all organisms adapted to their environment by means of hereditary and learned responses. "These adjustments may be very adequate or they may be so inadequate that the organism barely maintains its existence," he said. "Secondly, certain stimuli lead the organism to make the responses."[2] Watson believed that in a fully systematized psychology, both the response to a given stimulus and the stimulus that caused a given response should be predictable.

Although he was to become a confirmed environmentalist, Watson believed at this stage that adult behavior was an amalgam of (innate) instincts and (acquired) habits. In his view, heredity provided the capacity to perform individual acts, which could be grouped (shaped) to form more complex habits that depended on the types of environmental stimuli presented. But specific habits could not be formed unless the necessary component instincts had been inherited.

Individuals certainly differ enormously in the number and kinds of random activity which they may display upon the presentation of given stimuli. If appropriate random acts do not appear upon the incidence of the given stimulus, it is fruitless to attempt to establish habits respecting that stimulus, e.g., if the child fails to respond adequately to colors, pencils, chalk, and to the form and size of objects (when intensity and combination are sufficiently varied) it is useless to try to instill artistic habits. . . . It seems safe to conclude that all of the vocations are probably at bottom dependent upon particular hereditary types of organization, i.e., dependent upon the presence of random activity of proper kinds.[3]

So far, Watson was subscribing to contemporary evolutionary associationist's concepts of development, except in one respect—he rejected any notion that implied that a habit was acquired through conscious choice on the part of the organism.

Watson was influenced by Edward L. Thorndike, who was concurrently demonstrating that the behavior of both animals and children could be investigated experimentally.[4] In 1898, by dint of repeated trials with cats in puzzle boxes of his own invention, he was able to adduce experimental evidence supporting the 19th century Spencer-Bain thesis that learning occurred because a random act that caused pleasurable sensations would tend to be repeated, whereas a useless instinctive action would tend to die out.[5] Thorndike labeled this "learning by trial and accidental success." (It was later known more generally as "trial and error learning") and he restated it as the "law of effect" in 1911.[6] The importance of the concept was that it eliminated the need for rational thought on the part of the animal; Thorndike's contribution was to provide empirical evidence for what had previously been only a hypothetical construct.

By 1901, Thorndike was suggesting that all learning in infants, and some in older children and adults, occurred by "trial and success" and that the use of this principle might afford the only way to teach dull children. "In such cases the work of the teacher is naturally to stamp out the failures by making the pupil feel uncomfortable at them, and to stamp in the successes by approval, by making the pupil himself care, etc.," he said.[7] This was no new principle of education, but an age-old common-sense method of reward and punishment that originally was given a theoretical basis—the association of ideas—by Locke. What was novel was Thorndike's explanation for the occurrence of this type of learning—namely, that it did not require the intervention of thought or inference on the part of the pupil, but merely that the act should be successful or pleasurable. Watson went even further, suggesting that all took place reflexively without the active participation of the organism; Thorndike was reluctant to take this step.

Moreover, Watson did not believe that responses that were "satisfying" to the organism were likely to be repeated, nor those which caused discomfort to become extinguished. Thus he rejected the two postulates of Thorndike's "law of effect." To Watson terms like "annoyance" and "satisfaction" were mentalistic and therefore objectionable. He proposed that frequency of an act and recency of performance determined habit formation, or learning.[8] In this view the organism was entirely passive and at the mercy of his instincts and of environmental stimuli impinging on them. Watson's attempt to explain the occurrence of learning on totally mechanistic principles was a bold one, considering the fact that the experimental evidence supporting this idea was not very convincing.[9]

In 1915, Watson discovered a far more satisfactory mechanism to account for habit formation—Pavlovian conditioning (often called classical or respondent conditioning). Ivan Pavlov had shown that the presentation of food to dogs caused a reflex of salivation. He further showed that if a second stimulus, such as the ringing of a bell, were consistently paired with the presentation of food, the second stimulus acting alone eventually became capable of evoking a salivary response very similar to the original reflex flow. Conditioning was but a part of more extensive research on reflex action that had been carried out for some years by Pavlov and V. M. Bekhterev and even earlier by I. M. Sechenov, but Watson apparently became aware of the relevance of the Russian work to his own line of thinking only in about 1915.[10] From then on he unwaveringly adopted the conditioned or conditional reflex as the basic explanatory mechanism for all types of learning.[11]

Watson now considered human behavior to be due in part to hereditary reactions (emotional and instinctive) and in part to modes of response acquired through conditioning (habits). An emotion was a "hereditary 'pattern-reaction' involving profound changes of the bodily mechanism as a whole, but particularly of the visceral and glandular systems."[12] After observing a number of infants, he concluded that only three innate types of emotional reaction existed: those due to fear, rage, and love, "using *love* in approximately the same sense that Freud used *sex*."[13] All others were acquired or learned. Watson defined an instinct as a "combination of congenital responses unfolding serially under appropriate stimulation," that is, as a coordinated sequence of reflexes leading to observable actions or movements. Instincts and habits were composed of the same elementary reflexes, but in instincts the pattern and order were inherited, whereas in habit they were acquired.[14] Instincts and habits could not be distinguished by observing adult behavior, according to Watson, but only by previous knowledge of the infant's instinctive repertoire.

Suiting action to words, Watson made the study of infant behavior a major part of his experimental program from 1917 until his resignation from The Johns Hopkins University in 1920.[15] His experimental work was then discontinued until 1923, when he returned to the study of infant development at the Hecksher Foundation, in collaboration with Mary Cover Jones. Although his opportunities for research were restricted, he continued to write books and popular articles on behaviorism, including his harshly provocative *Psychological Care of Infant and Child*, published in 1928.

Observation of the newborn soon convinced Watson that conditioning began early in life, probably even while a child was only a fetus. Consequently, he began to discount the importance of instinctive behavior, now labeled "unlearned responses," in shaping personality. Instead, he stressed that differences in anatomic structure and early training could account for all possible varieties in later behavior. Watson did not deny that the infant had an extensive repertoire of unlearned responses at birth, but he insisted that the majority of these "instincts" rapidly became conditioned—modified by environmental factors, usually accidentally, but sometimes deliberately, as in training. As a result, later behavior was almost entirely learned, and the early environment was all-important.[16]

Sneezing, hiccuping and blinking were examples Watson observed of the few innate responses that remained unaltered throughout life. The rest—crying, smiling, turning the head, moving the hands, and so on— soon became attached to new stimuli. Thus, smiling was probably caused at first by kinesthetic and tactile stimulation. It could occur as early as the fourth day, either after feeding or when the infant was tickled or rocked. M. C. Jones studied smiling in 185 babies and found that conditioning factors were recognizable at the age of 30–80 days; when the experimenter smiled or said babyish words to the infant, he would begin to respond with a smile.[17] According to Watson, the child learned very early that he could control the responses of nurse or parents by smiling or by crying. Later, the infant became capable of more complex activities, such as reaching, grasping, crawling, sitting up, standing, walking, running, and jumping. Physical maturation also played a part in such activity, and the role of conditioning was less clear:

In the great majority of these later activities it is difficult to say how much of the act as a whole is due to training or conditioning. A considerable part is unquestionably due to the growth changes in structure, and the rest is due to training or conditioning. [18]

As mentioned earlier, Watson recognized only the three innate emotional reaction patterns of fear, rage, and love. Observation of babies reared in hospitals convinced him that only two stimuli, loud noise and sudden loss of support, caused "fear reactions" in the neonate. Babies were not naturally afraid of animals (contrary to popular belief). Watson and Rosalie Rayner set out to condition a fear of rats in Albert, an 11-month-old healthy baby whose mother was a wet-nurse at the Harriet Lane Home for Invalid Children. [19] A steel bar was struck behind Albert's head each time he touched the rat, which caused him to draw back, whimper, or cry. After seven of these combined stimulations, Albert began to cry as soon as he caught sight of the rat. Furthermore, a rabbit, a fur coat, cotton wool, and even a Santa Claus mask could now induce fear in him. According to Murphy and Kovach:

Despite its crudeness, this experiment immediately had a profound effect on American psychology, for it appeared to support the whole conception that not only simple motor habits, but important, enduring traits of personality, such as emotional tendencies, may in fact be 'built into' the child by conditioning. [20]

Watson fully intended to undo the damage by "deconditioning" Albert, but the child left the hospital before this could be attempted. In later, similar experiments, "deconditioning" was always carried out, although it proved to be more tedious than conditioning. [21]

The observation of young children seemed to Watson to support his contention that mental processes, including language and thought, were simply conditioned responses that had become internalized during development. This assumption allowed Watson to put behaviorism forward as a consistent theory to explain all mental, physical, muscular, and glandular activity. As a result, "consciousness" became redundant. Watson had become a radical environmentalist.

To render his theory more convincing, he described the acquisition of language in the young child. The crying and babbling of the newborn was at first reflexive and instinctive, but a sound that brought forth a response from the mother or caretaker was most likely to be repeated. In addition, imitation seemed to play a part in the forming of vocal habits.

The parents, of course, watch every new instinctive sound that approximates articulate speech and they immediately speak the word that is nearest the child's own vocal efforts (for example, "ma," "pa," "da"). The imitation here may be more apparent than real. That is, the parents by repeating the sounds constantly offer a stimulus for that which the infant's vocal mechanism is just set to utter. [22]

The parents' response to babbling acted as a conditioned stimulus and led to the consolidation of vocal habits. But these "do not become language habits until they become associated with arm, hand and leg activities and substitutable for them." In early infancy, there was no necessity for the child to develop language habits inasmuch as all its needs were anticipated. As the child became more physically active and the environment more complex, more specific modes of communication became essential for progress. The child looking for his rag doll might wander around uttering a meaningless word, such as "tata." An attendant, guessing the baby's needs, might hand him the rag doll and say, "Here is your tata." With frequent repetition, the word "tata" would become connected with the act of seeking the doll:

The putting on of conventional speech habits is thus an illustration of conditioned reflex level of functioning (vocal habit) plus later associative connection of the word when learned with the bodily habits connected with the object for which the word stands (true language habits).[23]

To Watson adult thought was merely "implicit" language. When we think, he suggested, we talk to ourselves. As a result of social pressure, the child gradually transforms his normal talking into a whisper and then into subvocal or "implicit" speech. (Here was another instance of the assumption of "continuity" between qualitative distinctive phenomena—in this case, between the yelling of a child and silent thought of adults). Watson acknowledged that in some, the transition was never complete: hence some adults talk aloud to themselves or cannot read without obviously articulating the words. Although most adults read and think silently, Watson thought it likely that some movements of the larynx, eyes or other speech mechanisms accompanied these cognitive functions. These movements would be so slight that they could be detected only with special instruments of a precision not yet available. Thus, Watson reduced thinking to a series of conditioned peripheral motor responses, with the cerebral cortex functioning as a passive connecting center, and not as an active site for the association and transformation of ideas.[24]

In sum, Watson's view was mechanistic, environmental, objective, and punctuated with assumptions about continuity.

Watson detailed his ideas in *Behavior: An Introduction to Comparative Psychology* (1914), then in *Psychology from the Standpoint of a Behaviorist* (1919), and finally in *Behaviorism* (1924). In *Behaviorism*, he emerged as a full-fledged environmentalist, unabashed by the paucity of experimental evidence to support his extreme views. "This will be remedied in the near future," promised Watson; but his influence was now limited by his being no longer a full-time psychologist. Perhaps this accounted for the anomaly of a man who was once dedicated to objectivity in psychology now allowing himself the luxury of speculation. Watson was to admit later that he was not especially proud of *Behaviorism*, which in reality was a hasty compilation of a series of lectures.

Similarly:

Psychological Care of Infant and Child was another book I feel sorry about—not because of its sketchy form, but because I did not know enough to write the book I wanted to write. I feel that I had a right to publish this, sketchy as it is, since I planned never to go back into academic work.[25]

As Watson made clear in *Psychological Care of Infant and Child*, conditioning normally occurred as a result of accidental parental acts—usually with disastrous consequences. The child learned to be fearful and shy, to depend on his mother, to pick at his food, to refuse to go to bed, or to exhibit tantrums at the slightest provocation because parents were not self-conscious about the rewards and

punishments they gave their child. They were not thinking about their task. Watson believed that none of these
things would happen if parents had foresight and trained
their children properly. Thoughtless mothers smothered
their children with kisses and cautions, instead of clearing
the nursery and backyard of dangerous toys and allowing
the youngsters to sort themselves out in relative safety
and to learn confidence and competence through their
own experience. Much of the book was a tirade against
the natural ineptness of mothers and a plea for systematic
training in childrearing. Although he had no evidence on
which to base predictions, Watson was convinced that his
methods, if applied conscientiously, would result in the
production of ideal citizens.[26]

Similarities and Differences
Between Freud and Watson

Watson's behaviorism and Freud's psychoanalysis may
have seemed different from each other, but their absolute
presuppositions were remarkably similar. Both were deterministic, stating that the actions of parents could cause
particular effects in the child. Both stated that the experiences of the infant and very young child could have
long-lasting effects. Both saw the mother as the critical
sculptor, whether she liked it or not, and made her responsible for her child's deficiencies of character, emotion,
or intelligence. Both invented hidden continuity out of
apparent discontinuity. Watson, for example, saw continuity between the yelling of the baby and the silent
thought of the adult; Freud saw continuity between the
sucking of the baby at the breast and the kissing of one's
sweetheart in adolescence. But the salient message that

emerged from both theories was that the careful handling of the infant and young child could ensure desirable adult character traits and prevent undesirable ones.

Both proposed the novel and persuasive idea that most, if not all, mental illness was caused by traumatic or unsatisfactory childhood experiences. It had been assumed by earlier investigators that heredity or "degeneracy" was responsible. Now American parents were told to regard their own behavior as responsible for later emotional breakdown in their offspring—even in children who had a "good" genetic background. This view increased the anxiety of many parents, but was flattering to mothers in that it reminded them of their important role in childrearing.

Watson, like Freud, considered sexuality or love in the child—between the child and his parents and between the child and his playmates—as an important factor in development. He adopted Freud's "libidinal energy" concept and wove it into his own developmental system. The result was a translation of psychosexual theory into behaviorist language. Indeed, Watson concluded that psychopathologists had a far more "sane, wholesome and adequate point of view" on sexuality, and on methods for enlightening children on the subject, than the average physician did. [27]

The belief that children were asexual was itself peculiar to the nineteenth century. As an outcome of the Romantic movement, it became fashionable to think of children as symbolic of purity, whereas a century earlier sexual precocity was admired, or at least tolerated. In the late medieval French court, a child's manipulation of his own sex organs or even those of others was not only accepted by adults, but even encouraged for the entertainment of all. [28] This casual attitude toward sexuality in the

young was later to disappear, partly because of S. A. Tissot's popular work on the dangers of onanism (1760).[29]
This was followed by a flood of medical literature on the
same subject, mostly but not exclusively emanating from
France.[30] Habitual masturbation was presumed to lead to
chronic physical and mental disease, and even to death.
Many of the suggested treatments were drastic—for
example, sedation with opiates, vasectomy, removal of
the clitoris, ligation of the spermatic arteries, circumcision
without anesthesia, and even castration.[31] Signs of early
sexual interest were not supposed to occur in the normal
child; if they did, they had probably been implanted by an
unscrupulous nurse or servant.

Freud's statements that sexual impulses were natural
characteristics of infancy, and hence that the asexual child
was abnormal, led twentieth century mothers to be concerned about acts that had made Victorian mothers proud.
The innocent, prudish child now became suspect. As
Watson put it, sex and love became synonymous, and
early libidinal manifestations were essential for the development of all human forms of love. However, neither
psychologist favored unlimited precocious eroticism. Indeed, Watson followed Freud very closely, advising the
discouragement of excessive sexual preoccupation in the
child. Some interest was thought natural, but too much
was considered potentially dangerous.

Despite the similarities between Freud and Watson,
they postulated quite different mechanisms to explain behavior. To Watson the "unconscious" was an impossibility
and most psychoanalytic terminology just nonsense.[32] He
made short shrift of the Oedipal conflict for he visualized
ideal early development, not as a series of psychosexual
crises, but as a smooth transition from simplicity to complexity of behavior. Conversely, the Oedipal phase was
pivotal to analytic theory, representing the climax of in-

fantile sexuality and a state of unconscious conflict whose satisfactory resolution was essential for further normal personality development. Indeed, so crucial was the concept that it merits further discussion.

According to the Freudian view, during the Oedipal phase, the child had to overcome his sexual attachment to the parent of the opposite sex and his jealousy of the parent of the same sex, who appeared as a sexual rival. A boy, fearing castration if he persisted, soon abandoned this hopeless contest with a stronger father, and instead identified with him. The process was more gradual in a girl; although she never quite lost her infantile attachment to her mother, she developed strong sexual affinity to her father during the phallic phase. But, because she feared the loss of maternal love, she too gave up her Oedipal involvement with her father. If all went well, the tumultuous Oedipal phase was followed by a period of sexual quiescence, the *latency period*, during which the child could begin the long process of detachment from the family. Unfortunately, much could go wrong during the Oedipal phase, in that both constitutional and environmental factors could prevent a satisfactory outcome. Freud held that to some extent everyone is bisexual. If a boy had stronger female tendencies, he might identify with his mother rather than with his father. A more masculine girl might have difficulty in identifying with her mother. Parents could intensify the Oedipal conflict by being too strict or too lenient about such sexual manifestations as infantile masturbation, by arguing among themselves and so confusing the child, by showing preference for a younger sibling, or by being too sexually attractive to the child. As one might imagine, parents who believed Freud became somewhat uncertain about parenthood. He had listed so many hazards associated with each stage of psychosexual development—like a marine map guiding a sailor in dangerous shoals—that almost every action by parent or child was suspect or potentially dangerous. Freud did not help parents because he rarely provided any guides to action. They were left on their own.

In contrast, Watson issued rigid, easily understood rules of parental conduct. The mother was not to hug, fondle, or kiss her infant. Parents must be objective and detached, leaving the child to discover the world for himself, insofar as this was consistent with safety. He must be told about sex in a matter-of-fact manner and in a language that he could understand. At no stage must euphemisms be used or the child be actively misled. If parents adhered to the tenets of behaviorism and trained their child accordingly, they could be confident that he would grow up happy and well adjusted. We find these convictions well expressed by Rosalie Rayner Watson at the end of her article, "I am the mother of a behaviorist's sons":

To conclude this little diary honestly, I must confess that my day dreams in respect to my sons often carry me years ahead, and like every fond mother, I predict their futures. I cannot see what choice of a profession they will make, but I sincerely believe that they will be happy individuals no matter what comes their way. They will be free of false standards, envies and jealousies, for they uo not exist for them now. They will not stand as moral judges against their fellow companions. They will work and get a kick out of it, and play and get a kick out of it. They will have no social inferiorities or superiorities, no overweening vanities, but instead a self-confidence which will carry them through many struggles. They will have strong bodies and healthy habits, and will fight their own fights. They will know that life is a stunning drama and, no matter what happens, around the corner lies a new adventure. They will find love because they can give it and, above all, they will keep a sense of humor about this rollicking universe and laugh up their sleeves once in a while—especially at themselves. This is my fondest dream for my two small pieces of protoplasm. [33]

The Influence of Behaviorism on Developmental Psychology

Psychologists did not respond with equal enthusiasm to all aspects of Watson's teaching; for example, many of his ideas on conditioning were unacceptable in their extreme form. In contrast, the research methods promoted by Watson met more general approval because they encouraged objectivity and were already popular among animal psychologists. The clinical, as opposed to the experimental, use of conditioning to modify behavior was not much used until the late 1930s and not extensively for another 20 years (under the rubric "behavior modification"). [34]

The very simplicity of early behaviorism attracted some and repelled others. Clark L. Hull, in his autobiography, gave some hint of his reactions to Watson's two major publications: *Behavior: An Introduction to Comparative Psychology* (1914) and *Psychology from the Standpoint of a Behaviorist* (1919).

Personally, while inclined to be sympathetic with Watson's views concerning the futility of introspection and the general virtues of objectivity, I feel very uncertain about many of his dogmatic claims. In this connection I recall the semifanatical ardor with which at that time some young people, including a few relatively ignorant undergraduates, would espouse the Watsonian cause with statements such as, 'Behaviorism has made a greater contribution to science than has been produced by psychology in its entire previous history.' This attitude on the part of some precipitated equally violent opposing claims. The zeal of both sides took on a fanaticism more characteristic of religion than of science.[35]

Probably no experienced psychologist accepted Watson's concepts in their totality, especially after he became an extreme environmentalist. He was then addressing himself mainly to the public through such organs as *Harper's Magazine* and *Collier's*. As expressed by Herrnstein: "Rather quickly after his resignation from Hopkins in 1920, Watson's writings took on a strongly missionary quality."[36] Some parents may have been converted to Watson because he backed the theme that later character was determined by early experience with evidence that sounded scientific. As always, it was difficult for the public to know to what extent the expert, in this instance Watson, should be believed. Certainly, parents were exposed to behaviorist ideas both in the official child-care literature and in popular magazine articles.[37] We shall examine some of these sources of information at the end of the chapter, but for now let us dwell a little longer on the reactions of psychologists to extreme behaviorism.

On the whole, this reaction was one of dismay that such a promising psychologist had gone off the rails. Many had admired Watson's earlier, more moderate stance, but could not follow him all the way. W. S. Hunter probably expressed a general opinion among probehaviorists when he stated that "some of Watson's pronouncements represented less the necessary details of behaviorism than his own prodigious effort to fill in the experimental gaps with hypotheses pending further work."[38] During the first 20 years of its official existence, behaviorism was a state of mind, a rebellion against the introspection of the structuralists, a justification for animal experimentation and infant observation, but not a well-defined theory. As Robert S. Woodworth observed in

1931, "it is a program rather than a system, and a hope rather than a program."[39]

Watson's position was that learning occurred through the modification of existing stimulus-response mechanisms by conditioning and that this process was the main determinant of behavior. He ignored central activity, instead thinking of the organism as responding passively to environmental stimuli. This mechanistic explanation, and the type of research it encouraged, did not satisfy even those most sympathetic to behaviorism. Both K. S. Lashley and E. C. Tolman, for example, admitted to becoming disenchanted with mere "muscle-twitch" psychology.[40] The neurophysiological investigations of Lashley seemed to show that the brain played a more active part than that allowed by Watson: "When viewed in relation to the problems of neurology, the nature of the stimulus and of the response is intrinsically such as to preclude the theory of simple point-to-point connection in reflexes."[41]

Watson had appeared as the champion of nurture versus nature in development. Yet his triumph was short-lived. True, he and other behaviorists eliminated the much-abused concept of "instinct" from the repertoire of academic psychology. In so doing, they temporarily held at bay the supporters of genetic theories of development, for "instinctive behavior" was the outcome of inherited adaptive patterns of activity. But because the environmentalists failed to provide a satisfying explanation for the occurrence of individual differences in reactivity, the belief in "instincts" was out, but two other possibilities were available: the concept of maturation, supported to some extent by neurological evidence; and the incorporation of organismic factors into learning theory.

It should not be imagined that in the 1920s and 1930s a majority of developmental psychologists were be-

haviorists. They subscribed to the general principle that
objectivity and detachment were essential to scientific
research but did not undertake much controlled experimentation, in contrast with the animal psychologists. According to Sheldon H. White:

S-R analyses of children's behavior did not become really prominent or widespread in American psychology until the middle
1950s. Yet, for several decades before this, the learning theories
had been overwhelmingly in the center of theoretical efforts in
psychology, coexisting with a sizable establishment of child
psychologists who took no substantial guidance from them. [42]

In the main, developmentalists were atheoretical; they felt
that no other course was justifiable until the norms of
human physical and mental growth had been more carefully mapped out. Much was known about the life history
of the rat, very little about that of the human being. Consequently, all existing theories of development—whether
derived from Hall, Watson, Piaget or Freud—seemed
premature. Instead of testing hypotheses emanating from
dubious theories, most researchers felt that they were better employed in obtaining the essential primary data. [43]
For a couple of decades, they deliberately ignored theory
and concentrated on carefully controlled general observation, which included longitudinal studies when the
money was available. (This last type of research, which
has had a checkered career since the early 1920s, will be
discussed in the next chapter.) John E. Anderson summed
up a prevalent attitude in a few words:

It would be unfortunate if too much preoccupation with a particular method or a preconception of what child psychology
should be rather than *is* were to cut off a manifold approach.
From today's studies, however inadequate they may be, come
the highly developed techniques of tomorrow. Science crawls
before it walks, and walks before it runs. [44]

Anderson was not opposed to experimentation; on the contrary, he considered that this approach and cross-sectional testing were the only two that were essentially scientific. But, to Anderson, controlled observation could also be classified as a form of experimentation:

If we regard the nursery school or the school itself as a laboratory situation relatively constant in its nature [and] select a certain type of behavior and observe each child for a *constant period of time* we secure results that show reliability or precision in proportion to the specificity of the behavior we undertake to observe and in proportion to the number of observations taken.[45]

This was the basis of the longitudinal method, which was not usually considered as experimental because no variable was deliberately manipulated. Nevertheless, to Anderson and to many of his contemporaries, observation was a properly scientific mode of inquiry and one that was expected to produce results useful for later theory building.

In short, the early behavioristic influence on developmental psychology was somewhat fleeting. Part of the original appeal of the viewpoint was its very simplicity; when this was found inadequate to account for all aspects of growth and behavior, developmentalists once again reverted to observation as their main source of theoretical inspiration.

Trends in Advice on Infant Care, 1900–1940

As noted in Chapter 1, at least since the beginning of the nineteenth century many experts, self-styled or otherwise, have proffered advice on childrearing in America. Some idea of changing trends, cultural as well as scientific, may be gained by noting the type of advice given to parents during the period in question. The reader should keep in mind that such sources reflected only some of the viewpoints of any professional establishment and were usually somewhat outdated with respect to research. For the first half of the twentieth century, an illustrative source was provided by the *Infant Care* bulletins published by the U.S. Department of Labor, Children's Bureau. The first edition appeared in 1914, and revised editions appeared in 1921, 1926, 1929, 1938, 1940, 1942, and 1945. In the 1950s Martha Wolfenstein wrote several articles analyzing the evidence of changing trends in child care, as illustrated by these government publications, and much of the following interpretation is derived from her writings. [46]

The 1914 edition emphasized the importance of initiating training and discipline as early as possible:

Habits are the result of repeated actions. A properly trained baby is not allowed to learn bad habits which must be unlearned later at great cost of time and patience to both mother and babe. The wise mother strives to start the baby right. [47]

This could be done only by establishing a daily schedule and sticking to it. Everything was to be done by routine, and activity was to be kept to a minimum. Parents were warned not to play with the infant—"however robust the child much of the play that is indulged in is more or less harmful." Fathers especially were cautioned in this respect:

It is a regrettable fact that the few minutes of play that the father has when he gets home at night, which is often almost the only time he has with the child, may result in nervous disturbance of the baby and upset his regular habits. [48]

The first *Infant Care* bulletin offered specific advice on many topics. No one, not even the mother, should kiss the baby on the mouth because of the danger of spreading infection. Pacifiers were considered too horrible to contemplate; they must be destroyed and "no such object should be permitted in the baby's mouth under any circumstances." The hands should be covered to prevent thumb-sucking, another habit, like the use of pacifiers, that led to deformity of the palate, infection, constant drooling, and facial disfigurement. If the more injurious practice of masturbation were suspected, more drastic measures were essential, even to the extent of tying the baby's legs and arms to the bed. Throughout the pamphlet there was notable emphasis on the value of early training:

It must not be forgotten that the period of infancy is a period of education often of greater consequence than any other two years of life. Not only are all the organs and functions given their primary education, but the faculties of the mind as well receive those initial impulses that determine very largely their direction and efficiency through life. The first nervous impulses which pass through the baby's eyes, ears, fingers, or mouth to the tender brain makes a pathway for itself; the next time another impulse travels over the same path it deepens the impression of the first.[49]

In giving this advice, Mrs. Max West, the author of this first edition of *Child Care,* was translating nineteenth-century associationism into simple language. Much of her advice closely reflected that given by E. Emmett Holt in *The Care and Feeding of Children,* a catechism that was very influential at the time.[50] Today the instructions given by Mrs. West, Holt, and later Watson seem strangely insensitive to the emotional needs of both mother and child. Yet, if one remembers the social context within which these recommendations were delivered, they make much more sense. Babies seemed unreliable then. Many of them became ill and died without apparent reason. So long as the precipitating causes of diseases such as tuberculous meningitis (always lethal) and infantile diarrhea (often lethal), remained conjectural, the best policy was surely to isolate the baby. Similarly one can find rational explanations for all the strange antics advocated in the name of scientific child care. (One of the most amusing statements from *Infant Care* is this: "A baby should be taught to blow its nose, to submit the tongue and throat to inspection, to gargle, and to regard the doctor as a friend whose visits are to be looked forward to with pleasure."[51])

Finally, it should be noted that *Infant Care* was an unusual nurture pamphlet, in that it was not addressed mainly to middle-class families but to less prosperous ones, in which infant mortality was greater. Thus, attention was paid to the health of the mother, who was assumed to be overworked and not to have much time for her baby. Her health was probably well below par, inasmuch as she would have had no antenatal or postnatal care.[52] All in all, the official pamphlet was intended to set out the absolute essentials of baby care—the kind of advice that might be heeded by a busy, tired woman with many children to mind and no nursemaid to help. Thus, we find the following warning:

An older child should be taught to sit on the floor or in his pen or crib during part of his waking hours, or he will be very likely to make too great demands upon the mother's strength. No one who has not tried it realizes how much nervous energy can be consumed in "minding" a baby who can creep or walk about, and who must be continually watched and diverted, and the mother who is taking the baby through this period of his life will need to conserve all her strength, and not waste it in useless forms of activity.[53]

In the 1929 issue of the bulletin, there was again a whole chapter on "Habits, training, and disciplines." A habit was still thought of as the result of repeated action, but the mechanism suggested now was the "law of effect," rather than associationism. "A baby, like a grown person, has a tendency to do again something that he has done before, if he has found satisfaction in doing it the first time."[54] Thumb-sucking and masturbation no longer were treated as dangerous activities; both would be outgrown in time. The stress was shifted to rigorous early bowel training: "Almost any baby can be so trained that there are no more soiled diapers to wash after he is six to eight months old."[55] By 1938, the advice was less severe and the authors of *Infant Care* (Ethel C. Dunham and Marian M. Crane) were suggesting that bowel training begin at six months, rather than the first month, as proposed in 1929. Both the 1929 and 1938 editions stated that early training in regular sleeping, eating, and elimination was character-building, and one can detect a behavioristic influence. In 1928, Watson had written:

It is quite easy to start habits of day time continence (conditional response) when the child is from 3-5 weeks old by putting the chamber to the child (but at this age never on it) each time it is aroused for feeding. It is often surprising how quickly the conditioned response is established if your routine is unremitting and your patience holds out.[56]

According to Watson, socially acceptable habits could and should be inculcated at a very early age:

The time was when we used to think it took generations to make
a well-bred person. Now we know parents can do it in a few
months' time if they start to cultivate the garden before the
weeds begin to grow.[57]

   To the behaviorist, childrearing was simplicity itself,
as long as one adhered to the rules of conditioning. This
view of the child as a responding organism, with no
"mind" of its own, was superbly exemplified in another
Children's Bureau pamphlet, *Are You Training Your Child to
be Happy?*, first published in 1930. The author, Blanche C.
Weill, may appear to today's reader to consider parents as
infantile or moronic, but she was suggesting the application of behaviorism in a straightforward way. It was then
believed that the baby would respond predictably to any
given stimulus; therefore, if the mother consistently used
a correct approach, the outcome could only be a happy,
well-adjusted child. Conversely, a defiant, unruly, or
emotionally disturbed child was the result of parental in-
eptitude, and nothing else. Let the pamphlet itself provide the flavor of this creed, which today seems naive:

Do You Have a Happy Baby?
Does he laugh and coo while you work?
Does he play quietly by himself while you work?
Does your little child like the food you give him?
Is he ready and willing to go to bed at bedtime?
Does he love the new baby?
Does he play happily with other children?
Then he is happy and good.

Does your baby cry all day?
Does he get mad and kick and scream?
Does your little child spit out the food he does not like?
Does he beg you not to put him to bed?
Does he tease the new baby?
Of course, you do not want these things.

We can help you make your baby happy, but you must help, too.

You must try very hard.

You must never stop trying.

You are tired and busy some day. Your baby is crying. You say, 'This one time does not matter. I will pick him up. Then he will stop crying.'

Then your smart little baby says to himself, 'Hurrah, I was the boss that time. I can be boss next time.'

Before you know it, he will cry again. Will you pick him up again?

Do you always give him what he wants?

Then he will not be happy long.[58]

Begin when he is born.

Feed him at exactly the same hours every day.

Do not feed him just because he cries.

Let him wait until the right time.

If you make him wait, his stomach will learn to wait.

His mind will learn that he can not get things by crying.

You do two things for your baby at the same time. You teach his body good habits and you teach his mind good habits.[59]

This message continued for over 50 pages. As in most behavioristic texts, the implication was that the well-trained baby would develop into an easy-to-manage child and a "good citizen." Consequently, the unyielding parental approach could be relaxed, within definite limits, as the child got older. Obedience should always be exacted for important matters, such as going to bed and getting up at set times, going to the toilet and eating meals regularly, and putting toys away. But allowances now had to be made for the increased activity of the child as an independent person. For example, he might not obey an order because he was too busy playing even to have heard it; or he might be incapable of carrying out a requirement, such as sitting still for a long time.

Punishment was also to be meted out with true behavioristic wisdom: "There is only one good reason to punish a child. That is to make him understand that he must not do the naughty thing again."[60] The best way of all was to keep the child from needing to be punished by starting him right as a baby—by paying attention to him only when he was good, by always keeping promises and speaking the truth, by never threatening even a baby with punishment that could not be carried out, and by keeping the older child too busy to have time to be naughty.

What then sounded exquisitely simple and rational depended entirely on the premises that a child could be shaped and that a parent could be consistently objective and untrammeled by emotional biases. The latter was a tall order, so much so that Watson could muse:

It is a serious question in my mind whether there should be individual homes for children—or even whether children should know their own parents. There are undoubtedly much more scientific ways of bringing up children which will probably mean finer and happier children.[61]

His was an extreme view but not quite without precedent. After the age of seven, the Spartan boy was reared away from home under rigid military discipline, and a not dissimilar fate has overtaken the British upper-middle-class child since the late nineteenth century. In America, this part of Watson's formula was not taken very seriously, instead compromises were adopted—namely parental education and nursery schooling.

Parental education is not a completely modern notion. The child-nurture texts of the nineteenth century were written with an educational intent, but it was usually assumed that parents, especially mothers, knew what they were about and needed encouragement rather than redirection. Similarly, in the child-study movement of the late nineteenth century, educators thought of parents as equal partners, who could provide information as well as receive it. In the early decades of the twentieth century, however, some progressive psychologists, sociologists and home economists decided that directed parent education might be the best way of reforming society.

Orville Brim has suggested that there were two major causes of the social movement to educate the American parent:

The first was the breakdown of cultural traditions in childrearing practices, which in turn was the result of still other antecedent social changes. The latter include the change in the status of women in our society toward increased autonomy in both their family and nonfamily roles; the decline in the frequency of intergenerational family relations, arising from the fact that now in our society most newly married couples establish residence apart from their parental homes; the increased contact through immigration and social mobility between members of different ethnic backgrounds and social classes who have contrasting cultural traditions of child care. . . .

However, it would be a mistake to conclude that parent education arose only in response to the needs of parents. The second fundamental cause of this social movement was the growing belief on the part of many persons that there existed better ways of rearing children than those prescribed by traditions. This belief was nurtured by the research on child development in both Europe and the United States, which . . . gave promise of providing a new body of scientific knowledge of the desirable ways to rear children. [62]

From 1914 the Children's Bureau was most active in publishing popular pamphlets on prenatal care, infant care, and child care. By 1925 about 3 million copies of *Infant Care* had been distributed to schools, women's clubs and doctors' offices and to individuals on request.[63] Presumably this pamphlet reached the widest and most nonspecific audience because of its broad circulation and low cost (10 cents in 1929).

However, projects organized specifically for parental education, that employed study groups and series of lectures, tended to be supported mainly by the better-educated sections of a community. This was particularly true of the Child Study Association of America, the most active of these organizations. Its aim was not simply to instruct parents but to encourage them to form their own decisions about appropriate modes of child care on the basis of information provided.[64] Thus, its pamphlets and its journal, *Child Study,* were far more intellectually demanding than the publications of the Children's Bureau.[65] During the 1920s the programs of the Child Study Association did emphasize the importance of behavior study and the discussion of behavior problems, but the orientation was not exclusively behavioristic. None of Freud's writings appeared in the bibliography of *Outlines of Child Study,* but interpretations of psychoanalytic theory by A. A. Brill and by O. Pfister were in vogue as were many works supporting genetic concepts of development.[66] The inclusion of a variety of psychological approaches to development was also evident in *A Selected List of Books for Parents and Teachers,* compiled by the Child Study Association in 1928.[67]

Parents were repeatedly told that they must become informed about the "new psychology." What did this term imply? First, it implied that through scientific inquiry novel ideas about child development were emerging and that they were pertinent to childrearing. Second, it implied that early experience was important in determining future character and behavior. This concept was made fairly clear in the introduction to *Guidance of Childhood and Youth* (1926):

There is implied the process of constant change or development, with the passing of time; there is implied the presence of innate impulses that drive to a variety of actions that may take no account whatever of the proprieties, of the comfort of adults, or even of the safety of the child himself. There is implied the hope that the conduct and attitudes of the growing child, though derived from native impulses, are nevertheless subject to modifications through experience, leaving for adults the responsibility of providing the suitable conditions and experiences.

From this point of view the child is considered as primarily neither moral nor immoral, but capable of acquiring both a form of behavior that is socially acceptable, and a set of attitudes that are essentially social and moral—or the opposite. [68]

The onus was thus on parents to understand their children and ensure that they learned good, rather than bad, habits. The training methods suggested were based on the theories of both Watson and Thorndike. The former emphasized conditioning; the latter gave the advice that: "Useful instincts must be given a chance to exercise themselves and become habits. Harmful instinctive responses must be inhibited through lack of stimulus, through the substitution of desirable ones, or through actual resultant discomfort, as best fits each special case."[69] The basic theme was not that all behavior was learned, but that all children, whatever their inherited characteristics, could be socialized with appropriate manipulation by parent or teacher.

Even if the mother could acquire the necessary expertise, could she sustain its application during the crucial first five years of her child's life? Some thought not and suggested that young children would benefit from attendance at nursery school. There they could gain a measure of self-reliance in an environment most suitable for their intellectual, social, and physical development. The school could provide special services such as regular medical examinations and psychological testing. Furthermore, the staff, equipped with greater scientific knowledge and objectivity than most parents, could advise parents about home care when necessary. Thus, the nursery school was regarded by some not only as an ideal environment for a 3- or 4-year-old child, but also as an adjunct to parental education. [70]

Since the 1920s enthusiasm for nursery education has waxed and waned, reflecting prevailing views as to whether home or school provided the more adequate environment for the young child. Many, perhaps most, of the beliefs so firmly held during the interwar years were to be repudiated in the late 1940s, when Freudian ideas of development finally came to the fore. But over one theme—the need for sex education beginning early in the child's life—there was no real dissent. It rapidly became commonly accepted that sexual matters should not be concealed from the child, but discussed in as much detail as he could understand. This was easier said than done; beginning in the second decade of the century there appeared numerous popular and technical books on the subject. [71] It is hard to know whether psychoanalytic or behavioristic theory provided the greater stimulus for this outpouring; perhaps it was the reflection of a cultural consensus.

Conclusions

The clearest concept to emerge during the 1920s and 1930s was that childrearing was not a simple or natural process, but one that should follow scientific principles. The new psychologies played havoc with traditional views of the child, his parents, and their interrelationships. No longer could the infant be regarded as an innocent who would become a happy and responsible adult if he came from healthy stock and had reasonably conscientious parents. No longer could parents be permitted to rear their children according to cultural patterns established over the centuries. Such methods were too haphazard and needed to be replaced by a definite system. The infant required training, and this must be according to specific rules, or he would acquire or retain antisocial habits. As the child's intellectual and physical capacities developed, nurture became more complex. Parents needed to learn the right ways of cultivating obedience, honesty, truthfulness, and good manners; of coping with fears, jealousy, destructiveness, and tantrums; and of encouraging curiosity, independence, and good work habits. Punishment should not be meted out according to the whim of the moment, but only along carefully prescribed lines. A good parent needed to be informed, insightful, consistent, objective, and restrained.

Basic to such demands from parents was the conviction that early experience determined later behavior. According to Freud, experience was the product of constitutional and environmental factors; but only the latter elements were stressed in behaviorism. Such a theme was attractive because it implied that the child was infinitely perfectible, given the appropriate environment. The function of science was to determine this ideal environment, and the duty of parents and teachers was to keep abreast of new findings. So powerful was the appeal of environmentalism that selected Freudian postulates were interwoven into the general framework. The genetic aspects of psychoanalytic theory tended to be ignored; those supporting environmentalism were used as additional scientific evidence.

While psychoanalysis was being adapted to American intellectual presuppositions, the chief supporters of Freud in America, the child guidance experts, were adapting his theories to fit practical needs. The importance of this group lay not in the purity of their interpretations of Freud, but in their role in incubating his concepts while most psychologists were concentrating on behaviorism. [72]

Notes and References

1. Watson, J. B. "Psychology as the behaviorist views it." *Psychol. Rev.* 20:158–177, 1913.

2. Watson, J. B. *Behavior; An Introduction to Comparative Psychology*, p. 10. New York: Henry Holt and Company, 1914.

3. Ibid., p. 186.

4. For a recent biography of Thorndike, see: G. Jonçich. *The Sane Positivist: A Biography of Edward L. Thorndike.* Middletown, Conn.: Wesleyan University Press, 1968.

5. Thorndike, E. L. *Animal Intelligence.* pp. 108–109. New York: Hafner Publishing Company, 1965. "The possibility is that animals may have *no images or memories at all, no ideas to associate.* Perhaps the entire fact of association in animals is the presence of sense-impressions with which are associated, by resultant pleasure, certain impulses, and that, therefore, and therefore only, a certain situation brings forth a certain act."

6. Postman, L. "Rewards and punishments in human learning," pp. 331–401. In L. Postman, Ed. *Psychology in the Making; Histories of Selected Research Problems.* New York: Alfred A. Knopf, 1962.

7. Thorndike, E. L. *Notes on Child Study,* p. 47. New York: Macmillan, 1903.

8. Murphy, G., and J. K. Kovach. *An Historical Introduction to Modern Psychology,* pp. 246–249. (3rd ed.) New York: Harcourt, Brace Jovanovich, Inc., 1972. Here it is pointed out that Watson

held that, whereas unsuccessful movements were legion, there was but one successful movement, which, however, over a series of trials would be repeated more frequently than any other. Thorndike's reply was that in many cases one successful movement was promptly learned, whereas an unsuccessful one, although repeated several times in the same trial, was eliminated.

9. Watson, J. B. *Behavior,* p. 269. "In general it must be admitted that recency is a much less potent factor in habit formation than is frequency. In certain habits such, for example, as those involved in the maze, its influence cannot very well be made out."

10. In his presidential address to the American Psychological Association in 1915, "Watson proposed that the conditioned reflex could take the place of introspection in psychology." (R. J. Herrnstein. Behaviorism, pp. 51–68. In D. L. Krantz, Ed. *Schools of Psychology.* New York: Appleton-Century-Crofts, 1969.) G. Murphy and F. Jensen stated that part of Bekhterev's writings on "objective psychology" were translated into French and German in 1913 and in this form stimulated Watson's own efforts toward an objective psychology. (Murphy and Jensen. *Approaches to Personality.* New York: Coward-McCann, Inc., 1932.)

11. The correct term, as used by Pavlov, is "conditional reflex." The word "conditioned" is a mistranslation of Pavlov's 1906 Huxley lecture, which he gave in German because he knew no English (Julian Jaynes, personal communication). Franks states that the terminology was correct in Pavlov's first book to be translated into English and that the misleading term "conditioned" crept into later translations. (C. M. Franks. Behavior therapy and its Pavlovian origins: Review and perspectives, p. 7. In C. M. Franks, Ed. *Behavior Therapy: Appraisal and Status.* New York: McGraw-Hill, 1969.)

12. Watson, J. B. *Psychology from the Standpoint of a Behaviorist,* p. 195. (2nd ed.) Philadelphia: J. B. Lippincott, 1924.

13. Ibid., p. 199.

14. Ibid., p. 273.

15. For further details, see Mary Cover Jones' recent biographical account of Watson as researcher and mentor, "A 1924 pioneer looks at behavior therapy" (*J. Behav. Ther. Exp. Psychiat.* 6:181–187, 1975).

16. Watson's later ideas (after 1924) may be found in *Behaviorism* (New York: W. W. Norton, Inc., 1924) and in *Psychologies of 1925; Powell Lectures in Psychological Theory* (C. Murchison, Ed., Worcester, Mass., Clark University Press, 1926, pp. 1–81). Watson also wrote articles for Harper's Magazine: "What is behaviorism?" (152:723–729, 1926); "How we think: A behaviorist's view" (153:40–45, 1926); "Memory as the behaviorist sees it" (153:244–250, 1926); "The behaviorist looks at instincts" (155:228–235, 1927); "The myth of the unconscious. A behaviorist explanation" (155:502–508, 1972. The treatment of the instinct doctrine by behaviorists between 1920 and 1935, and beyond, is discussed by R. J. Herrnstein in "Nature as nurture: Behaviorism and the instinct doctrine" (*Behaviorism* 1:23–52, 1927).

17. Watson, J. B. *Behaviorism*, pp. 122–123.

18. Ibid., pp. 135–136.

19. Watson, J. B., and R. Rayner. "Conditioned emotional reactions." *J. Exp. Psychol.* 3:1–14, 1920. At nine months, Albert reacted to loud noise by crying, but showed no fear when suddenly confronted with a white rat, a rabbit, a dog, a monkey, masks with and without hair, etc.

20. Murphy, G., and J. K. Kovach. *An Historical Introduction to Modern Psychology*, p. 246.

21. Watson thought that "reconditioning" or "deconditioning" could be used to remove accidentally acquired fears, as well as experimentally induced ones (*Behaviorism*, pp. 172–177). *Also:* M. C. Jones. "The elimination of children's fears." *J. Exp. Psychol.* 7:382–390, 1924. *And:* M. C. Jones. "A laboratory study of fear: The case of Peter." *Pedagog. Sem.* 31:308–315, 1924.

22. Watson, J. B. *Psychology from the Standpoint of a Behaviorist*, p. 319.

23. Ibid., p. 320.

24. According to Watson, the function of the cerebral cortex was analogous to that of the spinal cord in the reflex arc. As summarized by Murphy and Kovach (*An Historical Introduction to Modern Psychology,* footnote, P. 249, 1972) "Behaviorism undertook to get rid not only of 'mental' connections, but of emphasis upon the mechanisms of cortical connection. If the neurologist wishes to study brain connections, well and good; the psychologist is concerned with observable behavior." A notable exception was Karl S. Lashley, who remained a prominent exponent of physiological psychology.

25. Murchison, C., Ed. John Broadus Watson, pp. 271–281. In *History of Psychology in Autobiography. Vol. III*. New York: Russell and Russell, 1961.

26. For a popular article on the subject, see: R. R. Watson. "I am the mother of a behaviorist's sons." *Parents' Mag.* 5:16–18, December 1930.

27. Watson, J. B. *Psychological Care of Infant and Child*, p. 157. New York: W. W. Norton & Co., 1928.

28. Ariès, P. From immodesty to innocence, pp. 100–127. In *Centuries of Childhood. A Social History of Family Life.* (Translated from the French by R. Baldick.) New York: Vintage Books, 1962. For a psychoanalytic interpretation of some of Ariès's findings, see: D. Hunt. *Parents and Children in History: The Psychology of Life in Early Modern France*, pp. 159–179. New York: Basic Books, Inc., 1970. According to Ariès, modesty during childhood was first encouraged by both Catholic and Protestant pedagogues in the late sixteenth century.

29. Tissot, Simon-André. *L'onanisme, on Dissertation Physique sur les Maladies Produites par la Masturbation.* Lausanne: A. Chapuis, 1760. 231 pp.

30. Some indication of the content of these writings, and their countries of origin, may be found in: U.S. Army. *Index Catalogue of the Library of the Surgeon-General's Office.* Vol. 8, pp. 677–680. U.S. Government Printing Office, 1887.

31. For example, J. M. Chapman, "On masturbation as an etiological factor in the production of gynic diseases" (*Amer. J. Obstet.* 16:449–458, 578–598, 1883); T. Haynes, "Surgical treatment of hopeless cases of masturbation and nocturnal emissions" (*Boston Med. Surg. J.* 109: 130, 1883); and A. A. W. Johnson, "An injurious habit occasionally met with in infancy and early childhood" (*Lancet* i:344–345, 1860).

32. While at Johns Hopkins, Watson had been an "earnest student of Freud" and had taught his classes about psychoanalysis (as interpreted by Watson). He seems to have thought that Freud was expressing important truths in the wrong manner. For an indication of his early interest in Freud and his attempts to rephrase psychoanalytic theory in behavioral language, see: J. B. Watson. "Behavior and the concept of mental disease." *J. Philosophy, Psychology, and Scientific Methods* 13:589–597, 1916.

33. Watson, R. R. "I am the mother of a behaviorist's sons."

34. For a summary of the events leading to the present interest in and use of behavior therapy, see: *American Psychiatric Association. Behavior Therapy in Psychiatry. A Report of the APS Task Force on Behavior Therapy.* Washington, D.C.: American Psychiatric Association, 1973.

35. Boring, E. G., H. S. Langfeld, H. Werner, and R. M. Yerkes, Eds. *A History of Psychology in Autobiography, Vol. IV,* pp. 153–154. New York: Russell and Russell, 1952.

36. Herrnstein, R. J. *Behaviorism,* p. 65. In D. L. Krantz, Ed. *Schools of Psychology.* New York: Appleton-Century-Crofts, 1969.

37. To a large extent, pediatricians were advocating similar systematic methods of infant care. Watson, in the introduction to *Psychological Care of Infant and Child* (1928), had expressed his admiration of L. Emmett Holt's *The Care and Feeding of Children* (New York: D. Appleton, 1894) and his own desire to write a similar text on the psychological care of the young. Only circumstantial evidence is available to suggest what parents really did to their babies. Thus, Marjorie Honzig has noted that, when "thumb-sucking" was studied by the Berkeley group, a greater incidence of the habit was found in infants belonging to the families of higher socioeconomic status. Pediatricians had told these parents to leave their babies alone as much as possible. Other parents, who did not use pediatricians, continued to pick their infants up between feedings, and their babies showed a lower incidence of thumb-sucking. (Personal interview, February 21, 1973.)

38. Boring, E. G., Ed. *A History of Psychology in Autobiography, Vol. IV,* p. 172.

39. Woodworth, R. S., and M. R. Sheehan. *Contemporary Schools of Psychology,* p. 92. New York: The Ronald Press, 1931.

40. For an analysis of Lashley's later views on behaviorism, see: R. S. Woodworth and M. R. Sheehan. "Behaviorism: The nature of the mediating process," pp. 170–213. In *Contemporary Schools of Psychology.* (3rd ed.) New York: Ronald Press, 1964. For Tolman's views, see: E. G. Boring. *A History of Psychology in Autobiography,* Vol. IV, p. 173.

41. Woodworth, R. S., and M. R. Shehan. *Contemporary Schools of Psychology,* p. 173.

42. White, S. H. "The learning theory tradition and child psychology," pp. 657–701. In P. H. Mussen, Ed. *Carmichael's Manual of Child Psychology.* New York: John Wiley & Sons, Inc., 1970.

43. M. C. Jones, for example, gave up conditioning research, held a Laura Spelman Fellowship for two years for further interdisciplinary training, and then went to Berkeley with her husband, Harold Jones. In 1931, she began working on the Oakland Growth Study program, and has continued to do so ever since. She has sometimes been told—e.g., by Joseph Wolpe— that she should have carried on with conditioning and established a school of therapy. (Personal interview, February 21, 1973.)

44. Anderson, J. E. "The methods of child psychology," pp. 1–27. In C. Murchison, Ed. *A Handbook of Child Psychology.* Worcester, Mass.: Clark University Press, 1931.

45. Anderson, J. E. "Psychological methods," pp. 55–59. In *Second Conference on Research in Child Development.* Washington, May 5–7, 1927. Washington, D.C.: National Research Council, 1927.

46. Wolfenstein, M. "Fun morality: An analysis of recent American child-training literature," pp. 168–178. In M. Mead and M. Wolfenstein, Eds. *Childhood in Contemporary Cultures.* Chicago: The University of Chicago Press, 1955. See also: M. Wolfenstein. "Trends in infant care." *Amer. J. Orthopsychiat.* 23:120–130, 1953. Other articles analyzing changing trends in advice on infant care from 1890 to 1950 are C. B. Stendler, "Sixty years of child training practices. Revolution in the nursery" (*J. Ped.* 36:122–134, 1950) and C. E. Vincent, "Trends in infant care ideas" (*Child Develop*. 22:199–209, 1951).

47. West, Mrs. M. *Infant Care*, p. 59. *Care of Children*. Series No. 2. Bureau Publication No. 8. Washington, D.C.: U.S. Government Printing Office, 1914.

48. Ibid., pp. 59–60.

49. Ibid., p. 63.

50. As pointed out by E. A. Park and H. H. Mason in their biography of Luther Emmett Holt (in B. S. Veeder, Ed., *Pediatric Profiles*, pp. 33–60, St. Louis: C. V. Mosby Co., 1957), *The Care and Feeding of Children* was one of the 100 pre-1900 books chosen by the Grolier Club of America in 1946 as having "influenced the life and culture of the American people." See: D. A. Randall. Books that influenced America. *New York Times Book Review* 51:7,22, April 21, 1946.

51. West, Mrs. M. *Infant Care*, p. 77.

52. Extensive surveys of maternity and infant care in rural counties were carried out by the Children's Bureau after 1917. Five of these reports have been reprinted as *Child Care in Rural America* (New York: Arno Press, 1972). The reports give some idea of the primitive conditions under which childbirth could take place and of the types of families with which the Children's Bureau was especially concerned.

53. West, Mrs. M. *Infant Care*, p. 60.

54. *Infant Care*, p. 53, 1929. The author of this revision was Dr. Martha M. Eliot, Director of the Child-Hygiene Division of the Children's Bureau.

55. Ibid., p. 57.

56. Watson, J. B. *Psychological Care of Infant and Child*, p. 128.

57. Ibid., p. 114.

58. Weill, B. C. "Are you training your child to be happy?" p. v. *Lesson Material in Child Management*. Washington, D.C.: U.S. Government Printing Office, 1930.

59. Ibid., p. 1.

60. Ibid., p. 23.

61. Watson, J. B. *Psychological Care of Infant and Child*, pp. 5–6.

62. Brim, O. G. *Education for Child Rearing*, pp. 17–18. New York: Russell Sage Foundation, 1959.

63. Tobey, J. A. *The Children's Bureau: Its History, Activities and Organization*, p. 15. Baltimore: Johns Hopkins Press, 1925.

64. The objectives and methods of the Child Study Association of America are discussed by O. G. Brim, *Education for Child Rearing*, and by W. I. Thomas and D. S. Thomas, *The Child in America; Behavior Problems and Programs*, pp. 305–309 (New York: Alfred A. Knopf, 1928).

65. The original association began in New York in 1888 and was reformed as the Federation for Child Study in 1909 and as the Child Study Association of America in 1924. *Child Study* began publication in December 1923.

66. Federation for Child Study. B. C. Gruenberg, Ed. *Outlines of Child Study: A Manual for Parents and Teachers*, pp. 237–260. New York: The Macmillan Co., 1922.

67. Child Study Association, Parents' Bibliography Committee. *A Selected List of Books for Parents and Teachers*. New York: Child Study Association, 1928. Only one book by Freud, *The Problem of Lay-Analysis* (New York: Brentano's Publisher, 1927), was included, but there were a few texts interpreting psychoanalytic ideas to the layman.

68. Gruenberg, B. C., Ed. *Guidance of Childhood and Youth: Readings in Child Study*, p. v. New York: The Macmillan Co., 1926.

69. Ibid., p. 221.

70. By 1928, nursery schools had become established at some of the child welfare research stations—e.g., in Iowa, Minnesota, and New York—and these were used both to train parents to observe and handle their own children and to train potential parents. See: Thomas and Thomas. *The Child in America*, p. 320. Also: H. T. Woolley. "The nursery school: A response to new needs," pp. 49–70. In *Concerning Parents: A Symposium on Present Day Parenthood*. New York: New Republic, 1926.

71. *A Selected List of Books for Parents and Teachers* (New York: Child Study Association, 1928) contained 31 titles of books and pamphlets on sex education.

72. For a history of the child guidance movement, see: M.

Levine and A. Levine. *A Social History of Helping Services: Clinic, Court, School and Community.* New York: Appleton-Century-Crofts, 1970. 315 pp.

5

The Value of Recent Empirical Research

The major purpose of this book is to show the important role of empirical research in ensuring that hypotheses do not lead to inflexible practices in the rearing of children. As noted in Chapters 3 and 4, the influence of both Freud and Watson, combined with the American faith in the power of early experience, gave credibility to the view that the young child's treatment by his parents (especially his mother) had a serious influence on his adult personality. Here it seemed a good idea to specify the nature of that influence. Exactly what is stable? And how early can one predict adult intellect and personality? One purpose of the empirical research of the period 1930–1960 was to separate good from bad hypotheses about personality development.

Furthermore, Americans during the 1960s became concerned with the status of poor minorities. As blacks migrated to northern cities and as Spanish-speaking children moved from Texas and Puerto Rico into more northern suburbs, it became apparent that many were having difficulty mastering school work. The failure they experienced was not the same as that of middle-class youth. The lack of success in school of the Spanish-speaking child could not easily be attributed to family dynamics, but rather seemed to be due to cognitive problems. Some psychologists began to question the intelligence of these children because their IQ scores were lower than those of middle-class children. Others assumed that failure was due to lack of familiarity with the language style and demands of the school. Still others thought that the culture of poverty led to a debasement of self and, as a result, low expectation of success. The increasing realization that it was necessary for each person in our society to have a minimum of 12 years of schooling in order to attain some dignity, coupled with America's egalitarianism, forced attention to the importance of guaranteeing success in school for all and forced attention away from phobias, obsessions, and bed-wetting. To worry about a fear of dogs or enuresis in a doctor's child, while thousands of children were three grades below the normative expectation in reading, was a luxury the nation could not afford.

Finally, the apparent technological lead held by Russia threatened a part of America's pride and led to the decision that educational programs were at fault. At the same time Piaget's theory of cognitive development, which had long been confined to Geneva, spilled over into the American university. Many forces, therefore, conspired to focus America's concern on intellectual development. The older belief in continuity and early origins of adolescent behavior was not touched by this new movement. Freud's hypothesis that early experience influenced adult functioning was not given up. The focus of concern merely shifted from emotion to intellect. It was assumed that early experience influenced later intellectual development. Mothers became concerned about the effect of their treatment on their child's intellectual ability, and work and worry over entrance into a "good" college replaced concern over guilt and impotence. Let us now examine the research that addressed some of these issues and consider how empirical work helped to keep invalid conclusions from gaining complete ascendance.

Longitudinal Studies

In the 1920s, the Laura Spelman Rockefeller Memorial was instrumental in financing several programs at recently instituted child research stations, such as those at Iowa, Yale, Minnesota, Denver, and Berkeley.[1, 2] At first short-term studies were envisioned, but some were continued for several years, or even decades, so they became longitudinal in nature. Lawrence K. Frank, who with Beardsley Ruml was in charge of the Spelman funds, probably did more than any other person to initiate longitudinal research in human development. As Jean Walker Macfarlane, who has been a member of the Berkeley Institute of Human Development since the late 1920s has recently attested: "Lawrence Frank was a marvelous person to be running the show. He was so enthusiastic, so eager, so supporting, got everybody involved, and made them think what they were doing was important, so they worked like fools."[3] One of his aims was to promote the interdisciplinary investigation of physical growth and mental development in normal children, without any specific research bias such as profound behaviorism, psychoanalysis, or just collecting measures. For this reason, when he was seeking to establish a research program on the West Coast in 1926, he chose the University of California at Berkeley, rather than Stanford, where research in child psychology under Lewis Terman was devoted almost entirely to mental testing.[4]

Soon after their establishment, most of the centers for child development instituted longitudinal research programs. In some instances the initiation of such a program was the reason for the funding of the research center itself, as in the instance of the Center for Research in Child Health and Development at Harvard University, which began operation in 1932. A detailed account of the objectives of the program and of studies in progress was given by the director, Harold C. Stuart, seven years later, in 1939.[5] According to Stuart:

The project has become a coordinated research in the borderland fields of human biology and has as its central theme the more precise understanding of the phenomena of human development and their relation to problems of child health. Although there has been emphasis on problems of health and fitness, an attempt has been made to explore, insofar as possible, all major aspects of development in the same children and all forces which may have bearing upon the developmental progress of these children. With this evidence in hand, important interrelationships between the various aspects of development, or between any one of them and physical well-being, should be brought to light.[6]

Enough children were enrolled before birth to ensure that at least 100 of each sex could be studied for five years (the period was later extended). Observations were made and records kept of pregnancy, labor, and delivery and of the care and diet given the child at home. Regular visits to the center were required for pediatric, orthopedic, and dental observations, for anthropometric determinations, and for the making of X-ray and photographic records. In addition, mental and personality development was assessed by standard test methods and by observing some children at the center's nursery school or in the home. The hope was that the enormous amount of data thus obtained would, when finally analyzed, reveal previously unsuspected correlations or confirm correlations predicted by developmental hypotheses.

The difficulties of organizing, running, and financing such a program may easily be imagined. Because the main objective was the long-term observation of growth, rather than the testing of hypotheses, as much information as possible was obtained, irrespective of its immediate relevance. Limits were, however, set by considerations of time, expense, and the anticipated endurance of children and their parents. Over the years, inevitable staff changes made it difficult to obtain consistent observations and measures. In addition, it was difficult to introduce new techniques once a study was under way.[7]

The difficulty of introducing new techniques prevented longitudinal studies from being useful in determining the effects of early experience on later development, although this was the kind of problem for which they were ideally suited. By a quirk of fate, most of the longitudinal programs had already been in operation for a decade or more by the time the early-experience hypothesis became of general interest. These programs, originally set up to investigate maturational processes and the relation of physical growth to mental development, were ill-adapted to deal with the consequences of specific patterns of childrearing. As pointed out by A. L. Baldwin, "they were committed to a research design that involved the careful periodic description of a relatively unselected group of children from birth onward."[8] Yet to investigate the influence of early experience, there had to be enough specific independent variables (parental characteristics) to provide reliable antecedent-consequent relationships. Many of the unselected groups already in the programs did not meet these requirements, and it was usually too expensive to set up new longitudinal samples in midstream.

Fortunately, the situation was not as hopeless as it may sound upon retelling. Although some of the programs had investigated children only from school age, others, notably the one at Denver, had detailed data dating from infancy. At Denver, mother-child interactions were studied intensively from 1947 to 1955. In addition, the Menninger studies were set up in 1948, specifically to explore the dynamics of personality development. The guidance and growth studies at Berkeley and the Fels program at Yellow Springs, Ohio, also provided data on the infant.[9] In general, however, the long-established programs were geared to the investigation of intellectual growth (as measured by intelligence tests) and physical development processes that could rather easily be quantified. In this context, the programs of the 1930s led to the establishment of physical norms of development invaluable to the pediatrician, many of which are still in current use.

Criticism of the somewhat inflexible, and certainly expensive and time-consuming, longitudinal studies increased in the late 1950s, as developmental psychology became more based on experiment. But some types of inquiry were irreplaceable. As pointed out by J. Kagan, they "are mandatory if we are to ascertain the relative permanence—or lack of permanence—of various response tendencies—an issue that could not be theoretically predetermined."[10] For example, both scientists and laymen often assumed that intelligence was a genetic endowment that showed continuity through development. On this principle, efforts were made to show that infant intelligence-test scores (e.g., on the Gesell Scale) predicted IQ ratings at 6 or 10 years of age. It was thought that the responses being measured in infancy were qualitatively the same as those assessed later in childhood. Nancy Bayley doubted this assumption after analysis of the intellectual growth data obtained at Berkeley by 1949.[11] Infant test scores correlated poorly with those obtained at school age. These findings did not necessarily invalidate the notion that intelligence was genetically based, but they suggested that whatever was being measured in infancy was not well related to what was being measured in later IQ tests.

Longitudinal studies had the important effect of introducing caution in the interpretation of infant psychological tests which, since their introduction in the early 1930s, had been accepted as highly predictive of later intellectual ability. One consequence of this earlier belief had been that adoption agencies had encouraged keeping babies in institutions for months before adoption so that psychological information about their mental status could be collected. The assumption was that an infant could then be matched with the "right" adoptive parents. A similar belief influenced some legislatures—for example, that of Connecticut—to outlaw private adoptions that were not between relatives and to require the welfare commissioner to indicate the physical and mental status of each child.[12]

Doubts were cast upon the wisdom of such policies years before Bayley published her findings in 1949. By 1938, Marjorie Honzik was using findings from the Berkeley longitudinal studies to suggest that mental tests given to children before they reached the age of 2 were unreliable predictors of later intellectual performance.[13] In 1939, Anderson at Minnesota was saying the same thing.[14] Ten more years passed before enough children had gone through the Berkeley program to provide the convincing information published by Bayley. Gesell, however, continued to believe in the stability of mental growth. In an article published in 1954 he reported that studies done at Yale indicated that early predictions were usually borne out through childhood.[15] One possible explanation for this discrepancy between research findings was that Gesell based his early judgments not simply on psychometric tests but also on careful clinical appraisal of each infant: perhaps this enabled him to predict mental growth more accurately than most.

To add fuel to the fire, several reports had come out by the late 1940s on the potentially devastating emotional effects of early maternal deprivation. The Child Welfare League of America responded fairly promptly to the implications of such reports, and, by 1958, stated that assumptions in adoptive practice should take into account "current scientific opinion." For example:

Prediction of future development. On the basis of current knowledge, present methods of medical examination and psychological testing, it is not possible within the first year of life to predict with a high degree of accuracy an infant's future mental or physical development. Adoptive parents, like own parents, should be expected to be able to take some risk in regard to the later development of an infant.[16]

A similar definitive statement was made by the American Academy of Pediatrics in 1959:

Formerly it was customary in many agencies to perform psychometric evaluation of infants at about three months of age.

At times this necessitated retaining these children in foster-home care until they had been tested. *Today retention of the infant for testing is justified only when retardation is suspected.* [17]

Thus, the overenthusiastic application of early scientific reports was modified by later findings of longitudinal studies. The infant was indeed proving to be a complex organism to decipher and one whose future mental status could not so easily be predicted.

The data from such programs also led some to question other shibboleths. As a result of the popularization of Freudian ideas, thumb-sucking had become "a diagnostic sign for insufficient sucking satisfaction, disturbed emotional development, troubled mother-child relations, and a host of other ills." [18] Consequently, any mother whose infant sucked his thumb naturally felt worried and guilty, even to the extent of considering herself a failure as a parent. Yet in 1963 Martin Heinstein reported data showing that the highest incidence of thumb-sucking occurred among girls who had been breastfed by "warm," apparently well-adjusted mothers.

During the last 10 years, several of the longitudinal programs have matured and have permitted detailed assessments of the adults on whom vast amounts of developmental data had been collected. Three of the important reports were based on data from the Fels Research Institute in Yellow Springs, Ohio, and the Berkeley growth and guidance studies conducted at the University of California, Berkeley. In these studies, predictability was sometimes poorer than had been anticipated. Macfarlane, after a lifetime of commitment to the study of a large group of subjects growing up in the Berkeley, California, area, expressed her appreciation for the dynamic nature of growth, and said she realized how current life situations had the power to change the growing child. Good treatment during the first few years of life did not guarantee a mature adult.

We have been forced to the conclusion from our long study that the only way one grows up, matures, learns to accept, to be comfortable with one's self and to approach one's potential is by having maturing experiences along the whole lifespan.[19]

Reflecting upon difficulties inherent in predictions of later development, she concluded that:

It seems clear that we overweighted the troublesome and the pathogenic aspects and underweighted elements that were maturity inducing. . . . We unquestionably overestimated the durability of those well learned behaviors and attitudes that were characteristic and habitual response patterns over a substantial period of time. It appears that no matter how habitual these patterns were, if they were coping devices or instrumental acts that no longer were effective for desired ends in changed situations and with changing physiologies, by the vast majority they were dropped or modified. . . . We had not sensed that long continuous patterns would be modified or converted into almost the opposite characteristics. For example, it has been interesting to see how many of our over-dependents have converted their patterns into nurturant ones, yet not to an over-nurturant extreme since they are aware that what they want to foster in their children is confidence, not overdependence. . . . Some subjects seem to be "late bloomers" or "slow jellers" who took a long time, and a change of situation away from their community and family to work through early confusions or inhibitions and to achieve release to be themselves.[20]

Macfarlane acknowledged that early patterns of behavior are continually vulnerable to change and that the environment of children and adolescents exerts a powerful influence on their behavior. More specifically, she wrote:

We have found that much of personality theory based on pathological samples is not useful for prediction for the larger number of persons. Many of our most mature and competent adults had severely troubled and confusing childhoods and adolescences. Many of our highly successful children in adolescence have failed to achieve their predicted potential.[21]

Similarly, Kagan and Moss concluded that it was not possible to predict significant aspects of adult behavior and temperament in children younger than 10 years old.[22] Hence, empirical research was having its intended effect. It was making slight corrections in presuppositions and causing both scientist and citizen to begin to question beliefs that some had assumed to be beyond refutation.

Experimental Studies

Experimental research was also casting doubt on some psychoanalytic predictions about personality development. Before discussing some of these studies, so different in structure from the psychoanalytic ones, we must briefly discuss the concept of *operationalism*, which led to a tightening of research criteria.

THE INTRODUCTION OF OPERATIONAL CRITERIA FOR PSYCHOLOGICAL RESEARCH

The principles of operationalism had first been defined by the physicist P. W. Bridgman in the late 1920s. He proposed that any concept used by a scientist should be defined in terms of the physical operations required for its determination. The method was intended to ensure "full understanding and communication of all the conditions surrounding observation, particularly the conditions

connected with the observational procedure itself."[23]
Such a principle seemed an ideal solution to the problem
of defining psychological variables without including subjective concepts, so its use was endorsed by many leading
psychologists, including S. S. Stevens, E. G. Boring, B. F.
Skinner, and E. C. Tolman.[24] Not surprisingly, however,
psychological concepts were less easily adaptable to operational definitions than were physical concepts, and early
hopes that the use of operationalism would confer a strict,
universally acceptable meaning for all psychological constructs were only partially realized. The movement did
stimulate attempts to obtain objective definitions of mental and other biological factors that needed to be included
in a behavioral formula.[25]

Soon after operationalism was introduced into psychology, Clark Hull decided that the application of its
principles could render many Freudian concepts amenable to scientific investigation.

On the assumption that psychoanalysis leaves much to be desired in the matter of theoretical structure, does it follow necessarily that this is a permanent defect? Is it not conceivable that,
taking the present informal elaboration of postulates contained
in the literature as a guide and a point of departure, there may
be formulated at a fairly early date a workable postulate system
accompanied by operational definitions of critical terms, and
that from these two there may be derived coherent theorem sequences covering extensive fields of phenomena in psychopa-
thology, normal psychology, sociology, and anthropology?[26]

On such operational principles, Hull began a series of
seminars at the Yale Institute of Human Relations with the
aim of integrating psychoanalytic and learning theory, not
loosely, but systematically.[27] Most of the analysts present
were unenthusiastic and not very helpful, and it was left

to the learning theorists—N. E. Miller, J. Dollard, O. H. Mowrer, R. R. Sears, and others—to interpret Freudian concepts according to the behavioristic viewpoint.[28] Although interdisciplinary cooperation was not fully achieved, the attempt to achieve it was a sign of the growing reversal of earlier intellectual isolationism. Some experimentalists were now willing to absorb Freud, although admittedly very much on their own terms.

ATTEMPTS TO INVESTIGATE FREUDIAN POSTULATES EXPERIMENTALLY

For several years, efforts were made to confirm or refute Freudian postulates by experimental means. The neobehaviorists were not the only scientists involved; indeed, since at least the early 1930s, sporadic attempts had been made to design procedures to investigate analytic concepts.[29] A survey of the resulting literature was provided by R. R. Sears in *Survey of Objective Studies of Psychoanalytic Concepts*. Sears included as many published investigations that were related to Freud's theoretical formulations as possible, irrespective of the primary intent of the researchers.[30] Some of these investigators had not been in the least interested in psychoanalysis, but their results were pertinent to some aspect of the theory. Other workers had deliberately used observational or experimental techniques to investigate the empirical validity of Freudian concepts. The sources of evidence tapped by Sears were therefore somewhat varied. Thus, to evaluate the reliability of the theories of infant sexuality, he assessed the results of anthropological studies of observations of infants and of nursery-school children, of reports by adults of remembered childhood sexual behavior, and of longitudinal studies. One of Sears's conclusions was that "Freud's notion of the universal Oedipus complex stands as a sharply etched grotesquerie against his otherwise informative description of sexual development."[31] According to Sears, there could be no typical learning situation for children, and therefore no common or universal pattern of development in the Freudian sense because even within a culture no two families were alike.

Sears, as will be discussed later, thought that the studies of fixation and regression—studies emanating mainly from the animal laboratories—had been the most productive. He wrote:

The reasons for this lie in a complex of factors. In the first place, fixation and regression relate to overt behavior to a far greater degree than do the majority of Freud's concepts. . . . Experimental psychology has become far better able to cope with such behavioral processes than with the more intangible thought processes represented by such concepts as repression and projection. Secondly, fixation and regression are part and parcel of the learning process, and of all the variegated phenomena that have interested psychologists, learning has been the most extensively and successfully studied. In dealing with these two concepts, then, psychologists have had the relatively simple task of incorporating them into a vast and well charted body of facts and principles.[32]

A historical analysis of the experimental investigations of the Freudian concept of repression was provided by MacKinnon and Dukes in 1962 (see note 29). Again, a considerable amount of work was done, but the results were generally equivocal.

On the whole, few psychologists seem to have been convinced either way by the experimental findings of the thirties and early forties. Most psychoanalysts rejected them, because the requirements of experimentation so distorted the real-life situations implicit in Freudian theory that results were meaningless.[33] As pointed out in 1942 by Rapaport (one of the few psychoanalytic theorists to pay serious attention to the efforts at experimental verification), Freudian mechanisms—in this instance, the development of frustration—could be explained only with knowledge of the history—that is, the past experience—of the individual.[34] Experimentation dealt only with isolated, static portions of the subject's life. Furthermore, it entailed an oversimplification of analytic concepts. For example, the Yale group concluded that aggression was always the result of frustration, whereas to the analyst aggression was an instinctual drive, to be distinguished from aggressive behavior, which itself was not inevitably the consequence of frustration. In short, reduction to immediate operational postulates suitable for experimental testing was a singularly inappropriate fate for broad analytic concepts that were conceived, not only as interacting, but also as operating in a time continuum.

Nevertheless, the testing of analytic propositions by Hull's students and colleagues had some important consequences. One was that their studies of regression, fixation, frustration, and aggression drew attention to the possible relations between early experience and emotional development. The experimental evidence was not always very convincing, but it was suggestive and led to further research. Another consequence was the formulation of a social learning theory of development in which some (but not all) Freudian hypotheses were reframed in stimulus-response (S-R) language.

THE EMERGENCE OF SOCIAL LEARNING THEORY

Among the psychologists attempting to validate social learning theory, Sears appears to have been one of the most persistent. One of the problems he attacked was that of finding suitable variables for relating parental childrearing methods to children's later personalities.[35] This was a difficult undertaking, for there would be a lag between the measurement of the dependent variable—character traits of the child—and of the independent variable—the earlier behavior of the parents.

According to Sears, there were six main criteria for the selection of useful behavioral variables under such conditions. First, such a construct must be *economical:* it must include a variety of actions to reduce the number of definitions required. Second, it should refer to actions that were *important* to the welfare of the child or to the comfort of others in his environment. Third, the construct should have *universality* of application—it should be relevant in any cultural context. "Disobedience" would be an acceptable variable, whereas the construct "scuffing shoes" would be unsuitable, because of its limited cultural relevance. Fourth, a construct must be *nonevaluative,* that is, it must not depend on the value judgment of any specific cultural group. Fifth, it must be reducible to an *operational definition,* so as to permit the reliable replication of measurements; this criterion was often in conflict with the first, and a balance between the two must be sought. Sixth, and most important, "a construct must be demonstrably useful in the discovery of consistent *antecedent-consequent relationships.*" Because "a theory is composed of interlocking principles of the 'if x, then y' character," a construct would have to be able to serve as x or y if it were to be useful in the development of laws.[36]

Both antecedent and consequent variables should be chosen according to those six criteria. Sears realized that the recommendations would be difficult to follow unless clinicians and experimentalists cooperated in the search for significant constructs. The clinician, because he explored the total personality of his patients, could suggest relevant constructs; the experimentalist could decide whether these variables were suitable for manipulation, first by inspection, then by running pilot studies.

Sears hoped that systematic analyses of antecedent-consequent relationships in childrearing would provide the bases for an S-R theory of personality development.[37] But it proved impossible to obtain objectively sound data on mother-child relations extending over the whole period of infancy. Sears and his coworkers were faced with the problem, discussed earlier by Rapaport, that a strictly Hullian S-R system could not accommodate variables extending over time. As S. H. White has commented, "Hull's analysis of the force field surrounding a single S-R episode would not be applicable and, instead, we deal with the causal connections between antecedents and consequents."[38] Sears and his colleagues were relying on interviews of mothers of 5-year-old children to establish infant experiences. The child's response or behavior (at 5 years) could be objectively determined, but the independent variables (the parent's earlier attitudes towards the child) could be determined only retrospectively, usually by interviewing the mother—a method that had questionable validity.

Although not entirely successful, Sears's attempts to specify the influence of early experience on personality development had great heuristic value. He was writing in the early 1950s, at a time when developmental researchers felt excluded from the mainstream of psychological thought (which was then almost entirely behavioristic), because they did not use an experimental approach. Thus, in 1956, McCandless and Spiker stated that: "from discussions with child psychologists throughout the country, the writers have obtained the definite impression that child psychologists are concerned and somewhat troubled about the present and future status of their field."[39] One concern was an alleged deficiency in the quality of research conducted, another was an alleged lack of interest in theory on the part of developmentalists. A similar opinion was expressed by H. L. Koch in the fifth *Annual Review of Psychology* (1954). In the middle 1950s, several papers published in *Child Development* dealt with methods of raising the status of the field and of defining subjects of high research priority.[40] In this atmosphere of uncertainty Sears's program for investigating developmental processes was welcome. (While continuing in developmental research at Stanford, Sears has recently also addressed himself to the history of child development; see, Robert R. Sears, "Your ancients revisited: A history of child development," in *Review of Child Development Research*, vol. 5, ed. E. Mavis Hetherington, Chicago: University of Chicago Press, 1975.)

Infantile Stimulation and Optimal Intellectual Development

The hypothesis that early stimulation influenced intellectual development and that deprivation of variety in experience led to retardation came into prominence in the early 1960s. A strong incentive for its adoption was that it provided an explanation for relative intellectual retardation among poor and minority-group children and suggested methods for curing the problem. Although there was little empirical basis for the hypothesis, many psychologists, including Bettye Caldwell and J. McV. Hunt, thought it a sound working theory. In their view, given the urgency of the social problem, the available evidence should not be ignored; instead compensatory early education should be provided, its effects noted and then the underlying theory revised, if necessary. This is indeed what has happened. But, in the meantime, in spite of the tentative nature of the hypothesis, early stimulation was popularized as a necessity for all children and regarded by some as the prime cause of later intellectual proficiency.

The broad hypothesis was attractive, because it suggested practical solutions to urgent social problems. Since at least the autumn of 1957, the demand had been growing for increased scholastic competence in both elementary and secondary schools.[41] The educational system was criticized for failing to produce enough adults equipped with the necessary intellectual skills, chiefly mathematical and scientific, to cope with the demands of a society increasingly dependent on technological innovation. Furthermore, it became generally accepted that survival in this society required that everyone acquire a certain competence in such subjects as reading, writing, arithmetic, and logic. Acceleration of learning, especially among the poor, became a new demand on the schools. By the late 1960s, riots and conflagrations led to a social and political climate in which the special needs of the poor could no longer be ignored. But how could they be met? Testing showed that even in the first grade, minority-group and poor children had lower IQ scores than middle-class children. One hundred years earlier, this difference would almost certainly have been ascribed to heredity and therefore not considered remediable through the manipulation of environmental factors. Twenty years earlier, it was generally accepted that poor school achievement was due to delayed maturation or to emotional maladjustment. Up to a point, motivational and emotional factors were considered relevant in the 1960s, but far greater emphasis was given to the hypothesis that an intellectual deficit was the main problem and that this was the consequence of insufficient stimulation in early childhood. The corollary of this hypothesis was that relative cognitive retardation at the age of six or seven could be avoided by providing the necessary stimulating environment at some time before the child entered school. The major federal compensatory program, Project Head Start, was launched in 1965 on the assumption that three months of summer school would be of help to poor children who would enter school in the fall. Afterwards, the project was extended to cover the whole preschool year. Since then, specific intervention programs have been designed to reach the child at a progressively earlier age, for even "compensation" beginning in the preschool year did not achieve the results desired.[42]

We shall return to this subject, but we must first consider the cultural values and research findings that led to promotion of the early-stimulation hypothesis.

Factors Contributing to the Adoption of Early Stimulation Hypotheses

Of prime importance were findings emerging from studies done in animal laboratories from the 1950s on. These investigations attempted to test the validity of hypotheses derived from developmental theories, most frequently those of Freud and of Donald Hebb, and to explore the notion of "critical period."

CRITICAL PERIODS

The critical period concept involves the belief that there are circumscribed stages in early animal and human development when the organism must undergo specific experiences to continue developing normally. The concept further implies that if appropriate stimulation is lacking at the right time, compensation cannot occur later in life for by then the organism will no longer be appropriately receptive. The existence of critical periods in early development was suggested by knowledge of imprinting in some species of animals.

The phenomenon of *imprinting* in goslings, first observed by the naturalist O. Heinroth and studied in greater detail by Konrad Lorenz, was an ethological finding that stimulated interest among researchers investigating the significance of early experience.[43,44] Lorenz noted that a greylag gosling that was hatched and then kept by its own parents for a few days would not become attached to a human.

However, if a greylag gosling is taken into human care immediately after hatching, all the behavior patterns which are slanted to the parents respond at once to the human being. In fact, only very careful treatment can induce incubator-hatched greylag goslings to follow a grey goose mother. They must not be allowed to see a human being from the moment they break their shell to the time they are placed under the mother goose. If they do, they follow the human being at once.[45]

The attachment seemed to Lorenz to be permanent, the animals treating the human being (in this instance Lorenz) as a member of their own species. They remained affiliative to humans, even if later allowed to live for years with other geese. Lorenz saw imprinting as a form of knowledge acquired through a single impression to which the animal was receptive only during a "critical" period in development. No comparable attachment could form once the critical period was over.

To Lorenz, imprinting had nothing to do with learning.[46] He saw it instead as an innate form of adaptive behavior that would usually be successful because the first object seen would ordinarily be the parent. The idea that some animal behavior was innately, or structurally, determined was quite acceptable to European naturalists, although later many modified their views of "instinctive" action after contact with learning theorists.[47] Learning theorists considered the phenomenon of imprinting as a specific kind of learning in which social attachments were rapidly formed very early in life and were not susceptible to extinction.[48]

For several years Lorenz's findings were known only to other naturalists, probably because his early papers, in common with a majority of ethologic contributions, were published in German journals. English translations were not available until the 1950s, by which time ethological concepts were rapidly becoming of more general interest. Imprinting and the critical-period hypothesis, for example, were consistent with the Freudian postulate of specific psychosexual stages of development during which experience could determine future personality characteristics. As we have seen, this analogy was extended by John Bowlby, who viewed early human infancy as a critical period during which attachment to a permanent caretaker must occur to ensure normal emotional development and future capacity for socialization.[49] But in the late 1950s most psychoanalysts were still theoretically self-sufficient and not very impressed by Bowlby's borrowings from ethology.

Other developmental psychologists were more receptive, but indicated that further research was needed before generalization to humans was justifiable. One large body of observational data available was that provided by

J. P. Scott, mainly on the development of puppies. He suggested that these animals exhibited a critical period between the ages of three and 10 weeks after birth during which lasting attachments were formed easily with members of their own species or with humans.[50] Later, the puppies became fearful, could be socialized only with great difficulty, and no longer seemed to form deep attachments. Scott, like Bowlby, was firmly convinced that human infants had an equivalent critical period for socialization; but other animal researchers, such as Frank A. Beach and Julian Jaynes, advocated caution in extrapolating the animal findings thus far obtained.[51]

After 1960, the critical-period hypothesis was far more intensively debated and researched, in part because new data suggested that specific experiences during the "sensitive" stages of development might affect not only socialization but also later capacity to learn.

The phenomenon of imprinting provoked much animal research, because it appeared to be a circumscribed event that lent itself admirably to detailed investigation. Such investigation promised to throw light on the mechanisms whereby early experience might determine later development. But, interspecies comparisons had to be made with caution. Classical imprinting, including a following response and attachment behavior, could most clearly be observed in many types of young birds. How analogous was the behavior displayed by some young mammals, such as lambs and kids? Comparable behavior in humans was far more difficult to posit, because of their relative physical immaturity after birth. The more abstract concept of a critical period, for imprinting or any other type of early learning, was even more controversial.[52] If such periods existed, when and why did they begin and end? Such questions were not easy to answer empirically.

For example, during the 1950s Scott had thought that the period of socialization for puppies ended at 10 weeks of age, but further research findings caused him to doubt whether such a definitive cutoff point could be justified. In his own words:

The process of socialization begins at approximately three weeks of age, reaches its peak between six and eight weeks, and declines slowly thereafter. There is no definite cutoff point, but all evidence indicates that the process reaches a low level by twelve weeks or shortly thereafter. At first, I placed the end of the socialization period at seven to ten weeks, the time when the puppies are finally weaned from the breast and a gross change in social relationships takes place. However, all subsequent experimental evidence indicates that this is actually the peak of activity in the process and, while it declines rapidly thereafter, the capacity for socialization probably never declines completely to zero. A somewhat arbitrary time of twelve weeks can be set for the end of the period.[53]

If the capacity for socialization did not completely disappear, this would mean that the stage was sensitive, rather than critical. This developmental plasticity was probably more common in animals that had a long growth period. For example, it had often been observed that a young child can easily learn to speak a foreign language, but that if such learning were deferred until adolescence or later, fluency would rarely be achieved.

SUPPORT FOR THE CRITICAL PERIOD HYPOTHESIS. J. P. Scott was a leading advocate of the idea that critical periods determined the direction of social, intellectual, and emotional development, not only in animals, but also in humans. He had been impressed by the unusual later development of a lamb that he and his wife had raised on the bottle for the first 10 days of life. The animal, although pastured with other sheep at the end of the 10-day period, remained independent of the rest of the flock and instead became attached to people. She was a very indifferent mother when she finally had lambs of her own. Later, working mainly with dogs, Scott developed the critical-period hypothesis further, suggesting in 1962 that there were three types of critical-period phenomena: for primary socialization, for the acquisition of motor and problem-solving abilities, and for the effects of early stimulation. [54]

The idea that there was a critical period for primary socialization had already received much support. The imprinting phenomenon had been observed in many species of birds. Harlow had found that monkeys reared with cloth surrogate mothers did not develop normal sexual and social behavior, unless they were allowed some time to play with other infant monkeys. Bowlby's 1951 report to the United Nations consisted of a collection of all available evidence supporting the theme that infancy, especially the period between six months and two and one-half years, was a critical time for the development of affectional bonds. Bowlby was originally convinced—he later changed his mind somewhat—that if bonding did not occur in this critical period the individual became permanently incapable of forming close relations—in short, affectionless.

Unfortunately, it was and is almost impossible to separate emotional and intellectual development in humans. The infants described by Spitz were both emotionally unresponsive and intellectually retarded, but there was no means of knowing whether the intellectual retardation was secondary to emotional maladjustment, or vice versa, or whether the two conditions were simultaneously

caused by deprivation, illness, or malnutrition. Was there
one crucial factor—attachment to the mother—or was it
the variety of input provided by the caretaker that was
essential for normal intellectual emotional development?
Finally, was the critical-period concept useful in explaining the effects of maternal or sensory deprivation?[55]

QUESTIONS ABOUT THE VALIDITY OF THE CRITICAL PERIOD
HYPOTHESIS. Many researchers recognized the heuristic
value of the critical-period hypothesis but doubted its
applicability to post-natal human development in its absolute form. They preferred to think in terms of sensitive,
rather than critical, periods. For in embryology, where it
had originated, the critical period concept had a very precise meaning: the designation of a circumscribed stage in
embryonic development during which a developing organ
was susceptible to irreversible damage through the action
of extraneous physical, chemical or living agents. In 1921,
the embryologist Charles Stockard had elaborated a
theory of critical periods to explain experiments in which
he had chemically induced monstrous development in
fish embryos.[56] (See also note 52). More recently recognition of the teratogenic action of the rubella virus and of
thalidomide during specific periods of gestation supports
the concept of critical periods during human embryonic
development. But were psychologists justified in borrow-
ing the term, with its implications of irremediable damage, and applying it to post-natal behavioral development? As Riesen stated in 1961, "a thoroughgoing
critical-period hypothesis would demand an irreversibili-
ty of the effects of early deprivation."[57] Such a thesis could
not be rigorously investigated in humans, for appropriate
research was inconceivable. (Recently, however, linguists
and psychologists in Los Angeles have been studying the

further development of Genie, a girl who had spent the first thirteen years of her life isolated at home under conditions of extreme mental and physical deprivation. When found six years ago, she could neither stand, walk, nor talk. Since then she has made remarkable progress both physically and mentally, although she is still very different from her peers who have had a normal background.[58])

Even in animals, in which the hypothesis could be more rigorously tested, the evidence was only suggestive. To quote Riesen again, "thorough-going efforts to provide conditions for reversing the apparently irreversible *have* several times *succeeded.*" Even the positive effects of pre-weaning stimulation in rats did not necessarily indicate the presence of a true critical period for this form of stimulation, although the early findings did seem to support such an interpretation. Denenberg, after more extensive research on mice and rats, concluded that the data did not warrant the application of such a definitive concept:

In instances where the data are consistent with the hypothesis, further study has found that the 'critical period' is a complex function of the parameter of stimulus intensity. Research to date indicates that, for the rat and mouse at least, there may be as many 'critical periods' as there are combinations of independent variable parameters and dependent variable measures.[59]

Later, in 1968, Denenberg reviewed the experimental literature on the subject and again found that the age at which stimulation occurred was but one of many significant variables. Equally important were the amount of stimulation, its quality, the particular dependent variable measured, the particular quantitative parameters of the dependent variable, and the animal's experiences between initial stimulation and final testing.

SOME INFLUENCES OF THE CRITICAL PERIOD CONCEPT. Today it is more usual to think of "sensitive" than "critical" periods. The implication is that effects of deprivation during such a stage are not necessarily irreversible and that the effects of stimulation are not necessarily permanent. But, in the early 1960s, the more absolute concept was often taken for granted and used to lend support to the belief that maximizing sensory stimulation in early childhood would lead to optimal mental development. Furthermore, although the designation given to the concept was novel, its implications were not. Freud's psychosexual stages of infancy were also periods of specific experiences that would have profound and permanent effects on mental development. The same may be said for the earliest of Erik Erikson's "eight ages of man." Finally, the acceptance of such a concept has been the basis for many intervention programs, such as the powerful drive for parental education in the late 1920s and the more recent demand for early education programs for children.

Muriel Beadle wrote in 1971:

After birth, too, there are critical periods in physical, emotional, and intellectual development. Some of these can be pinpointed in time quite specifically; others, especially those pertaining to emotional and intellectual development, can as yet be bounded only generally.[60]

It may seem pedantic to argue that, given the present state of knowledge, we cannot talk of "critical," but only of "sensitive," periods. Indeed, the fact that the child learns to speak a language, perhaps the most complex skill to be acquired in a lifetime, is strong presumptive evidence that infancy and early childhood constitute a critical period for cognitive development, as far as language is concerned. Yet the weaker term is to be preferred, because it underlines the uncertainty about precise timing and about the specificity of events that must occur, or deprivations that must be avoided, to ensure optimal intellectual development.

The lack of definitive data, or of knowledge of the physiological changes that are part of a "critical" event, need not prevent the establishment of early education programs. Indeed, Bettye M. Caldwell has argued forcefully that such programs should be set up in spite of a lack of clear-cut information.

The strategy involved in offering the enrichment experience to children of this very young age group [between 6 months and 3 years] is to maximize their potential and hopefully prevent the deceleration in rate of development which seems to occur in many deprived children around the age of two to three years. It is thus an exercise in circumvention rather than remediation. Effectiveness of the endeavor is being determined by a comparison of the participating children with a control group of children from similar backgrounds who are not enrolled in the enrichment program. Unfortunately, it is too early for such projects to do more than suggest alternatives. The degree of confidence which comes only from research evidence plus replicated experience will have to wait a little longer.[61]

The controlled-intervention study would then itself act as a source of further data, at least about behavior.

Effective social action, however, can seldom await definitive data. And in the area of child care, the most clamorous demand for innovative action appears to be coming from a rather unlikely source—not from any of the professional groups, not particularly from social planners who try to incorporate research data into plans for social action, but from *mothers*. From mothers themselves is coming the demand that professionals in the field look at some of the alternatives. We need not be reminded here that in America at the present time there are more than three million working mothers with children under 6 years of age.[62]

As is so clearly pointed out by Caldwell, society may demand answers to questions for which there is no authoritative scientific reply. But such questions themselves stimulate further research, especially in child development, which is basically engaged in solving problems of constant human interest. In the early 1960s, when there was a general demand for improved school performance, studies in cognitive development, which had been in low gear, were greatly accelerated.

DONALD HEBB'S THEORY OF LEARNING

The idea that early learning might be qualitatively different from learning that took place later in life and the basis for it constituted but part of a novel synthesis of behavioral development set forth by Donald O. Hebb in *The Organization of Behavior.* Hebb proposed a learning theory that differed from the sensory-motor connectionist one advocated by the behaviorists and from the perceptual emphasis of the Gestalt field theory. His objection to the former was that it could not account for the autonomous cerebral activities, "something like *thinking*," that undoubtedly intervened between sensory and motor processes.[63] Gestalt psychologists denied that central connections influenced learning and thus could not account for a specific response to a specific stimulus. According to Hebb, there was a need for "a conceptual tool for dealing with expectancy, attention, and so on" and with "the main facts of perception, and of learning."

Hebb noted that, particularly in higher animals, two distinct types of learning could be recognized: the slow, primary class of learning of the infant and the faster, insightful learning of the more mature animal. Primary learning depended on perceptual experience and established a control over the autonomous activity of the infant's brain association areas. "The larger the association areas, the slower the establishment of such a control must be and the less rigid and more complex its final form."[64] Secondary learning was not an association between totally unrelated processes, a strengthening of facilitations, and consequently could proceed much faster.

Hebb's theory implied not only that perceptual experience was essential for primary learning but also that the better organized the activity of the central organization areas became during infancy, the faster the animal would be able to learn in maturity. *The Organization of Behavior* was a seminal work. It not only led to research investigating the effects of early experience on later intelligence, but also provided a conceptual model of the relation of behavioral processes (in this instance learning) to underlying neurophysiological activity. It provided an impetus for viewing the human organism in its biological context, which led to revivals of research about the anatomic and physiological correlates of behavior and of comparative studies.[65] In this respect, it should be mentioned that, when psychologists and zoologists who were engaged in the study of animal behavior at Cambridge, England, formed a Behavior Discussion Group in 1953, they spent the first year analyzing and debating *The Organization of Behavior.*[66]

Hebb proposed an important environmental influence on intellectual development at a time when genetic influences were generally considered the more powerful.[67] During the 1930s and 1940s, there was little in the way of theory of intellectual development (Jean Piaget's early writings on the subject stimulated only transient interest outside Geneva). Most research was empirical and consisted of observations of stabilities and changes in IQ scores of groups of children enrolled in longitudinal studies. In school-aged children, IQ scores tended to remain constant over the years; this tendency supported the concept of a strong genetic basis of intelligence. Two groups of Iowa studies, those of H. M. Skeels and those of G. D. Stoddard and B. L. Wellman, seemed to show that environmental change could cause an appreciable rise in IQ score, but severe criticism, such as that of Florence Goodenough, was directed at the design of these studies.[68]

Animal psychologists hoped that their findings would be relevant to, or would provide guidance for, human research, but some were probably rather startled by society's enthusiastic espousal of their still-tentative proposals.[69]

In *The Organization of Behavior*, Hebb set out a formulation that was soon to become implicitly accepted by many people:

There are then two determinants of intellectual growth: a *completely necessary* innate potential (intelligence A), and a *completely necessary* stimulating environment. It is not to the point to ask which is more important; hypothetically, we might suppose that intelligence will rise to the limit set by heredity *or* environment, whichever is lower. Given a perfect environment, the inherited constitution will set the pace; given the heredity of a genius, the environment will do so.[70]

He then added the crucial rider: "The essentials of this environmental influence cannot be specified." Since the early 1960s, a major aim of both developmental and educational research has been to determine these "environmental essentials." But during the 1950s interest in the effects of experience on learning was confined to small groups of experimentalists working with animals.

HEBB'S RESEARCH AND ITS INFLUENCE. These researchers set out to discover the behavioral consequences of early sensory deprivation, usually visual (inasmuch as its effects could be more accurately observed). According to J. McV. Hunt, the first visual-deprivation experiment was performed by O. H. Mowrer in 1936 to find out whether maturation was responsible for the development of eye movements in pigeons.[71] Mowrer stitched up the eyelids of newly hatched birds for six weeks. The results suggested that maturation accounted for the appearance of eye movements that accompany body movements, in that vestibular nystagmus (rapid eye movements associated with vestibular stimulation) occurred as soon as the sutures were removed. But object fixation seemed to require some learning, for it did not appear for at least three days after the stitches were removed.

Hebb also carried out an early study that "was originally expected to demonstrate the truth of the Gestalt theory of perception and to embarrass learning theory."[72] He reared 18 rats in complete darkness and then trained them to discriminate horizontal from vertical lines. Lashley had found that normal rats learned this discrimination in a mean of 21 trials, whereas Hebb's rats required a mean of 129 trials—six times as many. However, they finally performed as well as normal animals; this showed that the slowness of the original learning could not be attributed to structural defects. Gestalt theory would have predicted no difference between the experimental and the normal rats, which was one reason why Hebb decided that neither Gestalt theory nor learning theory fully explained perceptual functioning. Although rats recovered fairly fast from the effects of visual deprivation, it was not clear what would happen in higher animals, which have larger cortical association areas. A crucial experiment was reported by A. H. Riesen in 1947.[73] He reared two newborn chimpanzees in complete darkness for 16 months and found that they were extremely incompetent visually after this period of deprivation. Later, it was found that both animals had marked pallor of the optic disks, and one of the chimpanzees became almost totally blind. Apparently, some visual stimulation was required for perceptual development, and some was required for the persistence of structural integrity.[74]

During the 1950s Riesen extended this study, and other workers confirmed his findings in kittens and chimpanzees. By 1965, he considered three factors essential for the optimal development of perceptual capacities in the higher animal: normal neural maturation, adequate stimulation, and morphological change in neural tissue induced by stimulation. Prolonged stimulus deprivation might lead to irreversible neural cell atrophy. "Stimulation must be both quantitatively optimum and behaviorally consistent if adaptive capacities are to be adequate," he reported.[75]

RESEARCH INTO THE EFFECTS OF ENRICHED AND IMPOVERISHED ENVIRONMENTS

Rather startling findings were reported by Mark Rosenzweig and his coworkers at Berkeley, who began investigating the relations between learning and brain biochemistry in 1953. Experimenting with rats that had just been weaned, they were surprised to find that "different experiences not only affected the enzymatic activity, but also altered the weight of the brain samples."[76] These researchers had set out to discover whether differences in learning ability among strains of rats might be related to differences in some biochemical brain measure. The measure chosen was cholinesterase content (thought to be directly related to cerebral synaptic activity) and the results did show correlation between "brightness" in maze-learning of certain strains and greater content of cholinesterase in the brain.

However, it was possible that the chemical values were not fixed for given strains of rats, but rather varied according to whether the animals were tested, to the type of test, and to the amount of handling they received. As a check, some members of a litter were given "intensive informal experience," whereas the others were placed in a restricted environment. Exposure to different environments produced small, but statistically significant, differences in brain cholinesterase activity.[77]

Changes in anatomy of the brain were neither expected nor sought, because, since the late nineteenth century, it had been conventionally held that such changes could not be induced by learning. As expressed by Rosenzweig:

Brain anatomy was disregarded, since we had inherited the dogma of absolute stability of brain weight. Fortunately, we had to record the weights of our brain samples in order to measure chemical activity per unit of tissue weight. After about 2 years of contemplating the chemical effects, we finally realized that the weights of the brain samples were also being altered by the environmental manipulations.[78]

This suggested a new hypothesis: that anatomical and chemical changes in the brain induced by experience lead to the changes in learning ability that are associated with experience.

By 1960, the Rosenzweig group was reporting that differential experience caused variation in cerebral acetylcholinesterase (AChE) content in postweaning rats. (AChE is the enzyme that hydrolyzes the synaptic transmitter acetylcholine, ACh.) By 1962, the researchers were describing the even more exciting finding that cortical weight also varied with differential experience. In 1964, Marian C. Diamond, a neuroanatomist, reported that she had found "the depth of cortex of enriched rats to exceed that of their less-enriched litter mates by 6.2% in the visual region and by 3.8% in the somesthetic region."[79] The enriched rats were those that had been kept for 80 days in an enriched environment—one with greater complexity and training than that of their litter mates. With respect to problem-solving, the enriched and the less-enriched groups did not show any difference in scores on the simple initial problems, but when they were presented with the more difficult reversal discrimination problems the enriched animals were significantly superior.[80]

Earlier researchers—notably Hebb, the Forgayses, and B. Hymovitch, at McGill University—had shown that rats reared in an enriched free environment (usually a large enclosure containing many playthings) showed improved problem-solving abilities when tested after they had reached maturity.[81] In 1962, Donald G. Forgays and Janet Michelson Read reported that there was a "critical" period for such exposure and that this crucial time appeared to be immediately after weaning, when the rats were 21 days old.[82] However, the Berkeley group found no indication in their data of a critical period for the effects on either brain tissue weight or AChE activity from the age of weaning.[83]

Thus far, rat studies had shown that, if these animals were placed in an enriched environment at some time during infancy, they became better problem solvers than control animals on reaching adulthood. But the testing had been done soon after the termination of the period of enrichment, whereas, as pointed out by Denenberg, "a considerable time gap must exist between the termination of the enriched experience and the ultimate test for problem solving" to test Hebb's assumption that induced brain changes would be permanent.[84] Denenberg waited until the animals were one year old to give them problem-solving tests and again found that the experimental groups performed better than the controls.[85]

In the meantime, Margaret Wilson et al. had shown that kittens responded in much the same manner as rats, both to early stimulation and to an enriched environment.[86] At 90 days, kittens that had been handled in infancy (increased stimulation) were less emotionally reactive than nonhandled controls, but required more trials to learn an active avoidance response. The subjects that had been exposed to the complex environment made significantly fewer errors in the Hebb-Williams maze and were more active in initial testing in an open field.

Harlow had occasion to investigate the effects of environmental enrichment on rhesus monkey learning. For many years, he was quite satisfied with the achievements of his "normal" monkeys (i.e., animals that had been reared in partial social isolation), in that they performed better than animals belonging to other laboratories and as well as feral monkeys. However, to study nuclear family behavior he had been rearing some monkeys in a relatively enriched environment, assuming that this would make no difference in their intellectual development. Nor did it appear to until the socially enriched adolescents were faced with the most complex learning task in the Wisconsin battery of tests. Then, to Harlow's admitted surprise, these adolescents proved to be significantly superior to those reared in partial social isolation ($p = 0.001$).[87]

STUDIES ON THE EFFECTS OF EARLY STIMULATION

The notion that early stimulation, even of an apparently "noxious" nature, might have a beneficial influence on later behavior was first suggested by studies on the handling and shocking of preweaning rats. Much of the early work was carried out by Seymour Levine and V. H. Denenberg.

Levine initiated this particular line of inquiry after he had mused over the fact that the ministrations of a well-meaning but relatively large and powerful adult to a human infant must often be emotionally stressful.[88] Beginning in 1954, he and his coworkers subjected a group of newborn rats to mild daily electric shocks; a second group of infant rats was placed in the shock cages each day but not treated; and a third group was left in the nest and not handled at all. To the investigators' surprise, it was the last group of rats that behaved peculiarly on reaching adulthood, whereas the shocked rats could not be distinguished from those that had merely been handled. Variations of this experiment were conducted several times. In Levine's words: "Invariably it is the non-manipulated 'controls' that exhibit deviations of behavior and physiology when they are tested as adults. Significantly these deviations involve the organism's response to stress and they show up in most of the diverse aspects of that response."[89]

Other researchers were also somewhat taken aback by these findings, which seemed to contradict the Freudian postulate that trauma in infancy caused anxiety and induced neurotic reactions to emotional stress later in life. As far as the laboratory rat was concerned, it appeared that very early stimulation facilitated adaptation to stress later in life.

One interpretation of this phenomenon was that early stress rendered the rats less reactive to stress engendered by the presentation of novel stimuli in later life. Partial support for this hypothesis was provided by the finding that handling a 2-day-old rat resulted in the secretion of corticosterone from the neonate's adrenal cortex.[90] Further support was derived from studies that showed that rats stimulated in infancy had a lower blood corticosteroid content immediately after exposure to novel field tests in adulthood than did nonhandled animals.[91] A possible explanation for such events was that the corticosterone that was released in infancy acted on the developing brain, possibly on the hypothalamus, and caused permanent and usually adaptive changes.

DEPRIVATION STUDIES IN PRIMATES

Perhaps of greatest impact were the reports of abnormal social and sexual behavior in primates that had been reared in socially restricted environments since earliest infancy. The best known animal studies on the effects of maternal deprivation, those conducted by Harry Harlow at the primate laboratory of the University of Wisconsin, were not set up originally to investigate this problem, but rather to study learning processes in the rhesus monkey. Harlow decided to isolate infant monkeys a few hours after birth, not to see how they fared without maternal love, but to prevent them from catching diseases.[92] Not only was primate mortality reduced, but a far-reaching longitudinal program was launched. Noticing that the isolated infant monkeys became very attached to the soft gauze diapers left in their cages, Harlow and his coworkers decided to find out whether bodily contact or feeding was the more important factor in leading to mother–infant attachment. A bare wire surrogate mother and a surrogate mother covered with terry cloth were placed in the cages of eight isolated newborn monkeys. Four of the monkeys were "bottle-fed" by the wire mothers; the other four were "fed" by the cloth-covered mothers. The first group drank from their wire mothers, but spent most of the rest of their time clinging to the cloth-covered surrogates. The other monkeys mainly ignored the wire surrogates. As the monkeys grew older, they spent more and more time clinging to the soft terry cloth.

Harlow concluded that bodily contact was of far greater importance than feeding in forming the infant's attachment to its mother.

All our experience, in fact, indicates that our cloth-covered mother surrogate is an eminently satisfactory mother. She is available 24 hours a day to satisfy her infant's overwhelming compulsion to seek bodily contact; she possesses infinite patience, never scolding her baby or biting it in anger. In these respects we regard her as superior to a living monkey mother, though monkey fathers would probably not endorse this opinion.[93]

But the above prediction, made in 1959, had to be retracted in the early 1960s. When the partially isolated (they could see other monkeys) surrogate-reared infants were exposed to "normal life," at the age of about three years, they proved to be almost totally socially and sexually incompetent.[94] From the experimenters' viewpoint, the latter was the greater disaster, for the original plan had been to produce a group of disease-free animals for breeding purposes. Instead, the laboratory was full of neurotic monkeys that were to require prolonged psychotherapy, supplied by experienced but patient normal monkeys of the opposite sex, before they learned what mating was all about. Indeed, none of the deprived males ever learned, and only some of the females became pregnant. As if to vindicate Bowlby, those that produced offspring proved to be the most appalling mothers, not only ignoring and rejecting their infants, but also on occasion attacking and even killing them. "Month after month female monkeys that never knew a real mother, themselves became mothers—helpless, hopeless, heartless mothers devoid, or almost devoid, of any material feeling," Harlow reported.[95]

Generalizing from the rhesus monkey to the human demands that some reservations be held in mind. First, it is impossible to imagine any human being reared under conditions of total social deprivation, although recent reports of children being reared in attics come close.[96] Second, Harlow found that rhesus monkeys reared in total isolation for the first nine months of life did not show a basic learning deficit (although they did exhibit rather subtle deficits—see p. 188.)[97] The isolates took much longer to adapt to the test apparatus, probably because they were so fearful, but once they had done so they performed within normal limits. "Social deficiencies demonstrated by these same animals would appear to be attributable to emotional factors rather than intellectual deficiency," Harlow reported.

Nevertheless, the studies of Richard Davenport and Charles Rogers have shown that, although basic intellectual capacity may remain normal, intellectual performance may be impaired for years after restoration to a normal environment. Seven chimpanzees were reared in isolation from birth to the age of two years.[98] When these animals were seven to nine years old, their ability to perform spatial delayed-response tasks was compared with that of eight chimpanzees of the same age that had lived in the jungle until captured at about one year of age.[99] The restricted subjects were initially inferior but, with experience, their performance approached that of the animals born in the wild. Davenport and Rogers concluded from these findings that "restricted early rearing does produce, in the chimpanzee, behavioral characteristics which hinder learning at a later age. Among these, distractability is of major importance; however, with proper experience distractability may decrease." In the following year, 1969, the same investigators reported a further comparison of the two chimpanzee groups in nonspatial discrimination learning.[100] Again, the restricted animals were reported to be generally inferior to the free-born ones. But, after being given sufficient intraproblem practice, they eventually performed well; this suggested that their deficit was relative rather than absolute. The impression gained by Davenport and Rogers was that the restricted animals had great difficulty in performing a novel task, that is, in learning the rules of the game. They had a persistent tendency to be distracted by irrelevant details and to engage in responses that had nothing to do with the test, especially stereotyped repetitive behavior.

Compared with the behavior of free-born chimpanzees, that of the initially restricted animals was not adaptive. They could not cope with a novel situation without much extra training, although, if this was supplied, they eventually performed adequately. Consequently, the findings on rhesus monkeys and chimpanzees, if relevant to human behavior, are encouraging, in that they suggest that basic intellectual capacity is resistant to deterioration, even when early environment is impoverished and variety of stimulation is minimal. Apparently, the main result of early deprivation is not a fundamental cognitive deficit, but an emotional one that seems to be amenable to special training and individualized attention.

But the question remained as to whether the findings from animal behavior, even those observed in apes and monkeys, could be applied to humans. There were, and are, no easy guidelines; generalizations may be misleading. The thalidomide disasters with human mothers were testimony to this danger, inasmuch as the drug had been pretested with animals (although not at what was found in retrospect to be the "critical" period in gestation). Similarly, developmental hypotheses derived from animal studies had to be tentative. The crucial step of evaluating these ideas in human subjects, especially infants, posed far more problems than the clinical trials of drugs.

RESEARCH ON THE HUMAN CHILD

One of the most important incentives for the hypothesis that early experience influenced a child's later development came from Rene Spitz. The influence of early experience on later development could hardly be investigated by requiring parents systematically to neglect their infants. An alternative was to study children fortuitously being reared under conditions similar to those required experimentally, that is, one group experiencing specific deprivation matched with a control group raised under more normal conditions. As discussed in Chapter 3, Spitz observed a situation of this type that consisted of two sets of institutionalized infants—a "nursery" group cared for by their own mothers and a "foundling" group deprived of individual attention—and described the outcome in a series of papers published in 1945 and 1946.[101] He concluded that the progressive mental and physical retardation exhibited by the foundling children, compared with the apparently normal development of the nursery babies, was due to the action of the one differing independent variable—the amount of emotional interchange offered.[102]

The research design was not tight enough to warrant such a definite claim, but it was made, and the impact on both the scientific and the general community was enormous. The excitement and controversy generated by Spitz's papers were fanned by John Bowlby's report, *Maternal Care and Mental Health* (1951), in which he concluded that "maternal care in infancy and early childhood is essential for mental health." This was a provocative statement, and it now became imperative for psychologists to determine more precisely the effects of maternal deprivation and the reasons for any observable deviations from normal development.

The discovery that children reared in some institutions tended to be physically, emotionally, and intellectually retarded supported early-stimulation hypotheses. One interpretation of the findings was that they were due to relative sensory deprivation, particularly perceptual deprivation, rather than to the lack of a single constant caretaker. For some who accepted this hypothesis, it was but a short step to proposing that, by implication, increased early stimulation should accelerate intellectual development of most, if not all, children. This feeling was

well expressed by the journalist Maya Pines in the opening chapter of her book, *Revolution in Learning:*

Millions of children are being irreparably damaged by our failure to stimulate them intellectually during their crucial years—
from birth to six. Millions of others are being held back from
their true potential . . .
. . . The scientists who would raise the nation's intelligence
through early learning believe that few educators or parents
have yet heard their message. As with public health, their
methods could benefit the entire population. They could
increase the talents and artistic involvement of all children.
Poor children could be given specific training that would bring
them up at least to the level necessary for success in school.
Middle-class children might gain even more from early stimulation.[103]

Yet there were no data concerning humans that directly supported the increased-stimulation hypothesis,
and not many animal findings, either. Rats and kittens
handled in early infancy showed decreased emotionality,
rather than increased learning ability, on reaching maturity. The belief that early stimulation itself would benefit
children intellectually was an extension of Hebb's theory,
as yet unsupported by firm empirical evidence. Here we
shall survey the findings in children that made the various early-stimulation hypotheses attractive.

EVIDENCE SUPPORTING THE PROPOSITION THAT LACK OF EARLY
STIMULATION CAUSED MENTAL RETARDATION. Various reports
suggested that infants reared in some institutions showed
evidence of early relative physical and mental retardation.
Further studies by Wayne Dennis, reported in 1957 and
1960, on the causes of retardation among institutionalized
children in Beirut were instructive.

In the early 1930s Dennis was a firm believer in the maturational or biological regulation of early development —so much so that he and his wife reared a pair of twins under conditions of minimal social and sensory stimulation.[104] The results were equivocal: one child showed signs of mental retardation by the age of 10 months, but the signs were attributed to the effects of an intracranial birth injury.

Still favoring a maturational view, Dennis studied the development of babies in a foundling home in Beirut and later in two other institutions that received children from this home.[105] The infant to caretaker ratio in the foundling home (Institution I) was 10:1, so the babies received minimal individual attention. When tested on Cattell's Infant Intelligence Scale between the ages of two months and one year, these children showed significant motor retardation. Dennis interpreted this as "probably due to the paucity of handling, including the failure of attendants to place the children in the sitting position and the prone position. The absence of experience in these positions is believed to have retarded the children in regard to sitting alone and also in regard to the onset of locomotion." Most of the infants never crawled, possibly because they had not had the previous experience of the prone position, and instead they developed an unusual method of getting around by scooting on their bottoms.

When, however, the more retarded babies from Institution I were sent, usually during the early months of life, to the modern and well-staffed Institution III, their later development resembled that of normal home-reared children. In contrast, children from the foundling home sent to Institution II, where conditions were poor, continued to show motor retardation, to the extent that only 15 percent of children between the ages of three and four years were able to walk alone. Dennis concluded that "the retardation of subjects in Institutions I and II is believed to be due to the restriction of specific kinds of learning opportunities." He now felt that experience played an important part in behavioral development and that the maturational hypothesis was not sufficient.

The babies in Institution I were deprived of stimulation: they had few toys, they lay in cribs with covered sides (so that only the ceiling was visible), and they were hardly ever spoken to by their caretakers. Later, they exhibited extreme motor retardation, but there was little evidence of intellectual deficit. They scored poorly on Cattell's Infant Intelligence Scales, but achieved almost normal mental ability when tested at the ages of four and one-half to six years, although they had remained in an impoverished environment. Thus, these studies did not support the belief that early-stimulation deprivation would have permanent intellectual consequences.

EVIDENCE SUPPORTING THE PROPOSITION THAT INCREASED EARLY STIMULATION CAUSED INTELLECTUAL PRECOCITY. Studies on human beings that suggested the beneficial role of early stimulation did exist. For example, Geber in 1958 had noted the extreme psychomotor precocity of Ugandan infants.[106] During the first year of life, the motor development of these children was two or three months ahead of that of European babies. Geber attributed this to the constant stimulation provided by the mothers, who almost never left their babies alone. They slept, played, and went almost everywhere together. The infants' precocity, however, usually disappeared after the first year, when most were abruptly weaned. The few Ugandan children raised in European style did not display extreme precocity.

Interpretations of this study became controversial. Some took it to mean that African babies were precocious on all counts, others suggested that only motor development was accelerated, and a third group proposed that early precocity implied a lower eventual intellectual competence. (This last group assumed, on comparative principles, that the longer the period of maturation, the higher the ultimate attainment.) In view of their implications, studies on "African infant precocity" were reviewed by Neil Warren in 1972.[107] He came to the conclusion that the phenomenon of African infant precocity was not established by existing data, "in particular, the conclusion of precocity has always been based on comparison with test norms, whereas studies involving actual comparative samples do not find precocity."

In general, although the early-stimulation hypothesis was attractive, it was still not firmly supported by a rich corpus of data. In its strong form, the hypothesis implied that early infancy was a critical period for some types of learning. If particular experiences did not occur, a permanent intellectual deficit would be the consequence.

A recent cross-cultural study by J. Kagan and R. E. Klein produced data that suggested that "absolute retardation in the attainment of specific cognitive competences during infancy has no predictive validity with respect to level of competence on a selected set of natural cognitive skills at age 11."[108] Although infants observed in San Marcos, Guatemala, were moderately to severely retarded in cognitive function, the 10-year-old children seemed competent in both absolute and relative terms. But the authors stressed that these findings did not imply "that a similar level of retardation among American infants has no future implication for relative retardation on culture-specific skills." The passive, quiet San Marcos infant developed normally in his own environment, but might not do so if transferred to another culture during early childhood.

These authors distinguished between universal cognitive competences—such as the capacity for language, inference, deduction, symbolism, and memory—and culturally specific talents, such as reading, arithmetic ability, and the understanding of specific concepts. A neurologically intact child would always exhibit the former group of skills, although the age of their appearance would vary somewhat according to previous experience. The second group of competences, however, would not appear naturally and needed to be directly taught.

Conclusions

Most people probably accept the general thesis that infantile experience influences later development. But such a broad theme is not very helpful, and a continuing research problem is to find more specific interpretations. A. D. B. Clarke has expressed this rather well:

The crucial question, to pose the analogy, is how far the foundations determine the later structure and dimensions of the building. Do they determine that a particular building must inevitably result, or can it be modified and restructured as it proceeds? If early learning has the role merely of being the first course of bricks, then it is important. If the first course of bricks also determines completely the structure of all above it, then it is ultra-important. This, then, is our problem. [109,110]

We have attempted to review the evidence supporting the secondary hypothesis that minimal sensory stimulation in infancy will cause later intellectual retardation. In view of all evidence, this thesis does not appear to have been proven. However, within our culture, it is likely that lack of specific types of early experience can slow the development of some competences and produce a relative intellectual retardation.

Notes and References

1. Child development research was initiated at the University of Iowa in 1917, at the Yale Psycho-Clinic under the care of Arnold Gesell in 1911, at Minnesota University in 1925, at the University of Colorado in 1923, and the University of California at Berkeley in 1927. The dates are approximate and depend on one's definition of child development research. L. K. Frank considered that such research did not truly begin until 1924–1925. See: L. K. Frank. "The beginnings of child development and family life education in the twentieth century." *Merrill-Palmer Quart.* 8:207–227, 1962.

2. For an outline of child-study work supported by the various Rockefeller boards, see: R. B. Fosdick. *Adventure in Giving; The Story of the General Education Board*, pp. 259–265. New York: Harper Bros., 1962; Also, Lomax, Elizabeth. "The Laura Spelman Rockefeller Memorial: Some of its contributions to early research in child development." *J. Hist. of the Behav. Sci.* 13:283–293, 1977.

3. Jean MacFarlane, personal interview, February 21, 1973.

4. Ibid.

5. Stuart, H. C. Studies from The Center for Research in Child Health and Development: 1. The Center, the Group Under Observation, Sources of Information, and Studies in Progress. School of Public Health, Harvard University. In *Monogr. Child Develop.* 4(1), 1939.

6. Ibid., p. 1.

7. Jones, H. E. "Problems of method in longitudinal research." *Vita Humana* 1:93–99, 1958.

8. Baldwin, A. L. "The study of child behavior and development," pp. 3–35, In P. H. Mussen, Ed. *Handbook of Research Methods in Child Development.* New York: John Wiley & Sons, 1960.

9. Kagan, J. "American longitudinal research on psychological development." *Child Develop.* 35:1–32, 1964. This report was the result of a survey, conducted by the author in 1962, of selected longitudinal programs that had been active for long periods. At Yale, A. Gesell had been studying infants longer than anyone else, but he did not provide the statistical data more typical of the other studies. Another longitudinal program investigating preschool children was run by William Blatz at Toronto. Both Gesell and Blatz wrote numerous books on child-rearing during the 1930s and 1940s.

10. Kagan, J. "American longitudinal research on psychological development."

11. Bayley, N. "Consistency and variability in the growth of intelligence from birth to 18 years." *J. Genet. Psychol.* 75:165–196, 1949. *Also:* Bayley. On the growth of intelligence. *Amer. Psychol.* 10:805–818, 1955.

12. *General Statutes of Connecticut, Revision of 1958* (Vol. VIII, Sections 45–63, pp. 33–35, 1958) required the welfare commissioner to indicate the mental and physical status of a child up for adoption. However, as cited in *Connecticut Reports,* Supreme Court, 1968, 157c, 596, the facts support the conclusion of the trial court that there is no basis for setting aside the adoption decree for failure of the commissioner to indicate the physical and mental status of the child (case of Ciarleglio v. Shapiro).

13. Honzik, M. P. "The constancy of mental test performance during the preschool period." *Ped. Sem. J. Genet. Psychol.* 52:285–302, 1938.

14. Anderson, L. D. "The predictive value of infancy tests in relation to intelligence at five years." *Child Develop.* 10:203–212, 1939.

15. Gesell, A. "The ontogenesis of infant behavior." In L. Carmichael, Ed. *Manual of Child Psychology.* New York: John Wiley & Sons, Inc., 1946, pp. 335–374. Studies on the validity of infant tests were reviewed by Boyd R. McCandless, Psychological assessment in infancy and very early childhood, pp. 66–71. In M. Shapiro. *A Study of Adoption Practice, Vol. II.* New York: Child Welfare League of America, 1956.

16. *Standards for Adoption Service*, p. 19. New York: Child Welfare League of America, 1958.

17. *Adoption of Children*, p. 13. Evanston, Ill.: American Academy of Pediatrics, 1959.

18. Heinstein, M. I. "Influence of breast feeding on children's behavior." In M. C. Jones, N. Bayley, J. W. Macfarlane, and M. P. Honzik, Eds. *The Course of Human Development.* Waltham, Mass.: Xerox College Publishing Co., 1971, pp. 300–305. The full paper was published in *Children* 10:93–97, 1963.

19. Jones, M. C., et al., *The Course of Human Development*, pp. 407–408.

20. Ibid., pp. 409–440.

21. Ibid., p. 415.

22. Kagan, J., and H. A. Moss. *Birth to Maturity; A Study in Psychological Development.* New York: John Wiley, 1962. 381 pp.

23. Israel, H., and B. Goldstein. "Operationism in psychology." *Psychol. Rev.* 51:177–188, 1944.

24. Boring, E. G. *A History of Experimental Psychology*, pp. 653–663 (2nd ed.) New York: Appleton-Century-Crofts, 1950. In reply to the above article by Israel and Goldstein, which criticized the manner in which operationalism was used by psychologists, Boring persuaded the Psychological Review to conduct a symposium on the subject. The views of the contributors—Boring, Bridgman, H. Feigl, Israel, C. C. Pratt, and Skinner—were published in *Psychol. Rev.* 52:241–294, 1945.

25. The relative importance of operationalism to research is summed up by J. Kagan as follows: "The movement toward operationalism was provoked by the extremism of the introspective method and the almost total concern with mental constructs . . . and so was in many respects healthy, for it pruned bad research questions from the tree of science. . . . However, there is now a legitimate revolt against the serious strictures posed by operationalism among both philosophers of science as well as psychologists. As a result there is a gradual loosening of those bonds. Witness the renaissance of empirical work by hard-headed experimental psychologists on memory and thinking and the postulating of constructs which, at the moment, cannot be operationalized—concepts like memory space, imagery, and attachment. These concepts are not amenable to elegant operational definitions at the moment, but psychologists are less upset about this in 1970 than they were in 1950." (Letter, August 9, 1973.)

26. Quoted by Shakow and Rapaport in "The influence of Freud on American psychology." *Psychol. Issues* 4(No. 1, Monogr. 13): 140, 1964.

27. Ibid., pp. 136–142. *Also:* J. Dollard. "Yale's Institute of Human Relations: What was it?" *Ventures* 3:32–40, 1964. The ultimate goal, according to Neal Miller, was a basic science of human behavior. (N. E. Miller. "Liberalization of basic S-R concepts: Extensions to conflict behavior, motivation, and social learning." In S. Koch, Ed. *Psychology: A Study of a Science.* Vol. 2. New York: McGraw-Hill Book Co., Inc., 1959, pp. 196–292. Miller was interested enough in the topic of conflict behavior to undergo brief psychoanalysis with Heinz Hartman in Vienna.

28. This interpretation was exemplified by the systems proposed in J. Dollard, L. W. Doob, N. E. Miller, O. H. Mowrer, and R. R. Sears, *Frustration and Aggression* (New Haven, Conn.: Yale University Press, 1939); and Dollard and Miller, *Personality and Psychotherapy* (New York: McGraw-Hill, 1950).

29. For an historical analysis of the experimental investigation of "repression," see: D. W. MacKinnon and W. F. Dukes. Repression, pp. 662–744. In L. Postman, Ed. *Psychology in the Making.* New York: Alfred A. Knopf, 1962. *Also:* For reprints of experimental papers on repression, projection, fixation and regression, displacement, and identification, see: S. G. M. Lee and M. Herbert, Eds. *Freud and Psychology.* New York: Penguin Books, 1970.

30. Sears, R. R. *Survey of Objective Studies of Psychoanalytic Concepts,* pp. x–xi. A report prepared for the Committee on Social Adjustment. New York: Social Science Research Council, 1943.

31. Ibid., p. 136.

32. Ibid., pp. 138–139.

33. Ernest R. Hilgard, a psychologist, and Lawrence S. Kubie and E. Pumpian-Mindlin, both psychiatrists, encouraged attempts to validate psychoanalysis as a science. See: E. Pumpian-Mindlin, Ed. *Psychoanalysis as Science: The Hixon Lectures on the Scientific Status of Psychoanalysis.* Stanford: Stanford University Press, 1952.

34. Rapaport, D. "Freudian mechanisms and frustration experiments." *Psychoanalyt. Quart.* 11:503–511, 1942.

35. Sears, R. R., J. W. M. Whiting, V. Nowlis, and P. S. Sears. "Some child-rearing antecedents of aggression and dependency in young children." *Genet. Psychol. Monogr.* 47:135–236, 1953.

36. Ibid., p. 140.

37. Ibid., p. 233.

38. White, S. H. "The learning theory tradition and child psychology." In P. H. Mussen, Ed. *Carmichael's Manual of Child Psychology, Vol. I,* pp. 657–701. New York: John Wiley & Sons, Inc., 1970.

39. McCandless, B. R., and C. C. Spiker. "Experimental research in child psychology." *Child Develop.* 27:75–80, 1956. The authors were also arguing for more experimental research on problems oriented toward theory construction.

40. Gollin, E. S. "Some research problems for developmental psychology." *Child Develop.* 27:223–235, 1956. Also: H. E. Jones. "The replacement problem in child development." *Child Develop.* 27:237–240, 1956. (Jones made a plea for more fellowships in child development research.) And: I. E. Siegel. "The need for conceptualization in research on child development." *Child Develop.* 27:241–252, 1956.

41. One of the best known criticisms of public school education was that of H. G. Rickover, *Education and Freedom* (New York: Dutton, 1959). As expressed by L. D. Cremin (*The Transformation of the School. Progressivism in American Education, 1876–1957*, p. 347, New York, Random House, 1964), "when Russians launched the first space satellite in the autumn of 1957, a shocked and humbled nation embarked on a bitter orgy of pedagogical soul-searching."

42. During the last 10 years, there has been an outpouring of publications on preschool education—its aims, the various methods of teaching, and the outcomes. The Educational Resources Information Center (ERIC) began publication of the *Head Start Childhood Research Information Bulletin* in 1969. This journal provided abstracts of research studies related to Head Start, but discontinued publication after a year. The Westinghouse Report, *The Impact of Head Start* (Springfield Westinghouse Learning Corporation, 1969) suggested that most of the intervention programs did not lead to appreciable intellectual changes and that the cognitive gains revealed by some studies appeared to be only temporary.

43. For clarification of the concepts involved in the terms "ethology" and "comparative psychology," see: J. Jaynes. "The historical origins of 'ethology' and 'comparative psychology.'" *Animal Behav.* 17:601–606, 1969. Today, the study of animal behavior is usually called "ethology" in biology departments and "comparative psychology" in psychology departments.

44. Lorenz quoted an accurate description of phenomenon given by O. Heinroth in 1910. See: K. Lorenz. "Companionship in bird life, Fellow members of the species as releasers of social behavior." In C. H. Schiller, Ed. (Translated from the German.) *Instinctive Behavior. The Development of a Modern Concept.* New York: International Universities Press, Inc., 1957, pp. 83–128.

45. Ibid., p. 103.

46. Thus Ibid., p. 118: "To my mind, the most important result gained from our study of innate reactions to fellow members of the species is this: in the realm of animal behavior, we cannot identify all that is acquired with experience, nor all acquiring with learning. In many cases, for instance, the adequate object of an innate reaction is not recognized instinctively as such. The animal comes to know it through a unique process, which has nothing to do with learning." However, as pointed out by Slukin, in *Imprinting and Early Learning,* pp. 9–10, (Chicago: Aldine Publ. Co., 1964), Lorenz later changed his mind somewhat on this point, expressing the view in 1955 that imprinting tapered off into learning and that imprinting was definitely a type of conditioning.

47. In America, animal behavior was studied almost entirely in the context of learning theory for the first half of this century. Researchers were interested in the animal as a reactive organism; after contact with ethology, they also became concerned with the study of the animal as an active organism. See: R. L. Eaton. "An historical look at ethology: A shot in the arm for comparative psychology." *J. Hist. Behav. Sci.* 6:176–187, 1970. For a spirited indictment of the laboratory emphasis on learning, see: F. A. Beach. "The snark was a boojum." In T. E. McGill, Ed. *Readings in Animal Behavior,* pp. 3–15. New York: Holt, Rinehart and Winston, 1965.

48. For reviews of imprinting studies and interpretations thereof, see E. H. Hess, "Imprinting in birds" (*Science* 146: 1128–1139, 1964); Slukin, *Imprinting and Early Learning* (1964); P. P. G. Bateson, "The characteristics and context of imprinting" (*Biolog. Rev.* 41: 177–220, 1966); and H. Moltz, "Imprinting: An epigenetic approach" (*Psycholog. Rev.* 70:123–138, 1963).

49. Bowlby, J. A. "Symposium on the contribution of current theories to an understanding of child development. I. An ethological approach to research in child development." *Brit. J. Med. Psychol.* 30:230–240, 1957. Bowlby interpreted the infant's early smile as an action that endeared him to his mother and so increased his chance of survival.

50. Scott, J. P., and M-'V. Marston. "Critical periods affecting the development of normal and mal-adjustive social behavior of puppies." *J. Genet. Psychol.* 77:25–60, 1950.

51. Beach, F. A., and J. Jaynes. "Effects of early experience upon the behavior of animals." *Psychol. Bull.* 51:239–263, 1954. This article was a comprehensive review of animal studies involving some modification of early experience.

52. The critical-period concept seems to have been borrowed from embryology. In using this term in "Companionship in bird life" (*Instinctive Behavior,* pp. 105–106), Lorenz referred to experiments by H. Spemann in which the latter transferred ectoderm cells, destined to form ventral skin, to the dorsal area of the future neural tube, in frog embryos. If the experiment was done during a limited specific period, the grafted cells developed into spinal cord; if later, they continued to grow as dermal tissue, presumably no longer having the capacity of being "redetermined" as neural tissue.

53. Scott, J. P. "The process of primary socialization in the dog." In G. Newton and S. Levine, Eds. *Early Experience and Behavior. The Psychobiology of Development*. Springfield, Ill.: Charles C Thomas, Publisher, 1968, pp. 412–439.

54. Scott, J. P. "Critical periods in behavioral development." In N. S. Endler, L. R. Boulter, and H. Osser, Eds. *Contemporary Issues in Developmental Psychology*. New York: Holt, Rinehart and Winston, 1968, pp. 181–197. (This paper was originally published in *Science* 138:949–958, 1962.)

55. Caldwell, B. M. "The usefulness of the critical period hypothesis in the study of filiative behavior." In N. S. Endler, L. R. Boulter, and H. Osser, Eds. *Contemporary Issues in Developmental Psychology*. New York: Holt, Rinehart and Winston, 1968. (Reprinted from *Merrill-Palmer Quart.* 8:229–242, 1962.) As noted by the editors, "this paper was part of a symposium entitled, 'Is the critical period hypothesis useful?' presented at the 1961 meeting of the American Psychological Association. Other participants included Dorothy Eichorn, Harry Harlow, Austin Riesen and Robert R. Sears."

56. Scott, J. P. "Critical periods in behavioral development." In N. S. Endler, et al., Eds. *Contemporary Issues in Developmental Psychology*, pp. 181–197. See also: C. R. Stockard. "Developmental rate and structural expression: An experimental study of twins, 'double monsters' and single deformities, and the interaction among embryonic organs during their origin and development." *Amer. J. Anat.* 28:115–277, 1921.

57. Riesen, A. H. "Critical stimulation and optimum period." Paper Presented at the APA Convention. Washington, D.C.: American Psychiatric Convention, 1961. Riesen suggested that inasmuch as primates must learn more of their behavior than do other mammals, "their greater plasticity permits late modification of behavior that could more efficiently be developed under optimum sequences of experience. Thus, what are critical periods in phylogeny become optimum periods in higher primates."

58. See Fromkin, V., S. Krashen, S. Curtiss, D. Rigler, and M. Rigler. "The development of language in Genie: A Case of language acquisition beyond the critical period." *Brain Language* 1:81–107, 1974; and, Susan Curtiss. *Genie: A Psycholinguistic Study of a Modern-day "Wild Child."* New York: Academic Press, 1977.

59. Denenberg, V. H. "Critical periods, stimulus input, and emotional reactivity." *Psychol. Rev.* 71:335–351, 1964.

60. Beadle, M. *A Child's Mind: How Children Learn During the Critical Years from Birth to Age Five*, p. 61. New York: Doubleday & Co., Inc., 1970.

61. Caldwell, B. M. "What is the optimal learning environment for the young child?" In J. L. Frost, Ed. *Early Childhood Education Rediscovered.* New York: Holt, Rinehart and Winston, 1968, pp. 50–67.

62. Ibid.

63. Hebb, D. O. *The Organization of Behavior; A Neuropsychological Theory*, p. xvi. New York: John Wiley, 1949.

64. Ibid., p. 123.

65. Jerome Kagan has said that reading *The Organization of Behavior* was one reason he chose psychology for his career.

66. Thorpe, W. H., and O. L. Zangwill, Eds. *Current Problems in Animal Behavior*, p. xi. Cambridge: University Press, 1961. The introduction to this book gives some idea of the enthusiasm and of the problems generated by attempts at interdisciplinary research into animal behavior.

67. See the first chapter in L. H. Stott and R. S. Ball, "Infant and pre-school mental tests: Review and evaluation" (*Monogr. Soc. Res. Child Develop.* 30:1–151, 1965).

68. The belief in "fixed" intelligence and in predetermined development is discussed by J. McV. Hunt in *Intelligence and Experience*, pp. 10–64 (New York: Ronald Press, 1961). Unfortunately, the Iowa studies were not well controlled, and, as pointed out by Hunt, critics like Florence Goodenough derided the proposition that appropriate early education could cause significant IQ gains. H. M. Skeels continued his longitudinal studies, irrespective of criticism. His report on the adult status of the group of 13 children who were subjected to an early-intervention program, as opposed to the group of 12 children (one died before reaching adulthood) who received ordinary institutional care, is given in "Adult status of children with contrasting early life experiences. A follow-up study" (*Monogr. Soc. Res. Child Develop.* 31:1–56, 1966).

69. Rosenzweig, M. R. "Environmental complexity, cerebral change, and behavior." *Amer. Psychol.* 21:321–332, 1966.

70. Hebb, D. O. *The Organization of Behavior,* pp. 302–303.

71. Hunt, J. McV. *Intelligence and Experience,* p. 92. Also: "O. H. Mowrer. 'Maturation' vs. 'learning' in the development of vestibular and optokinetic nystagmus." *Ped. Sem. J. Genet. Psychol.* 48:383–404, 1936.

72. Hunt, J. McV., *Intelligence and Experience,* p. 92. *Also:* D. O. Hebb. *Organization of Behavior,* p. 81.

73. Riesen, A. H. "The development of visual perception in man and chimpanzee." *Science* 106:107–108, 1947.

74. A survey of animal studies showing the effect of prolonged visual deprivation on neural growth and function is given by A. H. Riesen in "Sensory deprivation" (*Progress Physiolog. Psycholog.* 1:117–147, 1966).

75. Riesen, A. H. "Effects of visual deprivation on perceptual function and the neural substrate." In J. de Ajuriaguerra, Ed. *Bel-Air II: Désafferentation Expérimentale et Clinique.* Geneva: Georg, 1965, pp. 47–66.

76. Rosenzweig, M. R., E. L. Bennett, and M. C. Diamond. "Brain changes in response to experience." *Scientif. Amer.* 226(2):22–29, 1972.

77. Rosenzweig, M. R., D. Krech, and E. L. Bennett. "Heredity, environment, brain biochemistry, and learning." *Current Trends in Psychological Theory.* Pittsburgh: University of Pittsburgh Press, 1961, pp. 87–110.

78. Rosenzweig, M. R. "Environmental complexity, cerebral change, and behavior." *Amer. Psychol.* 21:321–332, 1966.

79. Rosenzweig, M. R., D. Krech, E. L. Bennett, and M. C. Diamond. "Modifying brain chemistry and anatomy by enrichment or impoverishment of experience." In G. Grant and S. Levine, Eds. *Early Experience and Behavior. The Psychobiology of Development.* Springfield, Ill.: Charles C Thomas, Publisher, 1968, pp. 258–298. *Also:* M. C. Diamond, D. Krech, and M. R. Rosenzweig. "The effects of an enriched environment on the histology of the rat cerebral cortex." *J. Comparat. Neurol.* 123: 111–119, 1964.

80. Rosenzweig, M. R., *et al.* "Modifying brain chemistry and anatomy by enrichment or impoverishment of experience," p. 276.

81. Denenberg, V. H. *Readings in the Development of Behavior,* pp. 312–315. Stamford, Conn.: Sinauer Associates, Inc., 1972.

82. Forgays, D. G., and J. M. Read. "Crucial periods for free-environmental experience in the rat." *J. Comparat. Physiol. Psychol.* 55:816–818, 1962. *Also:* V. H. Denenberg. *Readings in the Development of Behavior,* pp. 329–332.

83. Rosenzweig, M.R., *et al.* "Modifying brain chemistry and anatomy by enrichment or impoverishment of experience," p. 273. *Also:* M. R. Rosenzweig and E. L. Bennett. "Experimental influences on brain anatomy and brain chemistry in rodents." In G. Gottlieb, Ed. *Studies on the Development of Behavior and the Nervous System. Vol. 4. Early Influences.* New York: Academic Press, 1977.

84. Denenberg, V. H. *Readings in the Development of Behavior,* p. 313.

85. Denenberg, V. H., J. M. Woodcock, and K. M. Rosenberg. "Long-term effects of preweaning and postweaning free-environment experience on rats' problem-solving behavior." *J. Comparat. Physiol. Psychol.* 66:533–535, 1968.

86. Wilson, M., J. M. Warren, and L. Abbott. "Infantile stimulation, activity, and learning by cats." *Child Develop.* 36: 843–853, 1965.

87. Harlow, H. F., M. K. Harlow, and S. J. Suomi. "From

thought to therapy: Lessons from a primate laboratory." *Amer. Scient.* 59:538–549, 1971.

88. Levine, S. "Stimulation in infancy." *Scientif. Amer.* 202(5):80–86, 1960.

89. Ibid., p. 81.

90. Denenberg, V. H., J. T. Brumaghim, G. C. Haltmeyer, and M. X. Zarrow. "Increased adrenocortical activity in the neonatal rat following handling." *Endocrinology* 81:1047–1052, 1967.

91. Levine, S., G. C. Haltmeyer, G. G. Karas, and V. H. Denenberg. "Physiological and behavioral effects of infantile stimulation." *Physiol. Behav.* 2(1):55–59, 1967.

92. Harlow, H. F. "Love in infant monkeys." *Scientif. Amer.* 200(6):68–74, 1959.

93. Ibid., p. 70.

94. Harlow, H. H. "The heterosexual affectional system in monkeys." *Amer. Psychol.* 17:1–9, 1962.

95. Ibid.

96. Fromkin, V., S. Krashen, S. Curtiss, D. Rigler, and M. Rigler. "The development of language in Genie: A case of language acquisition beyond the 'critical period.'" *Brain Language* 1:81–107, 1974.

97. Harlow, H. F., K. A. Schlitz, and M. K. Harlow. "Effects of social isolation on the learning performance of rhesus monkeys." In C. R. Carpenter, Ed. *Proceedings of the Second International Congress of Primatology*, Atlanta, Ga., 1968. *Vol. I. Behavior.* Basel: S. Karger, 1969, pp. 178–185.

98. Davenport, R. K., and C. M. Rogers. "Intellectual performance of differentially reared chimpanzees: I. Delayed response." *Amer. J. Ment. Defic.* 72:674–680, 1968.

99. Both groups had shared the same cages and test experiences after the age of 2 to 3 years, so early experience is the significantly different factor under investigation in this and the next study reported by Davenport and Rogers.

100. Davenport, R. K., C. M. Rogers, and E. W. Menzel. "Intellectual performance of differentially reared chimpanzees: II. Discrimination-learning set." *Amer. J. Ment. Defic.* 73:963–969, 1969.

101. Spitz, R. H. "Hospitalism: An inquiry into the genesis of psychiatric conditions in early childhood." *Psychoanalytic Study Child* 2:113–117, 1946.

102. Spitz, R. A. "The role of ecological factors in emotional development in infancy." *Child Develop.* 20:145–155, 1949.

103. Pines, M. "The battleground." *In Revolution in Learning.* New York: Harper & Row, Publishers, 1966, pp. 1–8.

104. Dennis, W. "Infant development under conditions of restricted practice and of minimum social stimulation: A preliminary report." *Ped. Sem. J. Genet. Psychol.* 53:149–158, 1938.

105. Dennis, W., and P. Najarian. "Infant development under environmental handicap." *Psychol. Monogr.* 71(7):1–13, 1957. *Also:* W. Dennis. "Causes of retardation among institutional children: Iran." *J. Genet. Psychol.* 96:47–59, 1960.

106. Geber, M. "The psycho-motor development of African children in the first year, and the influence of maternal behavior." *J. Social Psychol.* 47:185–195, 1958.

107. Warren, N. "African infant precocity." *Psychol. Bull.* 78:353–367, 1972.

108. Kagan, J., and R. E. Klein. "Cross-cultural perspectives on early development." *Amer. Psychol.* 28:947–961, 1973.

109. Clarke, A.D.B. "Problems in assessing the later effects of early experience." In E. Miller, Ed. *Foundations of Child Psychiatry.* New York: Pergamon Press, 1968, pp. 339–368.

110. The interested reader should see Clarke, Ann M., and A. D. B. Clarke. *Early Experience: Myth and Evidence.* New York: Free Press, 1976.

6

Conclusion

This brief text has attempted to put a selected corpus of developmental research into historical perspective by concentrating on one major aspect of inquiry—the importance of variation in early experience on the profile of intellect and motivation seen in adolescence and adulthood. We chose this theme for study because it provides one of the most obvious examples of the essential role that empirical research plays with respect to the beliefs and practices of the larger society. The preceding chapters were not intended to be a coherent history of all the major developmental themes or intriguing discoveries. We have not dealt in a major way with Piaget's enormous influence on contemporary developmental psychology; the current work on memory, perception, and problem-solving; the debate over genetic and environmental contributions to intelligence; nor the fascinating new investigations of the cognitive and perceptual development of the young infant. All this work is important and is part of the fabric of developmental psychology.

But the discoveries in these domains are still fresh and have not had a chance to affect old beliefs or produce new ones in the minds of parents and legislators.

If, as proposed by Freud and Watson, experiences during early childhood exerted a powerful constraint on the topography of adult behavior, it was society's responsibility to discover the crucial needs of the young child and to guarantee that all would have access to the resources necessary to gratify a child's needs. Such a challenge could not be avoided, and the scientific establishment responded to that mandate. We have tried to set the terms of the challenge in the varied ways in which succeeding generations of scientists sought to assess its validity.

In that process, further lines of inquiry were opened and much was learned about the child and his requirements, without any clear consensus on the early experience hypothesis. There is certainly agreement that a baby reared in a monotonous, abusive or malnourished environment will not thrive, but as yet no clear indication of the quality and amount of variety in sensory and social stimulation that is most beneficial to growth. Empirical study has shown that developmental retardation due to relative isolation or even physiological insult may not be permanent if the child is moved to a more beneficial environment. Much depends on the learning opportunities provided later for the older child. Harry Harlow and his colleagues found appropriate treatment for frightened and depressed isolates—play therapy with younger members of the same species—and without hazarding reckless analogies, it seems reasonable to suppose that the mind of the human infant is as plastic as that of the rhesus monkey.

The animal and human work has formed a rich background of "fact" that removes the debate from complete speculation, even though final answers are far from clear. There is a flexible attitude toward these themes.

To those who believe nature to be complex, the fact that there are no easy answers is a triumphant vindication of their conviction. The relative simplicity of behavioristic theory—the notion that the mind could be ignored or considered merely as the passive transmitter of environmental events—has been anathema to this group. Yet, as we have seen, behaviorism had at least two significant positive influences. It demonstrated to those who believed in the overwhelming importance of heredity that they had underestimated the extent to which environmental factors could shape development. And it provided a model for more objective research.

The grand theories of development were perhaps too ambitious, but they were useful. They stimulated debate and inquiry in specialized institutions and enlarged everyone's perspective of childhood. Before Freud, few if any credited children with sexual and aggressive emotions and conflicts. Before Watson, hereditary factors, such as "degeneracy," seemed the obvious cause of delinquency, insanity, and mental retardation. Before Piaget, no one sought to understand the mental constructions of the young child because it was believed they either were very much like those of adults or were not amenable to rational analysis. Not all the answers are in, but the boldness of theorists and the caution of empiricists have provided an immeasurably richer conceptual field within which to understand the behavior of children.

There is no easy way to differentiate sound from unsound theory. The early developmentalists believed that the best solution was to collect large corpora of data and see which available theory best accounted for the facts. The early growth studies, which were intended to solve the age-old nature-nurture controversy, showed only that the problem was unanswerable unless related issues, such as the influence of disease and malnutrition on early growth and final stature, were resolved first. Like all research, these studies did not lead to firm conclusions, but to the elaboration of a series of new questions, which were themselves so complex that many (such as the effect of early malnutrition on intellectual development) are still being debated.

The difference between then and now is not that the important questions have been answered, but that the inquiry is deeper. Progress is not linear. Some problems are shelved for decades in favor of more socially pressing or apparently more soluble ones. As Peter Medawar has stressed, research is "the art of the soluble." Scientists do not persist in grappling with overwhelming odds, but tackle problems that have a good chance of being solved. Much depends on whether appropriate methods are available or can be elaborated in a short period. In the 1930s the nature-nurture debate came to the fore because the intelligence test seemed a suitable toll with which to decide the learning potential of children. In time some became convinced that the results of such practices were misleading because the intellectual competence measured by the tests was strongly related to the values and information stressed by the majority culture.

Freud's ideas posed another dilemma. Psychoanalysts offered unusually broad, fundamental generalizations that led, for example, to the positing of a maternal deprivation syndrome. Experimentalists remained doubting

Thomases, believing nothing that was not supported by empirical evidence and offering alternative explanations for the apparently obvious. When Casler suggested that lack of adequate stimulation might be the principal cause of the "maternal deprivation syndrome," even the tough-minded were shocked by such a materialistic outlook that ignored "maternal love." Yet the distinction is important. If mental health depended on the presence of a constant primary caretaker for the first two years of life, then orphanages, foster homes, and day-care centers were intolerable in a humane society. If Casler was correct, multiple caretaking could be cautiously attempted.

The findings of developmental research yield possibilities. This was not obvious at the turn of the century, but it became so as empirical facts failed to support grand theories. Final outcomes cannot be predicted from the displays of infancy because not enough is known. We have not yet discerned the presence of long chains and broad combinations of causality in human development. Such models may be postulated, for they have heuristic value, but the extent to which they should be used as rational bases for intervention in real life is still problematic.

This difficulty is common to all scientific development. At what stage should a new drug or vaccine be marketed, or the adoption of a new device to remove smog be made compulsory? Usually final evaluations cannot be completed in laboratories and the crucial final testing of innovations occurs in the field. (The atomic bomb was no exception to this rule.) But in the physical and basic medical sciences, the preliminary evaluation of theory is a more private process than it is in psychology. The debates as to how much empirical research is necessary before application, how to interpret findings, and how to restructure hypotheses to fit facts, are more often conducted behind closed doors through professional media in a language that is not always comprehensible to the layman. Gradually, lumps and grooves are smoothed out of the model, leading to the final unveiling of a polished *fait accompli*. It may not be perfect, but it will be the best approximation possible.

In child development, events take a slightly different turn. Ideas circulate in simpler form, for they often have immediate relevance to the human condition and are expressed in terms that we all more or less understand. And if we do not, magazines and newspapers will attempt to translate them into simpler language. If, in addition, these ideas complement our presuppositions, they can become almost irresistible. Such was the case when the concept of maternal deprivation was introduced into our language soon after World War II. It confirmed the traditional belief in the vital and exclusive role of the biological mother. Today young parents leave their babies in infant-care centers—if not with gay abandon, then at least with less soul-searching—and it is difficult to believe that research findings made no contribution to this new attitude.

Parents have been presented, not with tightly structured models, but with a variety of alternative or complementary views of development from which they can draw their own conclusions. Rigid prescriptions are currently out of style, as are the grand theories that produced them. But there is no moratorium on ideas. Fortunately, private speculation is immune to outside interference. All sciences aim at objective evaluation of hunches, difficult as that mission is in the social sciences. We have tried here to show some of the penalties incurred through ignoring this useful role of scientific inquiry and the problems involved in trying to replace incorrect ideas with less incorrect ones.

A

Topical Syllabi
for Child-Study*

Anger

The phenomena wanted are variously designated by the following words: Wrath, ire, temper, madness, indignation, sulks, sours, putchiness, crossness, choler, grudge, fume, fury, passion, to be or fall out with.

1. Add any other *terms* or any euphemisms, or phrases you know or can get from children indicating their feelings.

2. Describe every vaso-motor symptom, such as flushing, paling about forehead, cheeks, nose, neck, or elsewhere. Is there horripilation, chill, shudder, tremor, prickly feeling, numbness, choking, twitching, swearing, if so where and how long. Are there any accompanying sensations of color, flushes, taste, smell, noises (question for each sense). Can blood pressure be tested?

*This is the first of the topical syllabi circulated by G. S. Hall (*Pedagogical Seminary*, 1894, 3:6–7).

3. Describe all changes of muscle-tension, scowling, grinding teeth, opening lips, setting of eye, clenching fists, position of arms and attitude of body. Is there nausea or a tendency to either contraction or relaxation of sphincter muscles which control anal or urinal passages.

4. Describe overt acts, striking (how, down, straight out, with fist or palm), scratching, biting, kicking. At what part are blows or attacks aimed.

5. What is the degree of *abandon* or loss of self control. Is it complete and is the rage entirely blind, or usually is some restraint shown in the intensity of blows or some consideration in the place attacked.

6. Describe long delayed anger, the venting of secret grudges long nursed and deliberately indulged.

7. Describe intensity curve of quick and slow children.

8. Describe reactions, physical, mental or moral, whether lassitude, contrition, and all verbal or acted signs of regret.

9. How do children speak of past outbreaks of anger in themselves, and of anger in others, and in general?

10. What treatment have you found good, and what palliatives do irascible children apply to themselves?

In description be photographically objective, exact, minute and copious in detail. Tell age, sex, family life, temperament, nationality of every child. Add to all a description of your experience with anger in yourself, and if possible get a few of your adult friends, whether good or ill tempered, to write theirs, or organize a little circle of friends, mothers, teachers, neighbors, to talk over the subject and to observe in concert. Above all get children of different age and temperament to talk confidentially, or better, to write their own ideas in response to such questions as, tell some things which make you angry; when do you get angry easiest; how do you feel and how act, how check it and how feel afterwards; write cases of others getting angry in detail, and state what you think about it generally.

This is a subject of obviously great importance for moral and even physical education, but there is almost no literature explored by concerted effort. The undersigned desires to investigate the subject and invites you to cooperation by sending him *any notes, however incomplete, upon any aspect of the subject.* Or, if preferred, you can start with these hints and work out your own data and print your conclusions.

Let us try the concerted method of work and in some way pool its results for the mutual benefit of teachers and for the good of the children we all live for.

B

Topical Syllabi

The following are titles of questionnaires circulated by G. S. Hall and his colleagues at Clark University between 1894 and 1915 (Hall, *Life and Confessions of a Psychologist*, 1923, pp. 382–388). If a questionnaire was written by someone other than Hall, the author's name is listed.

1. Anger, October 1894.
2. Dolls, November 1894.
   Dolls (supplementary questionnaire), A. C. Ellis, June 1896.
3. Crying and laughing, December 1894.
4. Toys and playthings, December 1894.
5. Folk-lore among children, January 1895.
6. Early forms of vocal expression, January 1895.
7. The early sense of self, January 1895.
8. Fears in childhood and youth, February 1895.
9. Some common traits and habits, February 1895.
10. Some common automatisms, nerve signs, etc., March 1895.

11. Feeling for objects of inanimate nature, March 1898.
12. Feelings for objects of animate nature, April 1895.
13. Children's appetites and foods, April 1895.
14. Affection and its opposite states in children, April 1795 [*sic*].
15. Moral and religious experiences, May 1895.
16. Peculiar and exceptional children, E. W. Bohannon, October 1895.
17. Moral defects and perversions, G. E. Dawson, October 1895.
18. The beginnings of reading and writing, H. T. Lukens, October 1895.
19. Thoughts and feelings about old age, disease and death, C. A. Scott, November 1895.
20. Moral education, N. P. Avery, November 1895.
21. Studies of school reading matter, J. C. Shaw, November 1895.
22. School statistics, T. R. Croswell, November 1895.
23. Early musical manifestations, Florence Marsh, December 1895.
24. Fancy, imagination, reverie, E. H. Lindley, December 1895.
25. Tickling, fun, wit, humor, laughing, Arthur Allin, February 1896.
26. Suggestion and imitation, M. H. Small, February 1896.
27. Religious experience, E. D. Starbuck, February 1896.
28. A study of the character of religious growth, E. D. Starbuck, February 1896.
29. Kindergarten, Anna E. Bryan and Lucy Wheelock, March 1896.
30. Habits, instincts, etc., in animals, R. R. Gurley, March 1896.
31. Number and mathematics, D. E. Phillips, April 1896.
32. The only child in a family, E. W. Bohannon, March 1896.
33. Degrees of certainty and conviction in children, M. H. Small, October 1896.
34. Sabbath and worship in general, J. P. Hylan, October 1896.

35. Questions for the study of the essential feature of public worship, J. P. Hylan, October 1896.
36. Migrations, tramps, truancy, running away, etc., vs. love of home, L. W. Kline, October 1896.
37. Adolescence and its phenomena in body and mind, E. G. Lancaster, November 1896.
38. Examinations and recitations, J. C. Shaw, November 1896.
39. Stillness, solitude, restlessness, H. S. Curtis, November 1896.
40. The psychology of health and disease, H. H. Goddard, December 1896.
41. Spontaneously invented toys and amusements, T. R. Croswell, December 1896.
42. Hymns and sacred music, T. R. Peede, December 1896.
43. Puzzles and their psychology, E. H. Lindley, December 1896.
44. The sermon, A. R. Scott, January 1897.
45. Special traits as indices of character, and as mediating likes and dislikes, E. W. Bohannon, January 1897.
46. Reverie and allied phenomena, E. Partridge, April 1897.
47. The psychology of health and disease, H. H. Goddard, May 1897.
48. Immortality, J. R. Street, September 1897.
49. Psychology of ownership vs. loss, L. W. Kline, October 1897.
50. Memory, F. W. Colegrove, October 1897.
51. To mothers, F. W. Colegrove, December 1897.
52. Humorous and cranky side in education, L. W. Kline, October 1897.
53. The psychology of shorthand writing, J. O. Quantz, November 1897.
54. The teaching instinct, D. E. Phillips, November 1897.
55. Home and school punishments and penalties, C. H. Sears, November 1897.
56. Straightness and uprightness of body, December 1897.
57. Conventionality, A. Schinz, November 1897.

58. Local voluntary association among teachers, H. D. Sheldon, December 1897.

59. Motor education, E. W. Bohannon, December 1897.

60. Heat and cold, December 1897.

61. Training of teachers, W. G. Chambers, December 1897.

62. Educational ideals, L. E. York, December 1897.

63. Water psychoses, F. E. Bolton, February 1898.

64. The institutional activities of children, H. D. Sheldon, February 1898.

65. Obedience and obstinacy, Tilmon Jenkins, March 1898.

66. The sense of honor among children, Robert Clark, March 1897.

67. Children's collections, Abby C. Hale, October 1898.

68. The organizations of American student life, H. D. Sheldon, November 1898.

69. Mathematics in common schools, E. B. Bryan, February 1899.

70. Mathematics in the early years, E. B. Bryan, February 1899.

71. Unselfishness in children, W. S. Small, February 1899.

72. Mental traits, C. W. Hetherington, April 1899.

73. The fooling impulse in man and animals (conjuring and sleight of hand), Norman Triplett, March 1899.

74. Confession, E. W. Runkle, March 1899.

75. Pity, March 1899.

76. Perception of rhythm by children, C. H. Sears, May 1899.

77. The monthly period, Anna L. Brown, May 1899.

78. Perception of rhythm, C. H. Sears, December 1899.

79. Psychology of uncertainty and gambling, C. J. France, February 1900.

80. Straightness and uprightness of body, A. W. Trettien, January 1900.

81. Pedagogical pathology, Norman Triplett, November 1900.

82. Religious development, G. H. Wright, January 1901.

83. Geography, F. H. Saunders, February 1901.

84. Feelings of adolescence, E. J. Swift, October 1901.

85. Introspection, E. J. Swift, October 1901.

86. Signs of nervousness, E. J. Swift, October 1901.
87. Examinations, W. M. Pollard, November 1901.
88. Sub-normal children and youth, A. R. T. Wylie, November, 1901.
89. English teaching, December 1901.
90. Education of women, December, 1901.
91. Heredity, C. E. Browne, December, 1901; (a) January 1902.
92. The conditions of primitive peoples and the methods employed to civilize and christianize them, J. W. W. Wallin, April, 1902.
93. Children's thoughts, reactions and feelings to animals, W. F. Bucke, November, 1902.
94. Reactions to light and darkness, November, 1902.
95. Children's interest in flowers, Alice Thayer, November, 1902.
96. Reactions to light and darkness (2) Theodate L. Smith, December 1902.
97. Superstition among children, S. W. Stockard, December 1902.
98. Ideas about the soul, L. D. Arnett, January 1903.
99. Children's prayers, S. P. Hayes, January 1903.
100. Religious experiences subsequent to conversion, E. P. St. John, January 1903.
101. Food and appetite, Sanford Bell, January 1903.
102. Development of the sentiment of affection, T. L. Smith, March 1903.
103. The health of teachers, W. H. Burnham, April 1903.
104. Moral and religious influence, Jean duBuy, May 1903.
105. Curiosity and interest, T. L. Smith, May 1903.
106. Birds and animals, October 1903.
107. Precocity and tardiness of development, October 1903.
108. Differences between young and old teachers, October 1903.
109. Predominance of female teachers, October 1903.
110. Dreams, October 1903.
111. Advertising, October 1903.
112. Stages of religious development, Jean duBuy, November 1903.

113. Nervous children, T. Kuma, November 1903.
114. Young people's christian organizations, J. N. Rodeheaver, November 1903.
115. The hygienic condition of normal schools, W. H. Burnham, December 1903.
116. Japan: A study in the pedagogy of missions, F. A. Lombard, November 1903.
117. The language interest in children, A. W. Trettien, December 1903.
118. Attention, A. A. Cleveland, December 1903.
119. Reaction of pupils to high school work, W. F. Book, January 1904.
120. Questions for members of young people's societies, W. B. Forbush and J. N. Rodeheaver, February 1904.
121. Crying, February 1904.
122. Defects in school education, M. W. Meyerhardt, February 1904.
123. Obstinacy, stubborness and obedience, February 1904.
124. Stuttering and other speech defects, E. Conradi, March 1904.
125. Keeping well, March 1904.
126. The subnormal or supernormal child, T. Kuma, May 1904.
127. Motherhood, November 1904.
128. Psychic reactions to sound, T. L. Smith, November 1904.
129. The development of the imagination, H. L. Brittain, January 1905.
130. The psychology of clothes, February 1905.
131. Peculiarly nervous children, B. C. Downing, October 1905.
132. Nervous children, B. C. Downing, October 1905.
133. Envy and jealousy, A. L. Gesell, October 1905.
134. Topics needing study on children of kindergarten age, T. L. Smith, October 1905.
135. The minister and his work, D. S. Hill, October 1905.
136. Emotional reactions to the moon, T. Misawa, January 1906.
137. The play interest of children, F. A. Judson, February 1906.
138. The early development of aesthetic interest, J. W. Harris, February 1906.

139. Fatherhood, R. N. Roark, February 1906.
140. Chess, A. A. Cleveland, 1906.
141. Adult education, T. Misawa, November 1906.
142. Spontaneous constructions and primitive activities in children analogous to those of primitive man, February 1907.
143. A syllabus for the study of "shock," W. F. Gard, March 1907.
144. Interest in philosophical and psychological subjects, E. I. Keller, October 1907.
145. Co-education, C. Reddie, November 1907.
146. The prophet of to-day, I. L. Willcox, November 1907.
147. The "social study" of the Negroes of the City of Worcester, G. T. Dominis, November 1907.
148. Sex differences in children of grammar and high school grades, December 1907.
149. Juvenile courts, W. G. Siddell, January 1908.
150. Psychology of shame, T. L. Smith, February 1908.
151. Drama in education, E. W. Curtis, February 1908.
152. The relations of mental and bodily factors in disease, C. A. Osborne, October 1908.
153. Special defects, A. Wiggam, November 1908.
154. Dancing, L. G. Barber, November 1908.
155. Psychology of suicide, Y. Nakamura, November 1908.
156. Ambition, H. M. Downey, January 1909.
157. Teaching of religion, E. S. Conklin, January 1909.
158. Some characteristics and tendencies of school children in the grades, Mrs. Eben Mumford, February 1909.
159. High school physics, H. W. Chase, March 1909.
160. Children and language, Genevieve Boland, October 1909.
161. A phase of adolescent development in girls, Lucetta Crum, October 1909.
162. Justice, November 1909.
163. Length of daily school session, P. K. Holmes, December 1909.
164. Literature in the grades, J. M. McIndoo, December 1909.
165. The psychological effect of music, H. P. Weld, December 1909.

166. School supervision, B. Roethlein, January 1910.
167. Teaching of mathematics, F. B. Williams, January 1910.
168. The belief in immortality, S. Spidle, October 1910.
169. Keeping well, E. Anastassoff, October 1910.
170. School superintendents, M. E. Wood, January 1911.
171. Suggestion and imitation, S. Yamada, February 1911.
172. Medical inspection, G. H. Shafer, February 1911.
173. A study of joy, sorrow, and qualms of conscience, G. D. Bivin, July 1911.
174. Justice, T. Ueda, September 1911.
175. The training of teachers in the United States: *Critic Teachers, School Superintendents, Principals and Directors of Training Schools, Departments in Colleges and Universities*, L. W. Sacket, November 1911.
176. Toys and playthings, Dorothy Drake, November 1911.
177. Psychology of adolescence in girls, Miriam Van Waters, November 1911.
178. Emotions in children and adolescents, F. E. Howard, November 1911.
179. Study in child mind, W. T. Sanger, October 1912.
180. Children's ideas of death, J. H. O., October 1912.
181. Food and drink experiences, H. F., November 1912.
182. Study in dreams, Raymond Bellamy, November 1912.
183. Toys, G. E. Freeland, December 1912.
184. Anger and fear, R. F. Richardson, January 1913.
185. The psychology of the story, E. C. Wilson, November 1913.
186. The model school in education in the United States, J. H. Purnell, December 1913.
187. The present status of the small college, F. M. McDowell, December 1913.
188. Public opinion and the teaching profession, G. A. Coe, March 1914.
189. How to teach the war, C. E. McCorkle, October 1914.
190. Dreams, Vance Randolph, November 1914.
191. Influence of politics in school affairs, R. N. Elliott, November 1914.
192. The junior high school, A. A. Douglass, November 1914.

193. The relation of the school and home, E. W. Moore, December 1914.
194. The psychology of industrial efficiency, S. K. Boyajian, February 1915.
195. The pedagogy of mathematics, A. O. Griggs, February 1915.

Examples of Problems
for Which Data
are Becoming Available*

We have received many inquiries as to our interest in various problems and the nature of the data we have accumulated. Such communications come from scientists working in many different disciplines and from graduate students who are contemplating a thesis problem. It is impossible in this brochure to describe in detail all the data we have or to enumerate all the problems, large and small, which are of interest to one or more members of the staff. However, perhaps a listing of a number of problems, comprehensive or circumscribed, will convey an adequate idea of the types of data available and the direction of interests, and will give the graduate student an idea of the kind of thesis problem he might be able to undertake with this material.

*Source: Pamphlet by Lester W. Sontag, the Fels Research Institute for the Study of Human Development, Antioch College, Yellow Springs, Ohio, 1946.

I. Studies of Development and Patterns of Development.

A longitudinal study of the distribution of subcutaneous tissue throughout the body.

A long-term study of the growth and development of the pelvis, with a consideration of its obstetrical significance.

A longitudinal study of the consistency of body-type in children.

Patterns and individual variations in physical development in puberty.

Posture as seen in photographs, physical examinations and posture X-rays.

A continuation study of the development of the arch of the foot and its relation to function.

A longitudinal study of sex differences and age changes in vision and hearing.

Phylogenetic aspects of variability in the appearance of ossification centers.

Symmetry in ossification, and its significance and relationships.

Type and frequency of skeletal abnormalities and anomalies, with special reference to growth changes.

Onset of ossification and eventual bone length.

Areal pattern of the appearance of ossification centers.

Developmental pattern of many structures as seen in the X-ray, e.g., sinuses, chest, heart, etc.

The fasting level excretion of thiamine, riboflavin, N^1-methyl nicotinamide, and ascorbic acid in school-age children.

A longitudinal study of the excretion of 17-ketosteroids by growing children.

Creatine and creatinine excretion by the growing child.

Relationship between urinary acid phosphatase and pubescence.

Acid-base balance in growing children.

Blood arginase levels in school-age children.

Blood ascorbic acid levels in school-age children.

Blood sugar levels in school-age children.

Salivary acid phosphatase in children.

Saliva pH values in school-age children.

Fractionation of urinary steroids in normal, pre-adolescent children.

Determination of the constancy of individual differences in range of autonomic reactivity: relation to chronological age and sex.

Determination of patterns of autonomic reactivity.

Individual differences in relaxability.

Relationships among fetal, infantile, child and adult measures of reactivity.

Relationship of fetal behavior to child behavior.

Relationship of individual differences in energy levels to biochemical factors.

Longitudinal study of the changes in personality organization.

Emergence of specificity of performance with tests of capacity.

Analysis of longitudinal development by means of case-study material.

Concept of maturity as reflected in interests.

Emergence of psychosexuality as revealed in interests and preferences, and as projected in apperception and fantasy.

II. *Studies of Influences on Development*

A. *Genetic or hereditary factors*

A comparative study of mothers' and children's skeletal development, as seen in X-ray.

Inheritance of facial angles, jaw formation and head shape.

Determination of the constancy of patterns of autonomic reaction: relation to age, sex, and familial background.

Determination of effects of heredity on intensity and patterning of autonomic reactivity.

B. *Environmental factors*

1. The prenatal environment

Prenatal protein and status of infant (size and condition) at birth.

Prenatal protein and progress (growth, illness) of the infant during the first year.

Calcium changes in the mother's condition during pregnancy and after.

Excretion of ketosteroids during pregnancy.

Effect of hypnotically induced anxiety of the mother upon fetal activity.

Relationship of maternal endocrine and vitamin status to fetal behavior.

2. The postnatal environment

Seasonal differences in the intercorrelation of weight, height and ossification.

Relation of illness patterns to physical growth.

Factors which influence the differential cell count in healthy children.

Cultural contribution to the developing personality pattern.

Effect of parent behavior on the personality of the child (as revealed by such measures as the Rorschach, personality ratings, etc.).

Significance of the parent personality in the child's life.

Differences in parent behavior as a factor of sibling patterns.

Serial changes in parent behavior.

Parent behavior and subsequent school adjustment of the child.

Effects of the school environment on personality development.

Factors correlated with IQ changes in individual development.

III. *Interrelationships Between Indices of Development*

Correlation of tuberculin and histoplasmin tests with serial chest X-ray findings in children (see description in text).

Relationships of changes in surface area to growth and size.

Relationship of sexual maturity to growth of bone, muscle and fat.

Differential tissue growth in individual cases, with nutritional, environmental, genetic, and medical aspects, as seen on the Fels Composite Sheet.

Relationship of sharp changes in growth rate and growth plateaus to other aspects of physical growth and skeletal development.

Relationship of differential tissue growth to body build, motor development and athletic performance.

Relationship of hormone status to physical growth and development.

Relationship of physical status to muscular fatigue.

Relationship of growth patterns to personality development.

Relationship of physical development to various measures of motor development and athletic performance.

Fusion patterns in the skeleton and their relationship to puberty.

Growth rates of children as related to nutritional status.

Plasma alkaline phosphatase as related to bone development in the child.

Effect of sodium heparinate on enzyme activity.

Activation of prostatic acid phosphatase.

Relationship among blood enzymes.

Salivary ammonia and dental caries.

Biochemical factors in the response of children to stress situations.

Relationship of range of autonomic reactivity to response in specific physical and emotional stress situations.

Relationship of autonomic instability to the ease of acquisition of new autonomic responses.

Relationship of quickness of physiological recovery from stress to general personality characteristics.

Relationship of physiological recovery from stress to biochemical factors.

Relationship of vitamin status to learning ability.

Determination of individual differences in muscular tension and biochemical and psychological correlates.

Patterns of performance on tests of capacity and their relationship to adjustment and maladjustment.

Blood protein levels as related to nutritional status in school-age children.

IV. *Technical and Methodological Studies*

Construction of a comprehensive atlas of the development of the major joints of the body.

Construction of posture scales for older children.

Comparison of load test and fasting level excretion as a measure of vitamin status.

An improved method for the determination of N^1-methyl nicotinamide in urine.

A comparison between photoelectric and haemocytometer red cell counts.

An improved method for the determination of creatine in urine.

A new reagent for the colorimetric determination of urinary steroids: 1) determination of androsterone, 2) determination of dehydroisoandrosterone.

A micro-filtration device for use in ascorbic acid determination.

Determination of steroid hormones in human blood.

Collection of micro samples of blood of children: an improved method.

Development of an index of autonomic reactivity: an approximation to maximal and minimal values of autonomic functions.

Development of efficient, simple stress situations to predict intensity and patterning of autonomic response to complex emotional stresses.

Utilization of skin resistance level as an index of muscular tension in BMR determinations.

Methodology in psychological measurement and observation.

Index

Abbott, Jacob, 6
Acculturation, 38
Adaptation
  brain chemistry and, 189
  genetics and, 30–31, 111
  habit and, 3, 29–31
  isolates and, 191–193
Adler, Alfred, 56
Adolescent phase, inception of,
  59–60
Adult
  experience and, 214
  neurosis, 47–48
  psychoanalytic theory and,
  152–153
  stereotype ideal, 63–64
Advice, journalistic, 71
Affection
  bonding and, 175
  denigrated, 124
  discipline and, 34, 57
Aggression, 34, 57
  frustration and, 165
  new consideration of, 215
Ainsworth, Mary Slater, 86–87

Albert, conditioning of, 116-117
Amnesia, 47
Anaclitic relationship, primacy of,
  85–86
Analyst, experimental
  psychologist and, 76
Anal personality, 49–50, 68–70
Anderson, John E., 128–129
Anderson, L. D., 158
Animal phobia, 56
Animal research, 84, 88–90, 92,
  110–111, 126
Annual Review of Psychology, 168
Anxiety, 55–56, 57, 94–95
Are You Training Your Child to be
  Happy?, 134
Asexuality, romanticism and,
  121–122
Associationism, 27, 28, 133
Atavistic behavior, 34
Atmosphere, toilet training, 71
Attachment
  critical-period and, 172–173
  instinct and, 85
  multiple mothering and, 86

Attachment and Loss, 86
Attitude, importance of, 71, 95–96
Autoeroticism, 46, 50
Autonomous cerebral activity,
    learning and, 180
Autonomy, developed, 73–74
Avoidance response, 187

"Baby biographies," 24–27
Babyhood, discipline in, 4–5
Baldwin, A.L., 155–156
Baldwin, James Mark, 21, 23, 24,
    25–27, 31, 36
Battered child syndrome, 81
Bayley, Nancy, 157
Beach, Frank A., 173
*Behavior: An Introduction to
    Comparative Psychology*,
    119, 125
Behavior
    atavistic, 34
    conditioned, 127
    controlled-intervention studies,
        179–180
    environment and, 6
    experience and, 141, 214
    instinct and, 111
    investigation of childhood, 15
    maturation and, 37–38
    neurophysiological activity and,
        181
    nuclear family and, 187–188
    observation of, 37, 128–129
    pattern stability, 90
    "proper," 64
    rationale for, 6–7
    reward-punishment technique,
        109
    surrogate mother and, 175
    "unconscious" and, 122–123
Behavioral scientist, nurture
    and, 3
Behaviorism, 30, 109–142, 215
    childrearing concept, 124–125,
        133–136
    cognition and, 127
    influence of, 215
    non-believer, 126–129

    popularized, 66
    psychoanalysis and, 120–121,
        140–142, 162
Behaviorism, 119
"Behavior modification," 125
Bekhterev, V.M., 114
Bell, Sylvia, 87
Beyond the Pleasure Principle, 57
Binet, Alfred, 21
Biogenetic law, *See* Recapitulation
Biology, evolutionary, 11–12
Bisexuality, parent and, 123–124
Boaz, Franz, 22–23
Bottle-breast dilemma, 68–71,
    85–86
Bottle feeding, new concepts, 97
Bowditch, Henry P., 21–22
Bowlby, John, 79–86, 92–93,
    95–96, 172, 173, 175, 194
Brain biochemistry, learning and,
    184–188
Brain weight, experience and,
    185–186
Breast feeding, 68–71, 85–86
Bridgeman, P. W., 161
Brill, A. A., 138
Brim, Orville, 137

Caldwell, Bettye M., 69–71, 87,
    168, 179, 180
Care and Feeding of Children, The,
    14, 131
Casler, L., 84, 217
Castration fear, ignorance and, 52
Cattel's Infant Intelligence Scale,
    196, 197
Cerebral synaptic activity, brain
    chemistry and, 185–186
Character forming, 2–3, 8–10,
    47–53, 63
"Character and anal erotocism,"
    49
Charcot, Jean Martin, 46
Child abuse, 81
Child care
    attitude and, 71, 95–96
    psychoanalysis and, 64–66,
        95–96

rationale for, 122–123, 131–134, 136–137
See also Childrearing
Child Care, 131
Child-centered America, 5
"Child conservation," 10
Child Development, 168
Child development, media and, 218
Child guidance, professional, 67
Childhood
  American, 2–15
  enlarged perspective of, 215
  sexuality, 52–53, 122–124
  traumatic experience,121
Childhood and Society, 67, 74
Child labor, 8–10
  economics of, 10
  growth and, 20–21
Child psychology
  challenge to, 214
  doubt, 167–168
Childrearing
  behaviorism and, 109–142
  changing, 119–122
  culture and, 76
  pattern, socio-economic, 71
  pediatrics and, 3
  personality and, 7, 151, 166–168
  practical advice, 67
Children
  behaviorist ideal, 124–125
  census of, 31–36
  deprived, 93
  institutionalized, 78–79
  kibbutzim and, 83
  sexual theory of, 52–53
  social beings, as, 26–27
  stimulus-response analysis, 128
  study of, 37–38, 128, 129, 193
  young animal and, 24–25
Child Study, 138
Clarke, A. D., B., 199
Classical conditioning, 113
Clinging response, 84–85
Cognition
  behavior and, 127
  universal competence, 199

Cognitive development, 73, 82
  attachment behavior and, 86
  critical periods of, 178–179
  environmentally delayed, 91–92
  mothering and, 77, 82
  university and, 152
Colic, breast feeding and, 68
Collier's, 126
Common Sense Book of Baby and Child Care, 67
Comparative embryology, 34–35
Conditional response, 133
Conditioning, 113, 127–128, 133
  accidental, 119–120
  maturation and, 63, 116
  prenatal, 115
Conscience developed, 75
Consciousness, psychical apparatus of, 61
Construct criteria, 166
Contented breast-fed child, 68–71
Continuity
  assumption of, 118–119
  development and, 47
  thought and, 117
Corticosterone, early stress and, 189
Counsel, human science, 2
Cowell, John W., 20
Crane, Marian M., 133
Critical-period
  concept exploration, 170–180
  imprinting in, 171–173
  learning, 198
  reversibility, 177
  socialization in, 173–176
  thalidomide and, 176, 193
  variation, 175
Culture
  changing, 135–138
  determinates, 24
  ego and, 73–74
  first concept and, 29
  infant care and, 129–130
  intelligence test and, 216
  libidinal impulse and, 52–53, 55

Dann, Sophia, 88–89
Darwin, Charles, 11
Davenport, Richard, 192–193
Death instinct, 57
Decision, parental, 1
Deconditioning, 117
"Degenerates," 15, 16
Denenberg, V. H., 177, 187, 188
Dennis, Wayne, 195–196
Dependence, remedial attention
    to, 6–7
Depression
  anaclitic, 79
  of hospitalized child, 93–94
  play therapy and, 214
Deprivation
  critical-period and, 176
  maternal, 77, 79, 217–218
  retardation and, 168–180,
    194–195
  study of, 77–78, 88–90, 91–92,
    183
Development
  biological stages of, 14–15, 38,
    73–76
  continuity concept of, 31–33
  day care and, 87–88
  emotion and, 152–153, 194
  enhanced, 64, 174
  environment and, 22, 75–76, 82,
    181–182
  experience and, 17, 35, 185–186,
    197
  infantile amnesia and, 47
  latency period, 53, 60–61, 123
  mental, 20–31, 153–154, 158
  normative, 37–38
  personality, 63, 73–76, 151–152,
    156
  predeterministic theory, 54,
    58–60
  psychosocial, 24–31, 46–56
  stimulation and, 82–93, 170
  study of, 129, 216
  theory of, 29, 45–46, 67–68, 129,
    215
Diamond, Marian C., 186
Directives, changing, 2

Discipline
  affection and, 4
  belief in, 62–63
  infancy and, 4–5
  routine and, 130
Disease, childhood and, 15, 132
Dukes W. F., 164
Dunham, Ethel C., 133
Dunlap, Knight, 51

Early stimulation, 170, 194–195,
    197–199
Early weaning, 97
Economics, 10, 15, 20
Education, 9–10, 27, 35, 152–153,
    169
  behaviorism and, 110
  perfectibility and, 64
Egalitarianism, education and, 152
Ego
  anxiety and, 57
  component, 73–74
  drive, 57–58
  id and, 75
Ego and the Id, The, 57
Elders, emulation of, 4
Emotion
  basic, 114
  intellect and, 152–153, 194
  continuing problem, 97
Empirical science, 1–2, 213
Enriched environment, deprived
    family and, 87–88
Enrichment program, 87–88, 179
Environment
  adaptive response to, 111
  behavior and, 6
  changing, 2
  development and, 75–76, 82,
    181–182
  ego need and, 73–74
  enrichment programming,
    87–88, 179
  instinct modification and, 116
  learning and, 164, 181
  maturation and, 38
  neurosis and, 53–55
  organism readiness and, 73–76

personality and, 36–38
psychoanalytic theory and, 140–141
variation, 29
Erection, early childhood, 47
Erikson, Erik H., 67, 73–76, 178
Eroticism, 122
Erotogenic zones, 48–51
Evil, propensities for, 5–6
Evolution, heredity and, 15
Evolutionary associationism, 28
Expectations, unrealized, 72
Experience
acculturation and, 36–38
behavior and, 141, 214
development and, 17, 35, 181, 185–186, 197
Indian infant, 91–92
maturation and, 160–161
stressful, 188–189
study of, 155–156
variation in, 213

Fact-Finding Report to the Midcentury White House Conference on Children and Youth, 73
Fact, speculation and, 214
Factories Inquiries Commission in England, 183, 20–21
Family continuity, 4–5
Fantasy, sexual, 46
Fear
liberation from, 17
parental, 71–73
Fear reaction, 116–117
First Three Years of Childhood, The, 26
Fiske, John, 10–14
Fixation, productive study of, 164
Following response, 84–85
Forgays, Donald G., 186
Frank, Lawrence K., 153
Freud, Anna, 67, 72, 75, 88–89
Freudian slip, 63
Freud, Sigmund, 35, 45–97, 138, 170, 214, 215
Frustration, 57, 165

Gaisford, Wilfred, 95
Gerber, M., 197
Genetic
adaptation, 30–31, 111
conditioning and, 36–37
development, 181–182
intelligence, 156–157
psychology, 32
psychoanalytic theory and, 140–141
Genie, childhood of, 177
Gesell, Arnold L., 36–38, 62–63, 67
Gesell Scale, prediction of IQ score, 157
Gestalt field theory, 180
perception, 183–184
Goldfarb, William, 78–79
Goodenough, Florence, 182
Gossip, prejudice and, 1
Growth
dynamics of , 159
stages of, 10, 12–13, 73–76
study, 19–24, 216
See also Development
Guidance of Childhood and Youth, 138–139
Guilt, creation of, 75

Habit
adaptation and, 3, 29–31
inheritance and, 111
language and, 117
law of effect, 133
socially accepted, 133–134
Haeckel, Ernst, 33, 50
Hall, G. Stanley, 9–10, 28, 31–36
Happy baby, 134–135
Harlow, Harry F., 84, 88–90, 92, 175, 187–188, 189–190
Harper's Magazine, 126
Hart, H. H., 6–7
Hartman, Heinz, 75
Hawkins, Dr. Bissett, 8
Head Start, Project, 170
Health
attainment and, 23
development and, 154

"Healthy" child labor, 10
Hebb, Donald O., 170, 180–184, 195
Hebb-Williams maze, 186, 187, 195
Heredity
  adaptive response and, 111
  cognitive growth and, 82
  growth rate and, 21
  nervous system and, 59–60
  neuroses and, 53–55
  revised attitude, 215
  See also Genetics
Heinroth, O., 171
Heinstein, Martin, 159
Herrnstein, R. J., 126
Holt, L. Emmett, 14, 131
Honzik, Marjorie, 157–158
Hope, fear and, 3
Hospital
  child depression in, 93–94
  maternity-unit routine, 95
Hull, Clark, L., 125, 162, 167
Hunt, J. McV., 168, 183
Hunter, W. S., 126
Hymovitch, B., 186
Hysteria, 46, 47

Id, unconscious and, 57–58
Ideal citizen, 120
Identity, 75
Ilg, F. L., 67, 94
Imprinting, 171–173
Inadaquacy engendered, 75
Independence, objective and, 53
Individuality, recognition of, 6–7
Industrial development, family and, 4–5
Infancy
  experimentation and, 110–111
  education and, 12–13
  indulgence of, 4
  observed, 24–38, 126
  plastic mind of, 215
  testing in, 157–158
  training advice, 129–140
Infant and Child in the Culture of Today, 67, 94
Infant Care, 130–133, 137–138

Infant monkey, research with, 88–90, 92
Infantile amnesia, development and, 47
Infantile sexuality, 35, 63
  adult analysis and, 46
  studies of, 163
"Infantile Sexuality," 47, 54
Inferiority engendered, 75
Inheritance, 27, 28, 127
  See also Genetic Heredity
Initiative, emergence of, 75
Innate idea, doctrine of, 27, 28
Instinct, 48–49, 85
  antisocial urges of, 65
  behavior and, 111
  defined, 114
  nurture and, 127
  perversion and, 55
Institution, custodial, 6–7
Integrity, feeling of, 74–75
Intellectual development
  deprivation and, 170
  determinant of, 182
  experience and, 153
  stimulation and, 168–180
  study of, 156
  See also Development; Growth; Learning
Isolate, learning by, 191, 192–193, 214
IQ test, invention of, 21
IQ score
  environmental change and, 182
  Gesell Scale and, 157
  socioeconomic class and, 152, 169

Jacobi, Abraham, 14–15
Jaynes, Julian, 173
Jones, Ernest, 49
Jones, Mary Cover, 115
Josselyn, Irene M., 67–69
Jung, Carl, 56

Kagan, Jerome, 90–93, 156, 161, 198–199

Kissing
  banned, 131
  erotogenic significance, 48
Klein, Melanie, 67
Klein, R. E., 90–93, 198–199
Koch, H. L., 168
Kris, Ernst, 75

Lamarckism, 28, 59
Language
  acquisition of, 25
  early learning, 174
  thought as implicit, 117–119
Latency period, 53, 60–61, 123
Lashley, Karl, 51, 127, 183
Law of effect, 112–113, 133
Learned response, environment
    and, 111
Learning, 164, 181
  biochemistry of, 184–188
Learning theory
  accommodation and, 30–31
  brain association area and, 181
  common sense and, 16
  imprinting and, 172
  organismic factor, 127
  perceptual function and, 184
  psychoanalytic theory and, 162
Levine, Seymour, 188
Libidinal impulse, social pressure
    and, 52
Libido
  energy of, 54
  mental development and, 57–58
"Little Hans," 66
Locke, John, 113
Lorenz, Konrad, 34, 171–172

McCandless, B. R., 167–168
Macfarlane, Jean Walker, 153,
    159–161
MacKinnon, D. W., 164
Malajustment, institutionalization
    and, 79–80
Marasmus, mothering and, 77–78
Masochism, 55
Masturbation, 47
  attitude change, 15–16, 121–122

infant, 51
  prevention of, 131, 133
Maternal Care and Mental Health,
    93, 194
Maternal deprivation, 75–97
  adoption and, 158–159
  cognitive experience and, 77
Maternal-deprivation syndrome,
    217–218
Maternal Physician, The, 5
Maturation
  biological, 36–38
  conditioning and, 116
  determinate, 14–15
  early experience and, 160–161
  environment and, 38
  experience and, 160–161
  eye movement and, 183
  popularized theory, 67–68
  precocity and, 197–199
Maxwell, James Clerk, 54
Maxim as truth, 1
Mead, Margaret, 81
"Meaning of infancy, The," 12
Mechanistic principles, 113
Medawar, Peter, 216
Media, child development and,
    218
Memory, physiognomy and,
    23, 27
Mental attainment, physique and,
    20–21, 23, 27
Mental development
  interdisciplinary investigation,
    153–154
  libido and, 57–58
Mental Development in the Child, 29
*Mental Development of the Child and
    the Race, The*, 29
Mental growth, stability of, 158
Mental health
  breast feeding and, 85–86
  freer sexuality and, 97
  maternal care and, 194
  war and, 73
Mental structure, 57–58
Mental process, understanding of,
    215

Mental retardation,
early-stimulation and,
195–196
Mind, 26
Mind, behavior theory and, 215
Mind of the Child, The, 28
Minorities
cognitive problem, 151–152
retardation and, 168
Mobility, changing concept and,
71
Modeling, 4, 30
Mortality, moral training and, 3
Moss, H. A., 161
Mother, social action and, 179–180
Mother–child bond
hospital and, 94–96
importance, 77, 84–86, 96,
189–191
reciprocal behavior and, 86, 156
Motherhood idealized, 63
Mothering, multiple, 84
Mother love, infancy and, 79–80
Motor movement model, 30
Mowrer, O. H., 183
"Muscle-twitch" psychology,
disenchantment for, 127

Narcissism, 57
Nature
complex, 215
power of, 91-93
toilet training and, 68–70
Nature-nurture controversy, 216
Nervous system
hereditary stimuli and, 59–60
readiness, 63
Neurosis
ego and, 57
environment and, 53–55
obsessional, 46, 68–70
sexual development and, 47–48
toilet training and, 68–70
Neurotic monkey, 191
*Notes on the Development of the
Child*, 26
Nourishment technique, sucking
and, 71

Nuclear family, learning and,
187–188
Nursery school recommended,
136, 139–140
Nurture
behaviorial scientist and, 3
complexity of, 141
nature and, 127

Object cathexis, 57
Observation justified, 24–38, 126,
128, 129
Obsession, 46, 68–70
Obstetrician "rooming in" and, 95
Oedipus complex, 52, 55–56, 58
behaviorism and, 122–123
reevaluated, 164
Onanism proscription, 122
See also Masturbation
Operationalism, 161–163
Oral personality, 48–49, 50, 71
Oral phase doubt, 85–86
Organization of Behavior, The, 180,
181, 182
Orphan, 93, 157
Outlines of Child Study, 138

Pacifier, 131
Papers on Metapsychology, 54
Parent
alternative for, 218
education of, 134–137
ego need and, 73–74
expectation, 2–3
fear of, 55–56
fixation on, 52
foster, 157
immaturity of, 66
importance confirmed, 17
inept, 120
moral development and, 63–64
new psychology for, 138–139
nurture and, 3
onus on, 66, 139–141
surrogate, teacher as, 10–11
Parent-child relationship, 71-73,
130, 151
Parent's Magazine, 65

Pavlov, Ivan, 113
Pavlovian conditioning, 133
Pediatrician, role of, 3, 70–71
Pediatrics
  advance of, 14–15
  attitude change, 94–95
  norms for, 156
Peer group socialization, 74
Penis envy, ignorance and, 52
Perception, 110, 183–184
Perez, Bernard, 26–27
Perfectability, education and, 64
Permissiveness, 71–73, 97
Personality
  absolutes, 91
  acculturation and, 36–38
  anatomy and, 101
  childrearing and, 7, 151,
    166–168
  development, 63, 73–76,
    151–152, 156
  ego and, 57–58
Personality in the Making, 73
Perversion, childhood impression
    and, 52–56
Pfister, O., 138
Physical growth, interdisciplinary
    investigation, 153–154
Physiognomy, ability and, 20–21,
    23, 27
Piaget, Jean, 24, 30, 31, 152, 182,
    213, 215
Pines, Maya, 195
Pleasure principle, 58
Porter, William, 22–23
Precocity, 197–199
Prejudice, cultural, 1
Preyer, Wilhelm, 24, 26–31
Productivity, nurture and, 3
Professional advice, demand
    for, 67
"Project for a Scientific
    Psychology", 60
Prosperity, values and, 6
Protestant ethic, 8–9
Psyche, infant needs and, 62–63
Psychoanalysis
  behaviorism and, 120–121,
    140–142, 162

child–care concept, 45–97
childrearing and, 64–66
dominance of, 73
empirical study of, 163
expectations of, 72–73
learning theory and, 162
popularity of, 71–72
precept of, 63
research and, 216
*Psychoanalytic Study of the Child,
    The*, 73, 94
*Psychological Care of Infant and
    Child*, 67, 115, 119
Psychological theory, reception
    of, 2
Psychologist
  experimental findings and,
    164–165
  role of, 73
Psychology
  new approach for, 109–112
  research evaluation, 217–218
"Psychology as the behaviorist
    views it," 110
*Psychology from the Standpoint of a
    Behaviorist*, 119, 125
Psychomotor precocity,
    stimulation and, 197–198
Psychosexual stage, 50–52
  critical-period theory and, 172
Psychosexual theory, behaviorist
    language for, 121
Psychosocial development, 24–31,
    46–56
*Psychosocial Development of
    Children*, 67
Puberty, 14–15, 47
Punishment, 141
Puritan concerns, 19

"Race," 21
  See also Heredity
"Race suicide," 16
Rapaport, David, 59, 75, 165, 167
Rationale for parent, maxim as, 1
Rational thought, evidence of, 22
Rayner, Rosalie, 116
Reaction-formation, 50
Read, Janet Michelson, 186

Reality "unknowable," 61
Recapitulation theory, 25–26, 28
  embryology and, 33–35
  infant and, 50–51
Reflex, elementary, 115
Regression, 164
Repetition compulsion, 57
Repression, 47–53, 55–56
Research, 151–201, 213–218
Respondant conditioning, 113
Response, predictable, 111
Retardation
  deprivation and, 168–180,
    194–195
  education and, 168–169
  remedial environment, 214
  social interaction and, 82–83
Retrospection, 167
*Review of Child Development
  Research*, 168
Revolution in Learning, 195
Reward and punishment
  accidental conditioning and,
    119–120
  concept, 109, 112–113
Ribble, Margaret, 77–78
Riesen, A. H., 177, 184
Rights of Infants, The, 77
Roberts, Charles, 22
Robertson, James, 94
Rogers, Charles, 192–193
Romanticism, asexuality and,
  121–122
"Rooming in," 94–95
Rosenbluth, D., 94
Rosenzweig, Mark, 184–186
Rousseau, Jean Jacques, 34
Rubella, 176
Ruml, Beardsley, 153

Sadomasochism, 55
Schedule, 130
School
  health care in, 13–14
  growth study in, 20–23
  as a laboratory, 129
Science
  function of, 2
  infant care and, 130–131

Scientific omniscient journalism, 71
Scott, J. P., 173–175
Sears, R. R., 163–168
Sechenov, I. M., 114
Seduction in early childhood, 46
*Selected List of Books for Parents and
  Teachers, A*, 138
Self-esteem, development of,
  73–74
Sensationalism, biological
  endowment and, 27–28
Separation, anxiety and, 94–95
Sex education, 140
Sexual development, adult
  neurosis and, 47–48
Sexual drive, 54–55
Sexuality
  childhood, 52–53, 122–124
  libidinal energy and, 121
  sublimation of, 48
Sexual theory, child's, 52–53
Shaping, 111, 115
Shinn, Millicent, 26
Simon, Theodore, 21
Skeels, Harold M., 83–84, 182
Sleep, faculties and, 25
Social experience, maternal
  deprivation and, 77
Socialization
  colonial promotion of, 3
  critical period and, 173–176
  personality and, 76
  retardation and, 82–83
Social learning theory, 73, 165–168
Social problem
  education and, 169
  parent and, 179–180
Social status, growth rate and,
  22, 152
Society
  heredity and, 15
  responsibility of, 6–7, 214
Socioeconomic class, IQ score
  and, 169
Speech, learning process, 117–118
Spencer, Herbert, 27–28
Spencer-Bain thesis, 112
Spiker, C C., 167–168
Spitz, Rene, 78–79, 175, 193, 194

Spock, Benjamin, 67
Stendler, Celia B., 63
Stimulation, development of, 82–93, 170
Stimulus-response
  language, 165
  mechanism, 127, 128
  personality and, 167
  reflex and, 111
Stockard, Charles, 176
Stoddard, G. D., 182
Stress
  corticosterone and, 189
  development and, 188–189
Stuart, Harold C., 154
Study, longitudinal, need of, 71–73
Sublimation, 47–50, 55
Substitute formation, 55–56
Superego, Oedipus complex and, 58
Surrogate mother
  behavior and, 175
  instinctual response to, 85
  rhesus monkey and, 190
Survey of Objective Studies of Psychoanalytic Concepts, 163
Survival, education for, 169
Suzzallo, Henry, 12

Tabula rasa, 12–13, 27, 28
Taine, Hippolyte, 25–26
Teacher
  nuture and, 3
  surrogate parent, 10–11
Temptation, training against, 4
Terman, Lewis, 154
Test, deprived children, 78–79
Thalidomide, critical-period and, 176, 193
Theory
  evaluation of, 215–216
  observation and, 128
  truth and, 1
Thorndike, Edward L., 16–17, 112–113, 139
Thought, language and, 117–119
Three Essays on the Theory of Sexuality, 50

Thumb sucking, 48, 131, 133
  well-adjusted mother and, 159
Tiedemann, Dietrich, 24–25
Tissot, S. A., 122
Toilet training, 62, 68–70
  atmosphere of, 71
  new concept, 97, 133
Tolman E. C., 127
Tradition, 4, 137–140
Training
  changing concept, 62–64
  receptivity to, 4
Trauma
  education and, 65
  hysteria and, 46
  parent and, 121
  stress adaptation and, 189
Trust, early experience and, 74–75
Twins
  development patterns, 37
  research of, 196
Two Year Old Goes to the Hospital, A, 94

"Unconscious," behavior and, 122–123
Unlearned response, 115
  See also Instinct
Unwanted children, 93

Variables, growth study, 21, 23
Volition, memory habit and, 30–31

Warner Francis, 23
Warren, Neil, 198
Watson, John B., 67, 109–142, 214, 215
Watson, Rosalie Rayner, 124
Weill, Blanche C., 134
Wellman, B. L., 182
West, Mrs. Max, 131
White, Sheldon H., 128, 167
Wilson, Margaret, 187
Wolfenstein, Martha, 130
Woodworth, Robert S., 126–127
Woman's traditional role, 4
Working mother, 76–77

Young, Robert M., 27